The Idea of the MODERN STATE

Edited by

Gregor McLennan, David Held

and Stuart Hall

Open University Press

Milton Keynes · *Philadelphia*

Open University Press
12 Cofferidge Close
Stony Stratford
Milton Keynes MK11 1BY, England
and
242 Cherry Street
Philadelphia, PA 19106, USA

First Published 1984

This book is derived from the Open University course D209:
The State and Society © The Open University 1984. Adapted and
revised material © the editors and contributors 1984.

British Library Cataloguing in Publication Data

The Idea of the Modern State.
  1. State, The
  I. Title   II. McLennan, Gregor   III. Held, David
  IV. Hall, Stuart, *1932 –*
  320.1′ 01   JC11

  ISBN 0 – 335 – 15021 – 7
  ISBN 0 – 335 – 10597 – 1 Pbk

Library of Congress Cataloging in Publication Data
Main entry under title:

The Idea of the modern state.
  Bibliography: p.
  Includes index.
  1. State, The.   I. McLennan, Gregor.   II. Held,
David.   III. Hall, Stuart.   IV. Title.
JC131.I34   1984   320.1′ 01   84 – 19019

Text design by Nicola Sheldon

Typeset by Getset(BTS)Ltd, Eynsham, Oxford
Printed in Great Britain by St. Edmundsbury Press,
Bury St. Edmunds, Suffolk

Contents

Notes on Contributors

Stuart Hall is Professor of Sociology at the Open University, formerly Director of The Centre for Culture Studies at the University of Birmingham and was Course Team Chairperson of the Open University Course on *The State and Society* (D209). He was co-author of *Policing the Crisis* (1929) and co-editor of *The Politics of Thatcherism* (1983).

David Held is Lecturer in Social Sciences at the Open University. His publications include: *Introduction to Critical Theory: Horteheimer to Habermas* (1980); *Habermas: Critical Debates*, edited with John B. Thompson (1982); *Classes, Power and Conflict: Classical and Contemporary Debates* (1982).

Gregor McLennan is Research Fellow in Sociology at the Open University. He is the author of *Marxism and the Methodologies of History* (1981) and co-editor of *On Ideology* (1977), *Making Histories* (1982) and *Crime and Society* (1982).

Tony Walton was formerly Lecturer in Philosophy of the Social Sciences at the Open University and is currently working in the Administration of the OU. He is preparing a book on Hegel's social and political theory.

Adam Westoby is Senior Lecturer in the School of Education at the Open University. His publications include *Communism Since World War II* (Harvester, Brighton, 1981).

Diane Elson is Tutor in Third World Studies for the Open University, NW Region. She has written several articles on the internationalisation of capital and the Third World, and is a member of the Editorial Board of *International Labour Reports*.

Roger Dale is Senior Lecturer in Sociology of Education at the Open University. He has written a number of articles on education and the State and on education and 'development'. He is co-editor of *Schooling and Capitalism* (1976) and *Education and the State* (1982).

David Beetham is Professor of Politics at the University of Leeds. His publications include *Max Weber and the Theory of Modern Politics* (1974) and *Marxists in Face of Fascism* (1984).

Editorial Preface

The character of our political future increasingly turns on the role to be played by the state. 'Quantitatively', its secular growth is one of the few really uncontroversial facts of the twentieth century. But it is not easy to say whether size in itself entails any particular *qualitative* outcomes. Without the state, many positive aspects of contemporary society – such as the provision of universal education – would be inconceivable. Yet this 'enabling' side of the state's growth almost inevitably brings in its train enhanced powers and possible dangers of centralization and coercive regulation. Whilst, empirically, there is evidence in abundance of the state's powers – both legitimate and questionable – and of its key role in representation and intervention, there is a need to pose some fundamental questions about the very character of the modern state, and to give them a sustained airing. How do we define the state? What is its relation to civil society? Is the state the product of the functional requirements of particular social systems? Is it the instrument of ruling classes? Can we even speak of *the* state as if it were a single, ahistorical entity?

It is to questions of this explicitly theoretical order that the essays in this collection are addressed. There can be no attempt to give theory any outright priority over more concrete studies in the area of state policy. All the same, in the plethora of important empirical work now appearing on political systems and social movements, the existence of a conceptual 'space' for basic reflection about the direction of the state in the modern world seems desirable and necessary.

This book aims to help contribute to that task. It is written and compiled in such a way that students and others with a general interest in political issues but who are relatively unfamiliar with specialized academic and political debates in the area will, by the end, have gained a solid working knowledge upon which they can form their own opinions on important but often difficult questions. In that sense, we have produced a textbook – a critical introduction – developed from the work presented in the Open University's well-received second level course, D209, *State and Society*. We hope that students and other readers will gain a sense of the range of *concepts* in state-analysis, of the rival *traditions* of state-theory, the different historical *types* of state, and the thinkers whose insights continue to frame today's intellectual and political arguments.

The first chapter sets down the major concepts we require to analyse the state in relation to the wider 'civil society'. These include: power, sovereignty, autonomy and representation. Chapter one also presents a summary assessment of the major historic trends in the functions and forms of the state in Europe. Chapter two focuses on four central perspectives of state-theory – those of liberalism, liberal democracy, Marxism, and political sociology. From Hobbes to Weber, Marx to Dahl, this chapter economically lays out the intellectual landscape and the background to most of the crucial writers and arguments. In the next essay, the complex and changing relationship between two of these traditions – Marxism and pluralism – is brought fully up to date, and a critical evaluation is made based on the coherence of each theory, and on their responses to two recently highlighted processes: corporatism and democratization.

Chapter four continues the prescriptive note by surveying some pertinent moral arguments which are voiced in contemporary political philosophy. Some of the arguments on the role of the state which have typically divided people are about the proper boundaries of state and civil society, about the *right* of the state to intervene in private and social life, or about the obligation of states to secure a socially *just* framework for its citizens. These are the kinds of issues which mobilize professors and presidents, writers and workers in the state sector; the whole future of state provision of welfare, for example, might depend on the ascendancy of one or other of these philosophical approaches.

It is important, then, to realize that the *kinds* of theories which come into existence or which prevail in the cultural battle of ideas, depend very much on the particular nature of the states which exist at any given time. Certainly, it is difficult to avoid thinking of *the* state as if it were timeless and place-less. In actuality there are states – in the plural – and vital differences exist even between states which can be grouped together for some purposes. In Chapter five detailed attention is paid to the ways in which *Communist* states have been categorized, and consideration is given to a number of positions, some from within, others outside the Communist movement in the twentieth century. One recurring problem here is the extent to which state-formation is a matter as much of *national* needs as of political ideology, and the next three essays take up the intricate relationship between nationalism, nation-states, and the international framework of state-development.

Chapter six dissects old and new versions of one pivotal idea of international expansion: imperialism; whilst Chapter seven discusses the influential 'world systems' approach, particularly as it is highlighted in the writings of Immanuel Wallerstein. The very future of the nation state is then succinctly and provocatively confronted in Chapter eight, whilst the final essay takes up the notion of human autonomy as one key means by which some long-standing theoretical and practical dilemmas may begin to be overcome.

The pieces described in the above summary, inevitably, do not exhaust the number of problems urgently requiring attention. But the book aims for an overall shape and coherence. For example, the longer, wide-ranging chapters near the start gradually give way to shorter, punchier chapters which nevertheless build on the perspectives laid out earlier. Whilst there is no single shared theoretical or political position across the various areas and approaches, we do hope to have produced a critical introductory text which can be connected to important issues of the day. We also hope to have covered some of the most central themes, perspectives, and problems of the modern state in a way which is both accessible and informative.

CHAPTER I

The state in question

Stuart Hall

The state is a *historical* phenomenon: it is a product of human association – of men and women living together in an organized way; not of Nature. Thus, there have been times when 'the state' as we know it did not exist. Clans and kinship groups in pre-history, semi-nomadic peoples today or even settled tribes with a very simple form of social organization, have all constituted what we would now call a *society*, without possessing a *state*. It must not be assumed from this that they are leaderless or lack the means of settling disputes. Order and social control can be maintained by many means other than that of a centralized authority or governmental organization. Custom can acquire the same constraining force over human behaviour as codified law. In some stateless societies, heads of households or chiefs of descent groups play a function in getting disputes settled, without forming the basis of a permanent or continuous system of rule.

This contrast with 'stateless societies' helps us to establish what the state *is*. Roberts has recently defined the state in terms of:

> . . . the presence of a supreme authority, ruling over a defined territory, who is recognized as having power to make decisions in matters of government [and] is able to enforce such decisions and generally maintain order within the state. Thus the capacity to exercise coercive authority is an essential ingredient: the ultimate test of a ruler's authority is whether he possesses the power of life and death over his subjects.
>
> (Roberts, 1979, p. 32)

This emphasizes the state's authority – its rightful claim to obedience from its subjects. All states depend on this particular *relationship* between rule and subjection. Rule is understood as the power to make decisions about the 'general arrangements' of a whole group. The test is within what boundaries and over which peoples the state can enforce its legal will. Within these boundaries, the state is the supreme authority.

Pre-histories of the modern state

The state is historical in another sense. It changes through time and in relationship to specific conditions and circumstances. From classical times onwards, there has existed in Western Europe an organized public power claiming authority and exercising a continuity of legitimate rule; though the actual term 'state' was not used for a long time with anything like its common modern meaning.

Out of the clans and tribes of early Greek civilization emerged a surprisingly 'advanced' form of state – the city-state or *polis*. This gave us the seeds of two very powerful ideas associated with the modern state: 'democracy' from *demos*, the rule of the people or the citizenry; and *polis*, the root of words like 'political' and 'politics'. Ancient Greece also provided two sets of reflections about the question of government and rule, widely regarded as the founding texts of political philosophy in Europe: Plato's *Republic*, and Aristotle's *Politics*.

The period of the Hellenic city-states lasted roughly from 800 BC to 500 BC. The early 'tyrants' broke the hold of the landed nobility over the government of the cities, and eventually the whole of the free citizenry, including the small and middle-sized farmers, were enfranchized. In the *polis*, all citizens belonged to the Assembly and could vote and participate directly in government: a 'direct democracy', sometimes consisting of 5000–6000 citizens, with little intervening administration or bureaucracy. However, the great slave population on which Athenian democracy rested had neither rights nor status of citizenship.

Later, the city-states were absorbed by the Athenian and other empires, which expanded as a consequence of territorial conquest. This expansion greatly tested Greek democracy. It proved difficult to extend the locality-based concept of citizenship to the 150 other cities which the Athenian Empire engulfed. After Alexander the Great, rule by a single ruler was inaugurated, with a royal line of succession. The royal ruler was later elevated to divine status and became, in his own person, a 'god'.

Rome, too, arose as a powerful city-state. But unlike its Greek counterpart it was never 'democratized'. The Roman *republic* (from the Latin *res publica*, or 'the things pertaining to the public realm': a term often used to signify what we would now call 'the state') was based on a Senate, dominated by aristocratic power. Later, its base was broadened to include the consuls, elected by assemblies of the whole people. Roman citizenship was defined by law, rather than by strict territoriality. Because it was not a 'direct democracy' it was easier to extend Roman citizenship to include the ruling classes of other cities and territories which fell to the Roman conquest. 'Civis Romanus sum': a Roman citizen was a citizen anywhere and everywhere.

The social basis of Roman civilization was the landowning class; the land was worked by a dependent and indebted peasantry, supplemented later by slave labour. The countryside was increasingly populated by small peasant farmers, free in status but 'propertyless'. The underclass of the cities were the 'proletarii' (origin of the term 'proletariat'). The size and scale of land transactions, the rules governing trade and the inheritance of private property, the definition of citizenship and the elaboration of distinctions between the land-owner's public role as citizen, and his 'private' role as head of the domestic household – *pater familias* – gave rise to Rome's other great contribution to the European state: a systemized code of 'Roman law'. Roman law helped to establish the distinction between 'state' and 'society', or between the *public* (pertaining to the state and public affairs) and the *private* (pertaining to relations of private association, 'civil society', and the domestic life of the patriarchal family).

Internal tensions arising from the skewed distribution of land, the demands of the 'landless', slave revolts, the problems of holding within a unified state the far-flung provinces which the Roman armies had conquered, challenges to senatorial power, pushed Rome into a more centralized form of rule. The Roman Empire arose as a new dispensation after Augustus Caesar. Yet the Roman state still rested on a system of civil laws, and the laws were still considered to derive in some unspecified way from 'the people' – though not in any sovereign 'will of the people' sense that we would recognize in modern democracies today.

This notion that state power was founded in law was crucial for the subsequent development of 'rule of law' arguments and 'constitutional government'. In the period of the Republic, Cicero formulated the basis of senatorial rule as 'We obey laws in order to be free'. But in the later Empire, when Emperors acquired full autocratic power and divine status, there was a notable shift formulated by the third-century (AD) philosopher, Ulpian: 'The ruler's will has force of law.' Yet law continued to embody an important ideal of rule and the state.

As the imperial frontiers of the Roman Empire were reached and closed, and the limited possibilities for economic growth on the basis of slavery became evident, Rome was gradually weakened: by 'dilution', as its 'Eastern' side grew at the expense of its Mediterranean 'West'; by rural unrest and slave rebellion; ultimately as a result of the barbaric invasions from the North. Late Rome pioneered a new labour system, on the very large estates, based on a system of 'free tenants' under direct patronage of the great agrarian landlords, and a peasantry (coloni) tied in a tenancy to the estate, and 'paying dues' in cash and kind. This element was later absorbed into feudalism.

When the Romans advanced northwards, they encountered the very different systems of government which organized the Germanic tribes. These wandered the outer hinterlands of the Roman Empire, began to settle on its frontiers and, eventually, formed part of the barbaric 'hordes' which sacked Rome and drove it into the Dark Ages. The Germanic peoples were essentially 'clan' societies – great kinship groupings, often tracing their membership matrilineally, owning and working land *in common*, with little private property: a communal, or 'primitive communist' mode of production. They were governed more loosely than Greece or Rome, through aristocratic-based councils with, below them, powerful assemblies of free warriors and, attached to them, retinues of soldiers in bands, often with their own 'chiefs'. These settler 'warrior communities', with their bonds of personal loyalty and their emphasis on military affairs and protection, contributed a second major element to feudalism. The German settlements placed considerable importance on popular *assemblies*. They also employed a different conception of law. In contrast with the formality of Roman law, Germanic law was said to belong to 'the people', the corporate inheritance of 'the folk' and a summary of their common customs. It was from these roots that the English later traced the origin of their 'parliaments' and the English system of common law.

Feudal states

European feudalism assumed a great variety of forms and it is possible only to outline the core relationships, and their consequences for state formation, which arose across Europe between 800 AD (the date of the coronation of Charlemagne, King of the Franks, as Emperor by the Pope). This was an attempt to recreate the imperial system of

Rome – long in serious decline – under the patronage of the
Catholic Church, and thereby to unify and centralize the fragmented
states of Western Christendom in a new Holy Roman Empire. These
countries and kingdoms, spreading from Spain to Germany, Northern France to Italy, were under the rule of a variety of counts, dukes
and princes owing allegiance to the Holy Roman Emperor. This
attempt to create a politically-unified Christian empire was offset by
the underlying system of social and economic relations.

The system had grown up of a ruler or lord giving his trusted
subordinates grants and rights of land ('benefices') in repayment for
gold and in the hope of continuing military services. There was also a
Germanic 'vassal' system, where leading warriors declared bonds of
personal loyalty and homage to their lord, in return for his protection.
Feudalism arose out of the fusion or synthesis of these two elements.
The lands became 'fiefs', granted on limited tenure only, in return for
military services. The vassal lords, in turn, exploited these tenures
economically through the labour of a dependent peasantry, tied to the
land, and required to give their labour services, rents and dues in
money and kind, in return for protection. This chain of mutual
obligation was exceedingly long because the lord could well, in turn,
be the vassal of some more powerful feudal lord who, in turn, was the
vassal of a noble, duke or king. The vast population at the base on
whom the whole pyramid rested were 'the objects of rule . . . but
never the subjects of a political relationship' (Poggi, 1978, p. 23).
The lord–serf relationship was the cell form of the feudal *economy*;
the lord–vassal relationship was the cell form of *political* rule.

This extended network of interlocking ties and obligations produced an inevitable 'fragmentation of each large system of rule into
many smaller, increasingly autonomous systems' (Poggi, 1978, p.
27). Power became both more personal and more local in focus. In
each area there were conflicting systems of loyalty – a 'social world
of overlapping claims and powers' (Anderson, 1974a, p. 149),
sometimes referred to as 'feudal anarchy'.

Basically (and with certain key exceptions, in Northern France and
in England, where the monarchy tended to be stronger and more
unified) the classical feudal monarch was different in degree, not in
kind, from his lords – *primus inter pares*. Though 'annointed of God'
he was *not* set off from them by divine status, but bound to them by
ties of reciprocal obligation. The most powerful lords constituted a
real source of alternative power with whom a feudal monarch had
constantly to reckon and whom therefore he regularly consulted,
since without them he could not raise taxes or an army. They became
his counsellors, his court and his council. Some rulers had to gain the

formal consent of popular assemblies to levy taxes. These were, in fact, early forms of 'parliament' which played an increasingly important role from the thirteenth century onwards.

The feudal state was thus constantly rent by these internal tensions between different and overlapping sources of power and authority. The monarchy tried to distinguish itself as a separate authority. The lords, however, used their lands and local military power to check the trend towards the centralization of royal authority. The feudal monarch was, therefore, never 'sovereign', only a *suzerain*: a particularly limited type of secular authority.

Within the loosely-knit fabric of feudalism emerged rival centres of power, with a very distinctive system of rule. The towns and cities fell outside the classical feudal system because of their independent *charters*. They had a different social and political structure because they were dominated by trade and manufacture, and centres of financial activity. Medieval towns were 'islands in the sea of feudalism' (Pirenne, 1969), with a large and wealthy merchant class, skilled craftsmen, artisans and wage-earning labourers. The larger among them evolved an autonomous system of rule – like the Italian *commune* – based on an oath of loyalty between a 'community' of equal citizens. The leading citizens won the right to administer themselves as a corporate body under charter, making them virtually self-governing. Within the towns, a system of representation by estates thus grew up, with each major status group – clergy, nobility and leading townsmen (burgers) – having rights of representation. Out of this evolved the variety of estates-based assemblies, parliaments, diets and town councils which became associated with the ruler or leading families of a city and its surrounding territory. The great towns and cities of Northern Italy and Flanders were examples of this type of development in late medieval society. The 'burgers' were the forerunners of that class of citizens who first exercised effective power in the medieval towns and were to form the basis of a nascent 'bourgeois' urban class.

The main source of rival authority to the feudal aristocracy was the Church. It spanned the whole period, disposed of immense wealth and institutional power, constituting a sort of rival network within and between states, claiming spiritual authority and therefore increasingly driven to compete with the secular feudal structure – kings, princes, dukes, the Holy Roman Emperor himself. It advanced claims to higher authority in secular as well as spiritual matters because, as St Augustine put it, what else is the history of the church but 'the march of God in the world' – a sentiment which put secular rulers very much in second place to the vicars of Christ on earth and their spiritual agents. From the twelfth century to the Reformation, when the universal claims of the Catholic church were challenged and broken, and 'national' churches finally emerged, linked with stronger and more unified national monarchies, there was an interminable struggle between the papacy and the rulers about the boundaries between spiritual and secular. The papacy's claim to a unique and sovereign spiritual power provoked, on the other side, the claim by the monarchy to a supreme, independent, secular authority. The latter was the germ of the modern conceptions of sovereignty.

Absolutism

Between the crisis of feudalism in the fourteenth century and the sixteenth century, there emerged, from the wreckage of medieval institutions, a new form of state, rooted in these independent, nationally-unified Renaissance monarchies in countries like France, Spain and England: modern *Absolutism*. This involved the strengthening of a unified territorial rule; the absorbtion of weaker and smaller territories into stronger and larger ones; the tightening of law, order and security throughout the kingdom; the application of a more 'unitary, continuous, calculable and effective' rule, with its power gathered under a single, sovereign head (Poggi, 1978, p. 61). Several factors contributed to its rise: the decline of feudal serfdom, the commutation of feudal dues into money rents, the growth of commerce and trade, the supplanting of feudal military obligations by the growth of new, professional, standing armies, the raising of taxation centrally and regularly by the state (provoking a tide of rebellions by the poor against the tax-gatherers).

The Absolutist state is the transition between the many varieties of feudal state and the 'bourgeois' constitutional state which emerged – first in England – in the seventeenth and eighteenth centuries. Within Absolutism, the movements of trade, commerce and capital undermined the dense local structures of feudalism, creating more unified, state-wide, national economies. The territorial boundaries increasingly coincided with the limits within which the state could effectively impose a uniform system of law, order and administration. Through 'mercantilism', the dominant economic doctrine under Absolutism, state and crown assumed a directive role in commercial enterprises. These states therefore increasingly acquired a 'national' character – like the proto-nationalism of, say, Elizabethan England. Relations between states increasingly became 'a formalized system of inter-state

relations' (Anderson, 1974b, p. 39), sustained through formal diplomacy and dynastic marriage alliances (though, as Anderson
reminds us, 'the long detour of marriage so often led back to the short
route of war' (1974b, p. 39)). The state bureaucracies were expanded
with offices filled by the aspiring nobility and others who clustered
within the court. Fluid alliances formed and re-formed in relation to
the Crown. The nobility sought office and favours in the royal court.
Absolute monarchies sometimes used them, sometimes forged alliances with other elements – eg. the mercantile classes – as a way of
containing the nobility's power. But these courts were adjuncts of the
monarch's rule, not participants in rule. The absolutist ruler 'ruled
from his court, not *through* it' (Poggi, 1978, p. 70). And law became
not 'a framework of rule', so much as 'an instrument for rule',
assimilated to the sovereign power of the throne.

In the sixteenth century, Jean Bodin sealed this development with
the doctrine of the 'divine right of kings'. Partnership-in-rule between
monarch and people, inscribed on the Estates system in later
feudalism, withered under Absolutism. In France, the Estates General
was not summoned between 1614 and 1789, and its calling set off the
process which ended in the French Revolution. In England, Stuart
kings' attempts to rule and raise taxes without Parliament precipitated
the English Revolution of the 1640s.

The constitutional or contractual state

Precisely because it fused and concentrated every element of rule
within one secular centre, and laid claim to an absolute sovereignty
which was secular and national, Absolutism helped to carve a path or
prepare the way through which the constitutional 'bourgeois' state
emerged. Both in England (where the main conflict occurred in the
seventeenth century) and in France (where it was delayed until the end
of the eighteenth century), sections of the gentry, along with the
emerging commercial classes, urban artisans and labouring classes,
were drawn into a 'mixed' struggle against the claims of Absolutism,
the power of the court, and the rigidity of mercantilism. Commercial
expansion of these new 'nation states' had undermined Absolutism.
And, in the wake of the revolts against these *ancien regimes*, modern
bourgeois development occurred at an increasingly rapid pace. By the
end of the eighteenth century, we find the British economy transformed by the growth of farming for the market, waged labour and the
laws of the 'free market' in full swing, the extensive sale and purchase
of land, fully-formed conceptions of private property, the general

dissolution of an old 'moral economy', the domination of agrarian capitalism. A new kind of bourgeois civilization began to appear. The classes connected with this development – the mercantile and commercial classes, and those sections of the landed classes increasingly treating their property as 'fixed capital' – emerged as new, powerful social formations in society. They gradually achieved a commanding presence in social and economic life, through their predominance in 'civil society'. They then began to struggle for a 'share of the action' of state power and rule. The principles of market and contract, which constituted the basis of their growing wealth, became, for the first time, the metaphor for a new conception of the state: a *contractual* state, where power was shared, the rights of the upper and middle ranks of society to participate in power along with the ruler was guaranteed by law and formalized in a constitutional system.

The long process towards widening the basis of the social contract was initiated in the Revolution of 1644 and the Parliamentary period in England, resulting in a moderate and mixed form of 'parliamentary monarchy'. It is under this constitutional system that industrialization occurred. Its final stages were the struggles to extend the franchise and to create a full democratic state in the nineteenth century. In France, Absolutism's demise was long-postponed. When it occurred, the popular classes – the real outsiders in this long shift of power – were directly involved in the struggle, and the programme of 'reform' consequently assumed its most 'radical' form with the Jacobin demand for 'liberty, equality, fraternity'. These were increasingly dominated by capitalist, rather than feudal, forms of economic and political relationship; with a novel type of social structure and a very different balance between the different classes; operating under new conceptions of rule, authority and power; and developing new, more 'contractual', liberal and constitutional forms of rule. This is the beginning of the 'bourgeois' revolutions and the threshold of the 'modern state'.

Development of the modern state

The idea of a 'modern state' is hard to date precisely, since the word 'modern' is open to different interpretations. The most useful definition is *not* in terms of a chronological timescale, but rather in terms of when particular features of the state which are still recognizable in contemporary societies first appeared. Those features include states in which power is shared; rights to participate in government are legally or constitutionally defined; representation is wide, state power is fully secular and the boundaries of national sovereignty are clearly defined. A state form of this type emerged very unevenly across Europe. It was already in existence in Britain by the eighteenth century, whereas there was nothing like it in Germany until towards the end of the nineteenth century.

In Britain, the *classical liberal* state evolved during the eighteenth and much of the nineteenth century, in the wake of the parliamentary interregnum and the 'Grand Compromise' of 1688. This spans the period of agrarian and early industrial capitalism, and Britain's rise to supremacy as a commercial and manufacturing power. The two things are organically connected, since the state was forced into a more liberal and constitutional path by the demands of the rising classes associated with these economic developments. This kind of state is called 'liberal' (a) in contrast with the rigidities of the *ancien regime*, and (b) because its main function was to guarantee the 'rights and liberties' of the individual. The organizational principles which enabled commerce and trade to expand – free trade, the laws of the market and contract – were also the principles on which the new relationships between state and individual were modelled. Individuals entered into a 'social contract' with the state in exchange for the defence of *their* rights and liberties, which they regard as 'natural'. This made individuals the *a priori* of the state, not *vice-versa*. These rights were of a very particular kind: the 'right' to buy and sell labour, to own and dispose of private property, to 'be at liberty' unless someone preferred a legal charge, to 'go about one's private business unmolested' (especially by the state), and to 'treat one's home as one's castle'.

Interference with these liberties could no longer be at the whim of crown or state, but had to be sanctioned *legally*. Even the state was subject to the law – i.e. rule by or 'the rule of law'. The liberal state had to be strong, in order to protect individuals' lives and property, uphold contracts freely made and defend the nation against external attack. But it had also to be small – not interfering across a wide range of activities. Especially, it must keep out of economic transactions and leave them to the free play of market forces (the origin of the doctrine of *laissez-faire*).

This 'liberal capitalist' state was, of course, *not* a democracy. The majority could not vote, assemble as they chose, 'publish and be damned', join a trade union, hold many posts if they were Dissenters, vote or dispose of property if they were women. The struggles by the majority of the ordinary people and the labouring classes to win for themselves these political and civil rights constituted the basis of the reform movements of the nineteenth century. These did not alter the fundamental form of the liberal state but they substantially modified it by deepening its popular base and its democratic content. In the end 'democracy' was grafted on to the liberal state, to create that hybrid variant which has to be distinguished from the classic liberalism: the *liberal–democratic* state. In the latter years of the nineteenth century, and the early years of the twentieth century, up to the First World War, the competition between industrializing world powers increased. There was a scramble between the imperialist powers. Britain lost her competitive lead: other nations began to industrialize faster and overtake her. There was a new drive to improve British competitiveness, modernize the society and make it more 'efficient'. Increasingly, the argument was advanced that the liberal, minimalist, *laissez-faire* type of state could not perform the task. Britain needed a more directive, interventionist state, able to act and plan organically on behalf of society as a whole.

This move towards *collectivism* was reinforced from *two* directions. The dominant classes supported it in the name of greater 'national efficiency'. The working classes, the poor and unemployed, supported it because they believed that only through the state would reforms be imposed on industrial capitalism which would improve their living conditions, provide greater economic equality and social justice. Egalitarian movements and socialists of very different complexions all thus demanded an enhanced role for the state. The reformers believed that, without state intervention, there would never be any proper provision for the poor, the unemployed, the aged and the sick. The socialists argued that, without state intervention, wealth would never be more equitably shared. The labour movement on the whole committed itself in this period to 'social' (i.e. in practice, state) ownership and control of the commanding heights of the economy. On the whole, it was the more evolutionary and reformist versions of these programmes which became institutionalized in the British labour movement.

Collectivist state policies were only slowly and unevenly implemented. The culmination of this 'reformist' tendency was not to be seen until the nationalization programme and welfare state measures of the post-war Labour government in 1945, despite movements in that direction between 1906–11 and during the two World Wars.

The 'origins' of the *welfare state* are rightly associated with the reforming social programme of the Liberal government of 1906–11; but its high point is found in the post 1945 Labour government. First Britain, then all other advanced capitalist societies, became 'welfare states' in the 1950s. The tendency was, of course, resisted by those committed to a 'liberal' view of the state, and by those who believed they would be 'overtaxed' to pay for it. But the beneficiaries – the majority classes – viewed it positively. And so, in fact, did the major political forces, for it became the basis of the 'post-war settlement': the tacit agreement between the two major political forces as to the basic political framework for post-war British society. This included state-supported welfare, benefits, housing, eduation; also full employment and a bigger role for the state in economic management (to avoid the disasters of the inter-war Depression). The 'settlement' came to be known by the names of the two leading partners to the political bargain: 'Butskellism', after Gaitskell (leader of the Labour Party) and Butler (the leading Tory reformer). Subsequently it has been associated with its chief mentor – Keynes. If the political reforms of the nineteenth century were the first step of reformism in modifying the liberal state, welfare was the second instalment: the widening of 'citizenship' to include some social and economic rights, and the end of strict *laissez-faire* – as well as a massive growth in the administrative state apparatus.

We must set against this the impact on British political attitudes and perceptions of the emergence, in Europe, of radically different tendencies in the same period. Evolutionary, reformist collectivism culminated in the welfare state. Revolutionary collectivism culminated in the formation of Communist states: the Bolshevik Revolution in Russia in 1917; the emergence of Communist China, culminating in the 1940s; and the extension of this type of regime into Eastern Europe after the war, largely under the shadow of Soviet occupation. In this model, the state and politics 'take command'. The state absorbs the major functions of civil society and economy, and sets about its positive transformation. It inaugurates a regime of national mobilization and strict regimentation. The latter feature in particular discredited the image of collectivism in Britain.

This was compounded by the parallel rise of the *fascist state*: Mussolini in Italy, Hitler in Germany, Franco in Spain, Salazar in Portugal. Paradoxically, fascist and Communist states seemed to share common characteristics. Both are one-party states. Both are dictatorial in form: 'fascist dictatorship' versus the 'dictatorship of the proletariat'. Despite their radical differences in politics and ideology, it was these shared features which permitted Orwell to synthesize them both into a common model: the image of *totalitarianism* which has haunted the liberal imagination since and was frozen in place after 1947 by the Cold War. This is the moment when the 'ascending curve' of positive attitudes to the state suffers a great reversal and the 'descending curve' imperceptibly begins.

This trend becomes clearer in the light of the 1960s and 1970s.

Primarily under 'social-democratic' (i.e. Labour) governments – but managed in not dissimilar ways when the Conservatives were in power – the liberal–democratic state became much more *interventionist*. It involved itself in every sphere of life. It established an active presence in the forbidden sphere of the economy. The state now owned state enterprises, was responsible for national economic policy, fine-tuned the economy through fiscal and other 'Keynesian' measures, regulated incomes and wages, and edged towards an alternative form of decision-making to that of Parliament – the process of *corporatist* bargaining between state, capital (the CBI) and labour (the TUC). The expansion of the state into the whole fabric of civil society and private life belongs *par excellence* to this period.

It is here that views about the modern liberal democratic state began to fracture and polarize. Reformists have generally supported the enhanced role of the state as an instrument of greater social justice and equality. Some 'rationalizers' believed a 'big state' was necessary to co-ordinate a complex economy and a sophisticated society. Some theorists believe that advanced capitalism cannot in fact survive without entering into partnership with a powerful state ('state monopoly capitalism'). Social democrats believe it shows that the state *can* be used to ameliorate the worst effects of capitalist competition, without destroying the system.

Others, however, have reacted vigorously against the whole corporatist trend. As British economic fortunes began to falter in the 1960s, and decisively as the world capitalist recession deepened after the mid-1970s, the interventionist state was exposed to a wider-ranging critique. It was inefficient and wasteful: a 'spendthrift' state. It was characterized by bureaucratic interference: the 'busybody' state. Too much welfare, it was said, had sapped the moral fibre of the nation: the 'nanny' state. It awakened expectations it could not afford to meet: the ungovernable state. It constituted a threat to the rights and liberties of the individual: 'creeping totalitarianism'.

What was proposed instead was a reversal of the whole trend: taking advantage of the crisis to 'roll back the state'. Hence the proposals to curb state intervention, cut state bureaucracy and public expenditure, reduce welfare, restore state-run enterprise to the private economy ('privatization'), break the trend to collectivism, restrict the power of the unions, and restore competitive individualism and the doctrines of free-market liberalism which constitutes the programme of the 'New Right'. This became the *dominant* trend in the British state in the 1980s. It represented a move to restore the ideal of the classical liberal state, but under advanced twentieth-century capitalist conditions: therefore, the *neo-liberal state*.

This schematic outline establishes a salient historial sequence. It charts a particular line of evolution with respect to the modern 'big state'. It suggests why the question of the state has become, once again, the principal point of contention in British politics, and in other liberal democracies.

Some elementary concepts

In his survey of *The Foundations of Modern Political Thought*, Quentin Skinner (1978) observed that 'by the beginning of the seventeenth century the concept of the State – its nature, its powers, its right to command obedience – had come to be regarded as the most important object of analysis in European thought' (Skinner, 1978, p. 349). He identified this moment with Hobbes, who determined in his work 'to make a more curious search into the rights of states and duties of the subject'. By the seventeenth century, 'we may be said to enter the modern world: the modern theory of the state remains to be constructed, but its foundations are complete'. What features and characteristics of the state led Skinner to argue that?

The first element is the notion of 'the powers' of the state – 'its right to command obedience'. Of course, states have duties towards their citizens, too – eg. to protect their lives and property or defend them against external attack. And citizens usually have 'rights', too – though these vary greatly from one type of state to another. But Hobbes's emphasis is the prior one. The state is itself a power – *the* central and supreme power – in the land. And it exercises the power by imposing its rule over us and commanding obedience. The state has many other functions: but fundamentally the state is about *rule*.

Rule may take many forms – monarchy, democracy, dictatorship, etc. But wherever the state is sovereign – the *supreme* power – it involves the *subjection* of its subjects to the powers of the state, its *domination* over them. Even in modern democracies, where the 'will of the people' is supposed to be sovereign, the government, once formed and in charge of the machinery of the state, nevertheless does constitute a power 'up there', separate from 'the people' who helped to form it.

The concept of the modern state, therefore, always entails a notion of *power*. State power can be exercised in many different modes. Administering society is every bit as much a part of the state's 'powers' as policing society. More broadly, 'state power' can be understood as the condensation of these different modes and processes of power into a single system of rule.

The state's relation to society is therefore *hierarchical* in form. Someone or some power 'up there' sets the rules of the game for us 'down here'. In some cases with our consent, in others not; but, regardless, the thrust of the exercise of the state's powers is downwards. This implies the power to set limits and establish constraints, as well as to intervene directly. Rules permit certain 'moves' to be made – and thus *exclude* some: otherwise we would have no need for them. They order and organize 'the play', and identify the norm and the deviant. The state both frames the rules of society (legislative) and applies them (executive). Part of what is implied by rule, then, must be this maintenance of a certain kind of *order* to the way society behaves. The state must have at its disposal, when all else fails, the power or capacity to *enforce* its will. As Hobbes remarked:

> For the laws of nature, [such] as justice, equity, modesty, mercy . . . without the terror of some power, to cause them to be observed, are contrary to our natural passions . . . And covenants without the swords, are but words, and of no strength to a man at all. (Hobbes, 1962 edn)

The powers of the state, then, include the power to employ *force* to oblige conformity to its rules, laws and regulations. Force is by no means the only way in which states govern. But no form of modern state so far encountered in history has totally renounced force or compulsion. Theorists sometimes overemphasize the centrality of force in the state, suggesting almost that the state is *nothing* but a coercive force. Actually, there are very few instances in history where a state has governed for any length of time by the imposition of naked force alone. Coercion and consent are not mutually exclusive but complementary. Even under military dictatorships, like that of General Pinochet in Chile, efforts are made to win at least a proportion of the 'hearts and minds' of the people. On the other hand, no state – even the most democratic – is without force as a backstop in the maintenance of public order, the policing of crime, the defence of the realm, the securing of conformity to the laws of the land. 'Of course,' the sociologist Max Weber observed, 'force is not the normal or the only means of the state . . . but force is a means specific to the state'.

Not only is state rule 'coercive' in one of its principal modalities. There is no point to the *right* to coerce obedience without the *capacity* to do so. State power is a matter of capacity first, of right afterwards. General Pinochet may have had no 'right' to expel Salvador Allende from power in 1973: but he did have the 'capacity' to seize power and overthrow the state. Even where the state is conceived as a contract, freely entered into by free individuals, people cannot be free to decide from day to day whether to be treasonable or not. The most consensual of states remains a power base.

That is why many theorists of the state, following Engels, made so much of the presence of 'armed bodies of men' – a specialized police, the 'enforcers' of order, separate from the rest of the population. This underlies Weber's famous observation that the state '(successfully) claims the monopoly of legitimate use of physical force within a given territory' (Weber, 1970, p. 77). Note 'monopoly'. It is essential, if the state is to be sovereign – *the* supreme power – that it can tolerate no other power within its jurisdiction, with a physical force capability greater than its own, which is not effectively under its jurisdiction or control. Rebellion is the rejection of the state. That is why modern states are so sensitive to the borderline between 'peaceful' and 'violent' protest, or between legitimate and illegitimate violence. It follows that a state wanting to damp down popular protest may well do so by representing opposition as 'violent' whether it really is or not.

This suggests that the key issue is not simply the state's violence or force, but the question of *legitimacy*. Of course, the state is physically capable of doing many things, including torturing prisoners, making troublesome citizens disappear, or even the wiping-out of whole ethnic groups. But what Weber had in mind was not what the state can get away with but what is considered right and proper in that society for the state to do: i.e. *legitimate* violence.

The issue of legitimacy covers the whole spectrum of what might be called sanctioned domination – of which physical force is only an extreme, special case. If the state regulates, directs, legislates and compels 'legitimately', it is because it can lay claim to the *authority* to do so. Authority is power which the state is licensed or 'authorized' to exercise.

The legitimacy of the state's powers to rule in modern society can arise in any of the following ways.

(i) The state can invoke the long, customary and traditional way in which this state has, in fact, ruled in the past. What Weber calls the ways of 'eternal yesterday' go a very long way in constructing constitutional legitimacy.

(ii) In times of extreme danger to or difficulty for the state, some person or group or force with exceptional or charismatic qualities may acquire the legitimacy to assume exceptional powers in the state: dictators, military leaders, leaders of popular movements which toppled the previous regime, war-time prime ministers, etc.

(iii) State powers are acquired legally. This is the principal mode of legitimacy in modern liberal democracies. The powers have been formally stated and claimed, enacted by the formally correct public procedure, embodied in the law, in formal regulatory rules, in a Constitution or some set of 'founding documents'. The *law* is an abstract system of rules, established for all to see and universally applicable: not made up for the occasion. Thus when powers are acquired legally, they carry the stamp of legitimacy. Legality and legitimacy have become closely intertwined in modern constitutional states. The fact that powers defined legally can be revoked by the same procedure suggests that they are not absolute and eternal but conditional, capable of amendment – and thus a check on the arbitrary use of state power. Legality does not, of course, guarantee either that the state *should* have such powers or *uses them properly*.

(iv) In modern liberal–democratic states, legitimacy involves the forms through which the citizens are represented or agree by formal electoral procedures that the state should exercise power. This means that any state which successfully monopolizes the claim that it 'gives the people what they want' is well placed to confer legitimacy on its own powers and policies.

The question of sovereignty

The concept of the modern state is closely tied up with the notion of sovereignty. Sovereignty means that the state is the *supreme* power, subject to the rule neither of some external power nor of a rival power within its own boundaries. In Russia, between the February and the October Revolutions in 1917, there were not one but two competing centres of power: the Kerensky government and the rival 'soviets' of workers, soldiers and peasants. This was a situation of 'dual power': the stability of the state was therefore clearly 'provisional'. The state 'cannot have rivals within its own territories as a law-making power and an object of allegiance' (Skinner, 1978, p. 351).

Other centres of power within a state must be *subordinated* to it: or, power must be *delegated* to them by the state – as the central state delegates certain powers to local authorities; or the state must license or, by its lack of legislation, 'permit' them to exist and function.

The state is not a single power; it has many centres of authority. But there must be a single chain or hierarchy of powers. Magistrates have a great deal of power in their own courts; but they must follow the precedents set by, and lodge appeals to, the courts above them in the legal hierarchy – in a unified chain of power to the House of Lords sitting as a judicial appeals committee. The modern conception of the state is unitary in this sense.

Sovereignty is also linked in complex ways with 'territory'. It has proved impossible to use the term 'state' in relation to a population without a permanent place of settlement. The attachment to land remains a powerful element in the complex of attitudes and feelings mobilized around sovereignty. Hence nationalism and nation lie close to the roots of the modern state. During the Falklands War (1982), for example, Enoch Powell argued that British sovereignty there inhered in the very inhospitable *soil itself*, even if not a single island settler remained. The state must be the 'sole bearer of Emperium (rule) within its own territories' (Skinner, 1978, p. 352).

On the other hand, the Basque people have a fierce loyalty to a particular region and territory of Spain, as the majority of the Northern Irish Catholics have to the Irish Republic; but in neither case are those territories their 'state'. 'Territory' and 'state' are therefore not the same. Yet territory matters for the definition of sovereignty, partly because the sense of 'belonging' – sentiments of loyalty – are important constituents of being members of a state; but mainly because of the need to establish the boundaries to power and legal rule. There must be some way of defining what parts are unified under the state, how extensive in space is its rule and where the boundaries to its rule end and the jurisdiction of other states begins. This is defined 'territorially' – even if, as is the case with most Empires, the territories are not adjacent to one another but may be flung far and wide across the globe.

The claims to sovereignty may not, of course, be strictly 'legal' at all, but founded in sheer possession of territory, or conquest *by force*. The greater part of Britain's nineteenth-century Empire was acquired by such means. But if rule is effectively established – if 'possession' is complete and unchallenged – the intruding power's *de facto* sovereignty will be recognized. Britain, having successfully defeated the Argentine occupation of the Falklands, remained the 'sovereign power' – the one 'having no rivals within [the territory] as a law-making power and object of allegiance' – whatever the (extremely complex) legal position.

A public and separate authority

Another of the 'distinctive modern ideas of the state' is of the state as a *public power*, separate from both the ruler and the ruled . . .'

Under Absolutism, ruler and state – person and public – were often indistinguishable. The modern notion of the public character of the state therefore arose in the course of the struggle *against* Absolutism. In the modern conception, the state is not supposed to be a secret, private affair. It is something operating in the world, universally known and acknowledged, carrying the force of an established legal authority, established for all to see by public processes. It therefore became necessary to distinguish between public *office* and the office-holder. The power of the state was redefined as an *abstract* power, distinct from its actual incumbents. Rulers come and go, but the authority of the state lives on: 'The King is dead. Long live the King!'. Office in the state can therefore be defined *impersonally*: in terms of roles, powers and functions.

This is part of the wider process by which the powers of the state have come to be seen as systematic, not arbitrary or capricious. The application of state power is not supposed to turn on the whim or caprice of the ruler – any more than, as Coke, the Chief Justice, put it during the seventeenth-century struggle of Parliament against the King, it would be right for the law to 'vary with the length of a Lord Chancellor's foot'. The most powerful lever to bring against a King who claimed divinity and on whose capricious whim there was therefore no constraint, was to insist that his rule must be responsible to and framed by the law. For the law gave the people a *public* criterion against which to measure the state's actions. This was embodied in the *constitutional* limits on rule, where the terms on which kings could or could not rule in the state were plainly set out and/or acknowledged in public custom and tradition.

The state apparatus

One particular characteristic of the modern state which fills out our conception of the state as a 'public power' is the growth of the institutional apparatuses of the state – the 'increasing apparatus of bureaucratic control', the 'distinct apparatus of power' in Skinner's terms. There has been a long-standing debate as to whether the terms 'government' and 'state' are interchangeable. The complex character of the state cannot be reduced to the ways in which the institutional machinery of government functions. The state embraces a much wider range of functions than the technical and administrative questions of how the machinery of government operates. The two terms involve very different levels of conceptualization. On the other hand, though the state may be an abstract and general force, its power has to

be *materialized* – i.e. it must acquire real, concrete, social organizational form, with real tasks, using and disposing of real resources,
through a set of practices in the apparatuses of the modern state
machine. This endows the power of the modern state with some
further distinctive characteristics – the phenomenon of bureaucracy
and the formation of the rational–technical administrative ethos of
large-scale government. State apparatuses acquire distinctive political
and policy characteristics of their own. They can become the power
bases for quite distinct interests, with a 'relatively autonomous'
effectivity of their own in terms of how the state works.

State and society

So far we have been considering what the state *is*. Now we must turn
to the relationship between the state and society. Where do the
boundaries of the state end and those of society begin? How are the
connections between 'state' and 'society' to be conceptualized?

The state is associated with public affairs – *res publica*: society,
especially in the liberal tradition, is linked with *the private*. By *public*
is meant everything which is directly owned, organized or admin-
istered by the state. The *private* is, by definition, everything which is
outside the direct control of the state; whatever is left up to the
voluntary, non-compulsory arrangements made between private
individuals. There are *two* quintessentially 'private' spheres in
modern society. One is the *family*, where personal, familial, emo-
tional and sexual relations have long been deemed to be a 'domestic'
matter into which the state should not intrude. The family, with its
authority unequally located in the male head of the household, was
once assumed to be the model for the state: the ruler as 'father to his
people'. The domestic sphere has long been thought of as a haven – a
'retreat from the public world'. The distinction has therefore acquired
a *gendered* character. The public is the sphere of work, authority,
power, responsibility, the management of the world by men; the
private is the 'domestic kingdom' where women and the feminine
virtues prevail. The private/public distinction is therefore rooted in a
particular sexual division of labour and one of the principal means by
which the exclusion of women from public affairs has been constructed and secured. The maintenance by the state of the public/private
separation is therefore sometimes taken to exemplify the *patriarchal*
aspects of the state.

The other 'private' sphere in liberal societies is that of the economy
and free market economic transactions. In the period of mercantilism

the state was massively involved in a directive role in economic life. But with the rise of the privately owned capitalist economy, operating on the basis of private property, free wage labour, money exchange, and the laws of the market, the idea emerged that the state should 'let the economy alone' (*laissez-faire*), allow the market forces to operate without state interference and leave economic transactions to be regulated through voluntary contract between private individuals alone. It was Adam Smith and the early Political Economists (and, after them, Marx) who coined the term *civil society* for this whole sphere of 'private' *economic* activity in capitalist societies.

The distinction is, however, by no means so clear cut as it once was. Consider the 'public schools' – which, however, are *privately* funded! This represents a different usage of the term 'public' from the distinction we have just considered. In this second usage, things are 'public' because they take place 'in the public arena'. They have been formally and institutionally established, like a public company; or take place out in society, in the sight of others, like a public gathering. In the same sense, public opinion represents the public views of ordinary people – yet outside the realm of state direction. The term 'civil society' has expanded to cover *all* forms of social intercourse or voluntary association, whether economic or not – provided only that they are not funded or controlled by the state. In modern liberal–democratic societies there are now a variety of mixed or hybrid public/private forms.

This confusion – public = state, and public = 'in the public arena' – arose in the eighteenth century. The rising commercial and professional classes first established a commanding presence and influence in civil society: through their private economic interests and commercial activities; by constructing a mass of privately-funded and controlled voluntary associations, clubs, chambers of commerce, scientific societies, libraries, charities, trusts, professional bodies, etc. These activities greatly enhanced their social power and authority and increasingly obliged the state to take account of them in more formal and 'public' ways. Needless to say, *men* predominated in these 'public' associations. They were men of substance, 'public persons'. Women were, by the same process, increasingly segregated into the 'separate domestic sphere'.

The boundaries between 'state' and 'civil society' are never fixed, but constantly changing. Public and private are not natural divisions, but socially and historically constructed ones. One of the ways in which the state expands its reach is to re-draw the public/private boundaries, and reconstitute the definition of the private, so as to make it legitimate for the state to intervene in areas which had hitherto been considered inviolable.

Is the state autonomous of society?

Because the 'separateness' of the state from society is institutionalized in the various apparatuses of government and the state machine, it does not follow that therefore the state is *autonomous* of society. If the state were autonomous, then it would be wholly outside the play of social forces and relationships, moving exclusively under its own impetus. In fact, the state arises out of society and is powerfully shaped and constrained by the social relations which surround it. At the same time, it constitutes an organized and condensed point of power sufficiently separate to act back on, intervene in and shape society in its turn.

Hence, the *relational* nature of the state: it is in constant interaction with society, regulating, ordering and organizing it. We have already stressed the necessity for the state to require obedience or impose obligation on its subjects. But we have also said that this process includes 'consent' – the general willingness of the population, despite many reservations, to support and conform to the state's rule. In liberal democracies, consent has actually been *formalized* in the franchise and representative government based on a territorial constituency of voters (plus certain social and civil rights, defined in law). In this case, the citizens formally help to *compose* and *constitute* the legislative part of the state, through the electoral process. Such a state clearly cannot be autonomous of society. Formal systems of popular representation do not, however, exhaust the responsiveness of the state to society. In such societies, *public opinion* is often the most sensitive barometer of public consent and shifts in popular attitude.

The state cannot stand totally outside the social, political, economic and cultural relations and institutions of which society is composed. One of its main functions is to preserve law and order; but the 'order' in a Communist state, with no private ownership, its fusion of economy and polity, is very different from that of western liberal capitalist societies, based on private property, wage labour, market exchange, and the formal separation of economy from politics. States do not just 'maintain order'. They maintain *particular forms of social order*: a particular set of institutions, a particular configuration of power relationships, a partiuclar social structure and economy. The 'empty' state – without social content – does not exist.

Since the state arises out of a particular configuration of socio-economic relations and institutions, it will' reflect in its internal operations the shape, structure and configuration of that social formation. A *feudal* society could not be governed by a *capitalist* form of state. A capitalist state is predicated on and adapted to a society which operates through money exchange: where the economy is judged in terms of its profitability, where revenues depend on the systematic raising of taxes, where the 'pyramid' of power is constructed out of the classes of modern industrial society, not feudal ranks; and the general spirit is not religious and Catholic, but secular and individualist in a democratic or 'egalitarian' ethos. Despite the formal separation of economy and polity, there are powerful reasons why the two will tend, to some degree, to correspond.

The state, then, is not autonomous of society. That does not mean that it is *wholly* determined in form and function by society. There *are* complex inter-relationships and inter-dependencies between the form of the state and the type of society. But the state has been vested by society with the ultimate power of supreme rule, and authorized to stand above society and govern it. It cannot be wholly *reducible* to society. Something is added, when power in society is organized into a separate and distinct instance of rule. From this perspective it seems clear that the state *constitutes* society as well as being constituted by it. States, then, are not autonomous of society. They are only 'relatively autonomous'.

This question of whether the state is autonomous of or reducible to society is one of the most important ways of differentiating different theories of the state from one another. Simple pluralist theories suppose the state to be largely autonomous. Inputs flow into the state from competing interest groups: the state acts as umpire between them. Its neutrality with respect to the different interest groups in society is guaranteed by its separateness and autonomy. Simple Marxist theories, on the other hand, see the state as the instrument of the dominant class. Its content, purpose and policy is identical with that of the dominant class. Its function is to administer society in their interests. Its 'separateness and autonomy' are an illusion, a trick, to fool the powerless into thinking that the state is neutral and above and beyond such sordid transactions. Theories of the state in general range widely between these two poles of 'autonomy' and 'identity'.

Representation and consent

The state, then, is in some way 'representative' of society. But representation is a slippery concept. The absolute monarch felt he was 'the father of his people' and had a duty to look after and care for their welfare, and represent their interests. But the common people had no *formal* rights of representation. Representation is never a simple, transparent process. An MP may listen to your views and try to 'represent them', as best she can, with those of others, in Parliament. But it would be naive to believe that she simply transmitted direct and without modification what you say and want. Politicians can 'represent' the people as wanting something – tough law and order policies, for example, or the return of hanging – which 'the people' didn't know they wanted until it was formulated for them.

The idea that the state should be defined in terms of 'representativeness' and 'consent' was not essential to the definition of the state until after the bourgeois revolutions of the seventeenth and eighteenth centuries. The fundamental break came with Hobbes, who started by assuming individuals as self-sufficient, possessive and self-interested units in a 'state of nature', prior to any state, and then he proceeded to explain the state as the result of a social contract between consenting individuals.

From this point onwards, government *with consent* stood at the centre of the modern conception of the state. In liberal theory, this was conceived wholly in individualist terms. The class of persons whose consent counted was strictly limited – even though conceded within a universal language of the 'rights and liberties of free-born Englishmen'. For Locke, 'individuals' meant propertied individuals – and men. It did not include women, the labouring poor or servants. 'By the term "free men" the Whigs always meant a man of independent means.' (Dickenson, 1977, p. 68)

'Consent' is a critical concept for all social contract and liberal theories of the state. But its meaning remains ambiguous. Need consent be positive and enthusiastic? Could consent be tacit, grudging, habitual – or even compelled? Reconciling the theory of individual rights and consent with the inalienable fact of state power has remained a thorny issue for liberal–individualist theories of the state ever since.

A state was necessary, Hobbes argued, 'to appoint in what manner . . . contracts between Subjects (as buying, exchanging, borrowing, lending, letting and taking to hire) are to be made' (*Leviathan*, ch. 24, p. 193, Macpherson, 1963, p. 96). The grounding of liberal theories of the state in free market societies and economies is clearly evident from this. Social contract theory raised these new socio-economic conditions of seventeenth-century society to the level of an abstract principle. Hobbes, however, could not explain how his individuals, outside society, in a state of nature, sufficiently possessed the 'socially acquired behaviours and desires of men' (Macpherson, 1963, p. 22) to enable them to formulate consent to the social contract. In fact, individuals are born, not into a void of Nature, but into already functioning societies, in definite social orders, within socially-formed relationships, with already established obligations to the state. Their consent must therefore also be socially formed and shaped. Moreover, consent is not necessarily spontaneous. We can be powerfully influenced by the state to consent. It can indeed be 'manufactured'.

In liberal democracies, consent and representation are often inextricably linked. The consensual basis of the state is sealed by the formal processes of representative government. Again, the 'representative' character of the state did *not* first appear with liberal democracy. The poor and the disenfranchized could always bring grievances or 'petition' the powerful. Absolute monarchs felt bound to recognize these representations – if for no other purpose than to protect their backs against rebellion, unrest and usurpation. The system of sending someone to 'represent' those who owed the king dues or wanted to petition him arose, giving rise in the thirteenth and fourteenth centuries to a welter of independent experiments in early forms of representative government, the basis of modern parliamentary government (Hexter, 1983). None of these forms, however, corresponded to the modern forms of democratic representation – on the basis of 'one person one vote'.

It was only with the work of radical democratic theorists like Rousseau, and later in the wake of the French Revolution and popular reform movements which developed in the context of industrial capitalism and modern class formations, that the demand for a state based on a *universal* system of representation, and grounded in a weak version of what Rousseau called the 'sovereign will of the people' or the *general* will, arose. This became the prototype for the *formal* processes of representative government. This liberal–democratic system of rule had to be grafted on to the 'liberal' state. The process was not initiated in Britain until the popular and working class reform movements of the early nineteenth century, and not completed until the enfranchisement of women in the twentieth century.

The state and social interests

Society is full of powerful and competing social interests. On whose side, then, is the power of the state harnessed? In whose interests does the state function?

Social interests are extremely tricky to define. Most interests conflict: workers need higher wages – but do not want to price themselves out of jobs. Interests are also historically determined: they
change with time and circumstances. History, indeed, produces 'new'
needs and thus new interests. There is no fixed, eternal list of abstract
needs which everyone has, simply as a result of 'being human'. Our
interests are socially and culturally defined. Moreover, interests
cannot be simply assigned to us on the basis of our collective identities
or social position. Not all the 'petty bourgeoisie' want to see the world
run like a corner shop. Not all the workers want a revolutionary
overthrow of society. Not all bosses follow to the letter their interests
in screwing the faces of the poor. Interests may *tend* to cluster in
particular ways as a result of our social or class position, our formation and outlook. But there is no fixed and unalterable agenda of
class interests which can be formally ascribed to social groups outside
the process by which interests are formed and changed, struggled
over, and transformed in struggle. And though material interests form
a particularly strong motive for action, they are not irresistible.
Unemployment will not necessarily drive *all* the unemployed to vote
for the Left. Problems cannot be resolved by the appeal to 'material
interests' alone – even though they are much too powerful to neglect.
'Hearts and minds' are interest-laden, too. These qualifications must
be borne in mind when we are analysing theories or explaining the
actions and strategies of groups in terms of the interests which they
are seeking to realize in relation to the state.

Theories of the state can also be categorized in terms of how social
interests and the state are conceptualized by them. In liberal theories,
the state, it is said, represents the interests of individual citizens. Its
function is to provide the conditions in which the life, limb and
property of individuals can be protected and the 'rights and liberties'
of the individual secured. In this variant, individuals are assumed to
be autonomous entities, driven by self-interest, and possessively
competitive by nature. The 'interest' they have *in the state* is to make
society open to these forces *but*, at the same time, to prevent this
breaking down into a destructive competition – Hobbes's 'war of all
against all'.

The pluralist account of interests and the state recognizes that
modern societies are *not* composed solely of competing individuals.
There are large social groups – classes, economic or other 'interest
groups' – who may have conflicting interests, which compete in
society. For the sake of a 'free society', such competition must be
allowed to proceed; but it must not be allowed to collapse into
violence as the means of resolving conflict. A 'power' is required

which will keep the competition peaceful, within a defined system of 'rules of the game'; but which will also pull some compromise solution together, which is likely to win the consensus of the largest number of people. This umpire is the state. (Of course, many more sophisticated pluralisms exist.)

The liberal–democratic or reformist approach argues that there must be something over and above particular interests which the state represents, i.e. that of society or the community *as a whole*. The guardian of this 'general interest' is the state. Reformism recognizes that where individuals, groups or classes are left free to compete for advantage, in liberal, free-market economies, one sector or class will accumulate the greater proportion of wealth, capital, profit and power. The state must therefore positively intervene to create the conditions of greater equality and social justice, without destroying the underlying competition framework.

But what if conflicting interests arise from the very structure of society itself? Marxist perspectives on the state argue that classes are the fundamental interest groups in society; that their interests inevitably conflict (the class struggle, not just peaceful competition); and these conflicts of interest are generated by the very structure of capitalist societies. Class interests are stubborn and structural. The power of the state will therefore be monopolized either directly by the dominant classes in society, or harnessed to expand, protect and advance *their* general interests. 'Wealth,' Engels once wrote of the democratic republic, 'wields its power indirectly.' (Engels, 1884 [1953 edn.]).

Marxist perspectives would see the state as a structural element systematically weighting the balance of advantage towards the general interest of the ruling class. Or, in another version, intervening so as to maintain or create the conditions for the whole system to run more profitably for those who already have advantage in it. There are several variants of the Marxist perspective, too.

Such broadly defined perspectives – liberal, pluralist, reformist, Marxist – will tend to inform almost all discussions of the state. Discussions of the state may strive objectively to test and refine these perspectives in the light of empirical investigation. But all such discussions will be informed by ideological and theoretical preconceptions.

References

Anderson, P. (1974a). *Passages from Antiquity to Feudalism.* London, New Left Books.

Anderson, P. (1974b). *Lineages of the Absolutist State*. London, New Left Books.

Dickenson, H. (1977). *Liberty and Property*. London, Methuen.

Engels, F. (1953 edn). *The Origin of the Family, Private Property and the State*. London, Lawrence and Wishart.

Hexter, J.H. (1983). 'The Birth of Modern Freedom', *Times Literary Supplement* 21 Jan.

Hobbes, T. (1962 edn). *Leviathan*.

Macpherson, C.B. (1963) *The Political Theory of Possessive Individualism*, Oxford, Oxford University Press.

Pirenne, H. (1969). *Medieval Cities*. New Jersey, Princeton University Press.

Poggi, G. (1978). *The Development of the Modern State*. London, Hutchinson.

Roberts, K. (1979). *Order and Dispute*. Harmondsworth, Pelican.

Skinner, Q. (1978). *The Foundations of Modern Political Thought* Vol. 1. Cambridge, Cambridge University Press.

Weber, M. (1970). H.H. Gerth and C.W. Mills (eds) *From Max Weber*. London, Routledge and Kegan Paul.

CHAPTER 2

Central perspectives on the modern state

David Held

The state – or apparatus of 'government' – appears to be everywhere, regulating the conditions of our lives from birth registration to death certification. Yet, the nature of the state is hard to grasp. This may seem peculiar for something so pervasive in public and private life, but it is precisely this pervasiveness which makes it difficult to understand. There is nothing more central to political and social theory than the nature of the state, and nothing more contested. It is the objective of this chapter to set out some of the key elements of the conflict of interpretation. [1]

In modern Western political thought, the idea of the state is often linked to the notion of an impersonal and privileged legal or constitutional order with the capability of administering and controlling a given territory. [2] This notion found its earliest expression in the ancient world (especially in Rome) but it did not become a major object of concern until the early development of the European state system from the sixteenth century onwards. It was not an element of medieval political thinking. The idea of an impersonal and sovereign political order, i.e. a legally circumscribed structure of power with supreme jurisdiction over a territory, could not predominate while political rights, obligations and duties were closely tied to property rights and religious tradition. Similarly, the idea that human beings as 'individuals' or 'as a people' could be active citizens of this order – citizens of their state – and not merely dutiful subjects of a monarch or emperor could not develop under such conditions.

The historical changes that contributed to the transformation of medieval notions of political life were immensely complicated. Struggles between monarchs and barons over the domain of rightful authority; peasant rebellions against the weight of excess taxation and social obligation; the spread of trade, commerce and market

Colonisation?

relations; the flourishing of Renaissance culture with its renewed interest in classical political ideas (including the Greek city-state and Roman law); the consolidation of national monarchies in central and southern Europe (England, France and Spain); religious strife and the challenge to the universal claims of Catholicism; the struggle between Church and State – all played a part.[3] As the grip of feudal traditions and customs were loosened, the nature and limits of political authority, law, rights and obedience emerged as a preoccupation of European political thought. Not until the end of the sixteenth century did the concept of the state become a central object of political analysis.

While the works of Niccolo Machiavelli (1469–1527) and Jean Bodin (1530–96) are of great importance in these developments, Thomas Hobbes (1588–1679) directly expressed the new concerns when he stated in *De Cive* (1642) that it was his aim 'to make a more curious search into the rights of states and duties of subjects'.[4] Until challenged by, among others, Karl Marx in the nineteenth century, the idea of the modern state came to be associated with a 'form of public power separate from both the ruler and ruled, and constituting the supreme political authority within a certain defined boundary'.[5] But the nature of that public power and its relationship to ruler and ruled were the subject of controversy and uncertainty. The following questions arose: What is the state? What should it be? What are its origins and foundations? What is the relationship between state and society? What is the most desirable form this relationship might take? What does and should the state do? Whose interest does and should the state represent? How might one characterize the relations among states?

This essay focuses on four strands or traditions of political analysis which sought to grapple with such questions: (1) *liberalism*, which became absorbed with the question of sovereignty and citizenship; (2) *liberal democracy*, which developed liberalism's concerns while focusing on the problem of establishing political accountability; (3) *Marxism*, which rejected the terms of reference of both liberalism and liberal democracy and concentrated upon class structure and the forces of political coercion; and (4), for want of a more satisfactory label, *political sociology*, which has, from Max Weber to Anglo-American pluralism and 'geopolitical' conceptions of the state, elaborated concerns with both the institutional mechanisms of the state and the system of nation-states more generally. None of these traditions of analysis, it should be stressed, forms a unity; that is to say, each is a heterogeneous body of thought encompassing interesting points of divergence. There is also some common ground, more noticeable in the work of contemporary figures, across these separate traditions. I shall attempt to indicate this briefly throughout the essay and in my concluding remarks. It is important to appreciate that, in a field in which there is as vast a range of literature as this, any selection has an arbitrary element to it. But I hope to introduce some of the central perspectives on the modern state.

A distinction is often made between normative political theory or political philosophy on the one hand, and the descriptive-explanatory theories of the social sciences on the other. The former refers to theories about the proper form of political organization and includes accounts of such notions as liberty and equality. The latter refers to attempts to characterize actual phenomena and events and is marked by a strong empirical element. The distinction, thus, is between theories which focus on what is desirable, what should or ought to be the case, and those that focus on what is the case. The political writings of people like Hobbes, Locke, and Mill are generally placed in the first camp, while those of, for instance, Weber are put in the second; Marx occupying sometimes one domain, sometimes the other, depending on the writings one examines. But it will become clear that, while this distinction should be borne in mind, it is hard to use it as a classificatory device for theories of the state. For many political philosophers see what they think the state ought to be like in the state as it is. Social scientists, on the other hand, cannot escape the problem that facts do not simply 'speak for themselves': they are, and they have to be, interpreted; and the framework we bring to the process of interpretation determines what we 'see', what we notice and register as important.

The essay begins with the thought of Hobbes which marks a point of transition between a commitment to the absolutist state and the struggle of liberalism against tyranny. It is important to be clear about the meaning of 'liberalism'.[6] While it is a highly controversial concept, and its meaning has shifted historically, I will use it here to signify the attempt to define a private sphere independent of the state and thus to redefine the state itself, i.e. the freeing of civil society – personal, family and business life – from political interference and the simultaneous delimitation of the state's authority. With the growing division between the state and civil society, a division which followed the expansion of market economies, the struggle for a range of freedoms and rights which were in principle to be universal became more acute. Gradually, liberalism became associated with the doctrine that freedom of choice should be applied to matters as diverse as marriage, religion, economic and political affairs – in fact, to everything that affected daily life.[7] Liberalism upheld the values of reason and toleration in the face of tradition and absolutism.[8] In this view, the world consists of 'free and equal' individuals with natural rights. Politics should be about the defence of the rights of these individuals – a defence which must leave them in a position to realize their own capacities. The mechanisms for regulating individuals' pursuit of their interests were to be the constitutional state, private property, the competitive market economy – and the distinctively patriarchal family. While liberalism celebrated the rights of individuals to 'life, liberty and property', it should be noted from the outset that it was generally the male property-owning individual who was the focus of so much attention; and the new freedoms were first and foremost for the men of the new middle classes or the bourgeoisie. The Western world was liberal first, and only later, after extensive conflicts, liberal democratic or democratic; that is, only later was a universal franchise won which allowed all mature adults the chance to express their judgment about the performance of those who govern them.[9] But even now, the very meanings of the terms 'liberalism' and 'democracy' remain unsettled.

Sovereignty, citizenship and the development of liberalism

Hobbes was among the first to try to grasp the nature of public power as a special kind of institution – as he put it, an 'Artificiall Man', defined by permanence and sovereignty, the authorized representative 'giving life and motion' to society and the body politic.[10] He was preoccupied, above all, with the problem of order, which resolved itself into two questions: Why is 'a great LEVIATHAN or STATE' necessary? and What form should the state take? Through a theory of human nature, sovereign authority and political obligation, he sought to prove that the state must be regarded as ultimately both absolute and legitimate, in order that the worst of evils – civil war – might be permanently averted.[11]

In so arguing, Hobbes produced a political philosophy which is a fascinating point of departure for reflection on the modern theory of the state; for it is at once a profoundly liberal and illiberal view.[12] It is liberal because Hobbes derives or explains the existence of society and the state by reference to 'free and equal' individuals, the component elements, according to him, of social life – 'men as if but even now sprung out of the earth and suddenly, like mushrooms, come to full maturity, without all kind of engagement to each other.'[13] It is liberal because Hobbes is concerned to uncover the best circumstances for human nature – understood as naturally selfish, egoistical and self-interested – to find expression. And it is liberal because it emphasizes the importance of consent in the making of a contract or bargain, not only to regulate human affairs and secure a measure of independence and choice in society, but also to legitimate, i.e. justify, such regulation. Yet Hobbes's position is also, as I shall attempt to show, profoundly illiberal: his political conclusions emphasize the necessity of a practically all-powerful state to create the laws and secure the conditions of social and political life. Hobbes remains of abiding interest today precisely because of this tension between the claims of individuality on the one hand, and the power requisite for the state to ensure 'peaceful and commodious living', on the other. [14]

In *Leviathan* (1651), Hobbes set out his argument in a highly systematic manner. Influenced by Galileo, he was concerned to build his 'civil science' upon clear principles and closely reasoned deductions. He started from a set of postulates and observations about human nature. Human beings, Hobbes contended, are moved by desires and aversions which generate a state of perpetual restlessness. Seeking always 'more intense delight', they are profoundly self-interested; a deep-rooted psychological egoism limits the possibilities for human cooperation. In order to fulfil their desires, human beings (though in different ways and degrees) seek power. And because the power gained by one 'resisteth and hindreth the power of another', conflicts of interest are inevitable: they are a fact of nature. The struggle for power, for no other reason than self-perservation and self-interest (however disguised by rationalization) defines the human condition. Hobbes thus emphasizes 'a generall inclination of all mankind, a perpetuall and restlesse desire of Power after power, that ceaseth only in Death'. [15] The idea that human beings might come to respect and trust one another, treat each other as if they could keep promises and honour contracts, seems remote indeed.

Hobbes desired to show, however, that a consistent concern with self-interest does not simply lead to an endless struggle for power. [16] In order to prove this he introduced a 'thought experiment' employing four interrelated concepts: state of nature, right of nature, law of nature and social contract. He imagined a situation in which individuals are in a state of nature – that is, a situation without a 'Common Power' or state to enforce rules and restrain behaviour – enjoying 'natural rights' to use all means to protect their lives and to do whatever they wish, against whoever they like and to 'possess, use, and enjoy all that he would, or could get'. [17] The result is a constant struggle for survival: Hobbes's famous 'Warre of every one against every one'. In this state of nature individuals discover that life is 'solitary, poore, nasty, brutish and short' and, accordingly, that to avoid harm and the risk of an early death, let alone to ensure the conditions of greater comfort, the observation of certain natural laws or rules is required.[18] The latter are things the individual ought to adhere to in dealings with others if there is sufficient ground for believing that others will do likewise.[19] Hobbes says of these laws that 'they have been contracted into one easy sum, intelligible even to the meanest capacity; and that is, *Do not that to another which thou wouldest not have done to thyself*.[20] There is much in what he says about laws of nature that is ambiguous (above all, their relation to the 'will of God'), but these difficulties need not concern us here. For the key problem, in Hobbes's view, is: under what conditions will individuals trust each other enough to 'lay down their right to all things' so that their long-term interest in security and peace can be upheld? How can individuals make a bargain with one another when it may be, in certain circumstances, in some people's interest to break it? An agreement between people to ensure the regulation of their lives is necessary, but it seems an impossible goal.

His argument, in short, is as follows: if individuals surrender their rights by transferring them to a powerful authority which can force them to keep their promises and covenants, then an effective and legitimate private and public sphere, society and state, can be formed. Thus the social contract consists in individuals handing over their rights of self-government to a single authority – thereafter authorized to act on their behalf – on the condition that every individual does the same. A unique relation of authority results: the relation of sovereign to subject. A unique political power is created: the exercise of sovereign power or sovereignty – the authorized (hence rightful) use of power by the person or assembly established as sovereign.[21] The sovereign's subjects have an obligation and duty to obey the sovereign; for the position 'sovereign' is the product of their social contract, and 'sovereignty' is above all a quality of the position rather than of the person who occupies it. The contract is a once-and-for-all affair, creating an authority able to determine the very nature and limits of the law. There can be no conditions placed on such authority because to do so would undermine its very *raison d'être*.

The sovereign has to have sufficient power to make agreements stick, to enforce contracts, and to ensure that the laws governing political and economic life are upheld. Power must be effective. Since, in Hobbes's view, 'men's ambitions, avarice, anger and other passions' are strong, the 'bonds of words are too weak to bridle them . . . without some fear of coercive power'.[22] In short: 'covenants, without the sword, are but words, and of no strength to secure a man at all'.[23] Beyond the sovereign state's sphere of influence there will always be the chaos of constant warfare; but within the territory controlled by the state, with 'fear of some coercive power', social order can be sustained.

It is important to stress that, in Hobbes's opinion, while sovereignty must be self-perpetuating, undivided and ultimately absolute, it is established by the authority conferred by the people.[24] The sovereign's right of command and the subjects' duty of obedience is the result of consent – the circumstances individuals would have agreed to if there had actually been a social contract. Although there is little about Hobbes's conception of the state which today we would call representative, he argues in fact that the people rule through the sovereign. The sovereign is their representative: 'A Multitude of men, are made *One* Person, when they are by one man, or one Person, Represented'.[25] Through the sovereign a plurality of voices and interests can become 'one will', and to speak of a sovereign state assumes, Hobbes held, such a unity. Hence, his position is at one with all those who argue for the importance of government by consent and reject the claims of the 'divine right of Kings' and, more generally, the authority of tradition. Yet, his conclusions run wholly counter to those who often take such an argument to imply the necessity of some kind of popular sovereignty or democratic representative government.[26] Hobbes was trying to acknowledge, and persuade his contemporaries to acknowledge, a full obligation to a sovereign state. As one commentator usefully put it:

> Hobbes was not asking his contemporaries to make a contract, but only to acknowledge the same obligation they would have had if they had made such a contract. He was speaking not to men in a state of nature, but to men in an imperfect political society, that is to say, in a society which did not guarantee security of life and commodious living (as witness its tendency to lapse into civil war). He was telling them what they must do to establish a more nearly perfect political society, one that would be permanently free from internal disturbance.[27]

A strong secular state was offered as the most effective, appropriate and legitimate political form. The right of citizens to change their ruler(s) was, accordingly, regarded as superfluous.

The fundamental purpose of sovereignty is to ensure 'the *safety of the people*'. By 'safety' is meant not merely minimum physical preservation. The sovereign must ensure the protection of all things held in property: 'Those that are dearest to a man are his own life, and limbs; and in the next degree, (in most men) those that concern conjugall affection; and after them riches and means of living'.[28] Moreover, the sovereign must educate the people to respect all these kinds of property so that men can pursue their trades and callings, and industry and the polity can flourish. At this point Hobbes suggests certain limits to the range of the sovereign's actions: the sovereign should neither injure individuals nor the basis of their material wellbeing, and should recognize that authority can be sustained only so long as protection can be afforded to all subjects.[29]

There are a number of particularly noteworthy things about Hobbes's conception of the state. First, the state is regarded as pre-eminent in political and social life. While individuals exist prior to the formation of civilized society and to the state itself, it is the latter that provides the conditions of existence of the former. The state alters a miserable situation for human beings by changing the conditions under which they pursue their interests. The state constitutes society through the powers of command of the sovereign (set down in the legal system) and through the capacity of the sovereign to enforce the law (established by the fear of coercive power). The state does not simply record or reflect socio-economic reality, it enters into its very construction by establishing its form and codifying its forces. Second, it is the self-seeking nature of individuals' behaviour and patterns of interaction that makes the indivisible power of the state necessary. The sovereign state must be able to act decisively to counter the threat of anarchy. Hence it must be powerful and capable of acting as a single force. Third, the state, and practically all it does, can and must be considered legitimate. For the 'thought experiment', drawing on the notions of a state of nature and social contract, shows how individuals with their own divergent interests come to commit themselves to the idea that only a great Leviathan or state or 'Mortall God' can articulate and defend the 'general' or 'public' interest. The sovereign state represents 'the public' – the sum of individual interests – and thus can create the conditions for individuals to live their lives and to go about their competitive and acquisitive business peacefully. Hobbes's argument recognizes the importance of public consent (although he was not always consistent about its significance), and concludes that it is conferred by the social contract and its covenants.

Hobbes's arguments are extraordinarily impressive. The image of an all-powerful Leviathan is a remarkably contemporary one; after all, most states in the twentieth century have been run by 'Mortall Gods', people with seemingly unlimited authority backed by the armed forces. (Consider the number of dictatorships that now exist.) Moreover, the idea that individuals are merely self-interested is also a depressingly modern one. Such a conception of human beings is presupposed in the economic and political doctrines of many writers today.[30] But the impressiveness of some of Hobbes's views should not of course be confused with their acceptability. Hobbes's account, for example, of sovereignty, obligation and the duties of citizens are all contestable, as are his general doctrines about human nature. The constitutive role of the state (the degree to which the state forms society), coercive power (the degree to which such power is or must be central to political order), representation (the degree to which a sovereign authority can claim to articulate the public interest without forms of democratic accountability), and legitimacy (the degree to which states are considered just or worthy by their citizens) – all have been and still are subject to debate.

John Locke (1632–1704) raised a fundamental objection to the Hobbesian argument that individuals could only find a 'peaceful and commodious' life with one another if they were governed by the dictates of an indivisible sovereign. He said of this type of argument: 'This is to think that Men are so foolish that they take care to avoid what Mischiefs may be done them by *Pole-Cats*, or *Foxes*, but are content, nay think it Safety, to be devoured by Lions'.[31] In other words, it is hardly credible that people who do not fully trust each other would place their trust in an all-powerful ruler to look after their interests. What obstacles are there to the potential 'violence and oppression', as Locke put it, 'of this Absolute Ruler'?[32] What would make such a system of rule compelling and trustworthy?

Locke approved of the revolution and settlement of 1688, which imposed certain constitutional limits on the authority of the Crown. He rejected the notion of a great Leviathan, pre-eminent in all social spheres, an uncontested unity establishing and enforcing law according to the sovereign's will. For Locke, the state (he spoke more often of 'government') can and should be conceived as an 'instrument' for the defence of the 'life, liberty and estate' of its citizens; that is, the state's *raison d'être* is the protection of individuals' rights as laid down by God's will and as enshrined in law.[33] Society, conceived of as the sum of individuals, exists prior to the state, and the state is established to guide society. He placed a strong emphasis on the importance of government by consent – consent which could be revoked if the government and its deputies fail to sustain the 'good of the governed'. Legitimate government requires the consent of its citizens, and government can be dissolved if the trust of the people is violated. What Locke meant by 'consent' is controversial,[34] but whatever position one takes on this question the contrast between the views of Locke and Hobbes remains remarkable. Moreover, while Locke did not develop a systematic doctrine about the desirability of a mixed form of government or a division of power within the state, he has been associated for many generations with such a view.[35] He accepted that the state should have supreme jurisdiction over its territory, but was critical of the notion of the indivisibility of state power and suggested an important alternative conception.

It is interesting that the ideas of social contract and the state of nature can yield a variety of political positions. Locke, like Hobbes, saw the establishment of the political world as preceded by the existence of individuals endowed with natural rights. Locke, like Hobbes, was concerned to derive and explain the very possibility of government. Locke, like Hobbes, was concerned about what form legitimate government should take and about the conditions for security, peace and freedom. But the way in which he conceived these things was considerably different. In the important second of the *Two Treatises of Government* (which was published for the first time in 1690), Locke starts with the proposition that individuals are originally in a state of nature, a '*State of perfect Freedom* to order their Actions, and dispose of their Possessions, and Persons as they think fit, within the bounds of the Law of Nature, without asking leave, or depending upon the will of any other Man'.[36] The state of nature is a state of liberty but not 'a state of license'. Individuals are bound by duty to God and governed only by the law of nature. The law of nature (the precise meaning of which is difficult to pin down in the *Two Treatises*) specifies basic principles of morality – individuals should not take their own lives, they should try to preserve each other and should not infringe upon one another's liberty. The law can be grasped by human reason but it is the creation of God, the 'infinitely wise Maker'.[37]

Humans – in fact, Locke spoke here only of men – are free and equal because reason makes them capable of rationality, of following the law of nature. They enjoy natural rights. The right of governing one's affairs and enforcing the law of nature against transgressors is presupposed, as is the obligation to respect the rights of others. Individuals have the right to dispose of their own labour and to possess property. The right to property is a right to 'life, liberty and estate'.[38] (Locke also uses 'property' in a narrower sense to mean just the exclusive use of objects.[39])

Adherence to the law of nature, according to Locke, ensures that the state of nature is not a state of war. However, the natural rights of individuals are not always safeguarded in the state of nature for certain 'inconveniences' exist: not all individuals fully respect the rights of others; when it is left to each individual to enforce the law of nature there are too many judges and hence conflicts of interpretation about the meaning of the law; and when people are loosely organized they are vulnerable to aggression from abroad.[40] The central 'inconvenience' suffered can be summarized as the inadequate regulation of property in its broad sense, the right to 'life, liberty and estate'.[41] Property is prior to both society and the state; and the difficulty of its regulation is the critical reason which compels 'equally free men' to the establishment of both. Thus the remedy for the inconvenience of the state of nature is an agreement or contract to create, first, an independent society and, second, a political society or government.[42] The distinction between these two agreements is important, for it makes clear that authority is bestowed by individuals in society on government for the purpose of pursuing the ends of the governed; and should these ends fail to be adequately represented, the final judges are the people – the citizens of the state – who can dispense both with their deputies and, if need be, with the existing form of government itself.

In Locke's opinion, it should be stressed, the formation of the state does not signal the transfer of all subjects' rights to the state.[43] The rights of law making and enforcement (legislative and executive rights) are transferred, but the whole process is conditional upon the state adhering to its essential purpose: the preservation of 'life, liberty and estate'. Sovereign power, i.e. sovereignty, remains ultimately with the people. The legislative body enacts rules as the people's agent in accordance with the law of nature, and the executive power (to which Locke also tied the judiciary) enforces the legal system. This separation of powers was important because:

> It may be too great a temptation to humane frailty apt to grasp at Power, for the same Persons who have the Power of making Laws, to have also in their hands the power to execute them, whereby they may exempt themselves from Obedience to the Laws they make, and suit the Law, both in its making and execution, to their own private advantage, and thereby come to have a distinct interest from the rest of the community, contrary to the end of Society and Government.[44]

Thus, an absolutist state and the arbitrary use of authority are inconsistent with the integrity and ultimate ends of society. Locke believed in the desirability of a constitutional monarchy holding executive power and a parliamentary assembly holding the rights of legislation, although he did not think this was the only form government might take and his views are compatible with a variety of other conceptions of political institutions. Moreover, it is not always clear who was qualified to vote for the assembly: it sometimes appears simply as if 'the people' (minus women and slaves of both sexes!) are entitled, but it is almost certain that Locke would not have dissented from a franchise based strictly on property holding.[45]

The government rules, and its legitimacy is sustained, by the 'consent' of individuals. 'Consent' is a crucial and difficult notion in Locke's writings. It could be interpreted to suggest that only the continually active personal agreement of individuals would be sufficient to ensure a duty of obedience, i.e. to ensure a government's authority and legitimacy.[46] However, as one critic aptly put it, 'Locke took much of the sting (and interest) out of this view by his doctrine of "tacit consent", according to which individuals may be said to have consented to a government in any society subsequent to the supposed contract simply by owning property, or by "lodging only for a week", by "travelling freely on the highway" and indeed even by being "within the territories of that government".'[47] Locke seems to have thought of the active consent of individuals as having been crucial only to the initial inauguration of a legitimate state. Thereafter consent follows from majority decisions of 'the people's' representatives and from the fact of adherence or acquiescence to the legal system; for what property now is, and what protection and security people can enjoy, is specified by law.[48] The government, by virtue of the original contract and its covenants, is bound by the law of nature and, thus, bound to guarantee 'life, liberty and estate'. The price of this is a duty to obey the law, an obligation to the state, unless the law of nature is consistently violated by a series of tyrannical political actions. Should such a situation occur, rebellion to form a new government, Locke contended, might not only be unavoidable but just.

One commentator has summarized Locke's views well:

> God, the Creator, determined the ends of man, his creature . . . God gave men reason to understand their situation on earth and, above all, their duty within this situation. He gave them senses as channels through which they could apprehend this situation. Government and social order were contrivances devised for them through their own reason and sense experience to improve this situation. It was a *subordinate practical convenience*, not a focus of value in itself.[49]

The duties of the state are the maintenance of law and order at home and protection against aggression from abroad. In Locke's famous words: 'Wherever Law ends Tyranny begins'. Free from tyranny, people would enjoy the maximum scope to pursue their own privately-initiated interests. The state should be the regulator and protector of society: individuals are best able by their own efforts to satisfy their needs and develop their capacities in a process of free exchange with others.

Political activity for Locke is instrumental; it secures the framework or conditions for freedom so that the private ends of individuals might be met in civil society. The creation of a political community or government is the burden individuals have to bear to secure their ends. Thus, membership of a political community, i.e. citizenship, bestows upon the individual both responsibilities and rights, duties and powers, constraints and liberties. [50] In relation to Hobbes's ideas this was a most significant and radical view. For it helped inaugurate one of the most central tenets of European liberalism; that is, that the state exists to safeguard the rights and liberties of citizens who are ultimately the best judges of their own interests; and that accordingly the state must be restricted in scope and constrained in practice in order to ensure the maximum possible freedom of every citizen. In most respects it was Locke's rather than Hobbes's views which helped to lay the foundation for the development of liberalism and prepared the way for the tradition of popular representative government. Compared to Hobbes, Locke's influence on the world of practical politics has been considerable.

Locke's writings seem to point in a number of directions at once. They suggest the importance of securing the rights of individuals, popular sovereignty, majority rule, a division of powers within the state, constitutional monarchy and a representative system of parliamentary government – a direct anticipation of key aspects of British government as it developed in the nineteenth and early twentieth centuries, and of central tenets of the modern representative state. But, at best, most of these ideas are only in rudimentary form and it is certain that Locke did not foresee many of the vital components of democratic representative government, for instance, competitive parties, party rule, and the maintenance of political liberties irrespective of class, sex, colour and creed. [51] It is not a condition of legitimate government or government by consent, on Locke's account, that there be regular periodic elections of a legislative assembly, let alone universal suffrage. [52] Moreover, he did not develop a detailed account of what the limits might be to state interference in people's lives and under what conditions civil disobedience is justified. He thought that political power was held 'on trust' by and for the people, but failed to specify adequately who were to count as 'the people' and under what conditions 'trust' should be bestowed. He certainly never imagined that such power might be exercised directly by the citizens themselves, i.e. in some form of direct or self-government. While Locke was unquestionably one of the first great champions of liberalism he cannot, in the end, be considered a democrat (even if we restrict the meaning of this term to support for a universal franchise), although his works clearly stimulated the development of both liberal and democratic government, what we may call 'liberal democracy'.[53]

Power, accountability and liberal democracy

If Hobbes and Locke saw the state as a regulator and protector, it was above all because of fears about the problems and dangers individuals faced if left to their own devices. People could not live adequately without a guiding force, although Locke added that the guiding force – the trustee of the people – could not be fully trusted either: there must be limits upon legally sanctioned political power. This latter argument was taken significantly further by two of the very first advocates of liberal democracy: Jeremy Benthem (1748–1832) and James Mill (1773–1836) who, for my purposes here, can be treated together. For these two thinkers, liberal democracy was associated with a political apparatus that would ensure the accountability of the governors to the governed. Only through democratic government would there be a satisfactory means for choosing, authorizing and controlling political decisions commensurate with the public interest, i.e. the interests of the mass of individuals. As Bentham wrote: 'A democracy . . . has for its characteristic object and effect . . . securing its members against oppression and depredation at the hands of those functionaries which it employs for its defence'. . .'.[54] Democratic government is required to protect citizens from despotic use of political power whether it be by a monarch, the aristocracy or other groups. Bentham's and Mill's argument has been usefully referred to as the 'protective case for democracy'.[55] Only through the vote, secret ballot, competition between potential political leaders (representatives), elections, separation of powers and the liberty of the press, speech and public association could 'the interest of the community in general' be sustained.[56]

Bentham and Mill were impressed by the progress and methods of the natural sciences and were decidedly secular in their orientations. They thought of the concepts of social contract, natural rights and natural law as misleading philosophical fictions which failed to explain the real basis of the citizen's commitment and duty to the state. This basis could be uncovered by grasping the primitive and irreducible elements of actual human behaviour. The key to their understanding of human beings, and of the system of governance most suited to them, lies in the thesis that humans act to satisfy desire and avoid pain. In brief their argument is as follows: the overriding motivation of human beings is to fulfil their desires, maximize their satisfactions or utilities, and minimize their suffering; society consists of individuals seeking as much utility as they can get from whatever it is they want; individuals' interests conflict with one another for 'a grand governing law of human nature', as Hobbes thought, is to subordinate 'the persons and properties of human beings to our pleasures'.[57] Since those who govern will naturally act in the same way as the governed, government must, to avoid abuse, be directly accountable to an electorate called upon frequently to decide if their objectives have been met.

What, then, should be the government's objectives? Government must act according to the principle of utility: it must aim to ensure, by means of careful calculation, the achievement of the greatest happiness for the greatest number – the only scientifically defensible criterion, Bentham and Mill contended, of the public good. It has four subsidiary goals: 'to provide subsistence; to produce abundance; to favour equality; to maintain security'.[58] Of these four the last is by far the most critical; for without security of life and property there would be no incentive for individuals to work and generate wealth: labour would be insufficiently productive and commerce could not prosper. If the state pursues this goal (along with the others to the extent that they are compatible), it will therefore be in the citizen's self-interest to obey it.

Bentham, Mill and the Utilitarians generally provided one of the clearest justifications for the liberal democratic state which ensures the conditions necessary for individuals to pursue their interests without risk of arbitrary political interference, to participate freely in economic transactions, to exchange labour and goods on the market and to appropriate resources privately. These ideas became the basis of classical nineteenth-century 'English liberalism': the state was to have the role of the umpire or referee while individuals pursued, according to the rules of economic competition and free exchange, their own interests. Periodic elections, the abolition of the powers of the monarchy, the division of powers within the state plus the free market would lead to the maximum benefit for all citizens. The free vote and the free market were *sine qua non*. For a key presupposition was that the collective good could be properly realized in many domains of life only if individuals interacted in competitive exchanges, pursuing their utility with minimal state interference. Significantly, however, this argument had another side. Tied to the advocacy of a 'minimal' state whose scope and power was to be strictly limited, there was a strong commitment in fact to certain types of state intervention, for instance, the curtailment of the behaviour of the disobedient, whether they be individuals, groups or classes.[59]

Those who challenge the security of property or the market society undermine the realization of the public good. In the name of the public good, the utilitarians advocated a new system of administrative power for 'person management'.[60] Prisons were a mark of this new age. Moreover, whenever *laissez-faire* was inadequate to ensure the best possible outcomes, state intervention was justified to re-order social relations and institutions. The enactment and enforcement of law, backed by the coercive powers of the state, and the creation of new state institutions was legitimate to the extent that it upheld the general principle of utility.

Bentham and Mill were reluctant democrats. In considering the extent of the franchise they found grounds for excluding, among others, the whole of the labouring classes and female population, despite the fact that many of their arguments seemed to point squarely in the direction of universal suffrage. Their ideas have been aptly referred to as 'the founding model of democracy for a modern industrial society'.[61] Their account of democracy establishes it as nothing but a logical requirement for the governance of a society, freed from absolute power and tradition, in which individuals have endless desires, form a body of mass consumers and are dedicated to the maximization of private gain. Democracy, accordingly, becomes a means for the enhancement of these ends – not an end in itself, for perhaps the cultivation and development of all citizens. As such it is at best a partial form of democratic theory.[62]

The 'highest and harmonious' development of individual capacities was, however, a central concern of James Mill's son, John Stuart Mill (1806–73).[63] If Bentham and James Mill were reluctant democrats but prepared to develop arguments to justify democratic institutions, John Stuart Mill was a clear advocate of democracy, preoccupied with the extent of individual liberty in all spheres of human endeavour. Liberal democratic or representative government was important for him, not just because it established boundaries for the pursuit of individual satisfaction, but because it was a key aspect of the free development of individuality: participation in political life (voting, involvement in local administration and jury service) was vital to create a direct interest in government and, consequently, a basis for an involved, informed and developing citizenry. Mill conceived of democratic politics as a prime mechanism of moral self-development.[64] He likened periodic voting to the passing of a 'verdict by a juryman' – ideally the considered outcome of a process of active deliberation about the facts of public affairs, not a mere expression of personal interest.

John Stuart Mill's absorption with the question of the autonomy of individuals and minorities is brought out most clearly in his famous and influential study, *On Liberty* (1859). The aim of this work is to elaborate and defend a principle which will establish 'the nature and limits of the power which can be legitimately exercised by society over the individual'.[65] Mill recognized that some regulation and interference in individuals' lives is necessary but sought an obstacle to arbitrary and self-interested intervention. He put the crucial point thus:

> The object . . . is to assert one very simple principle, as entitled to govern absolutely the dealings of society with the individual in the way of compulsion and control, whether the means used be physical force in the form of legal penalties or the moral coercion of public opinion. That principle is that the sole end for which mankind are warranted, individually or collectively, in interfering with the liberty of action of any of their number is self-protection. That the only purpose for which power can be rightfully exercised over any member of a civilised community, against his will, is to prevent harm to others.[66]

Social or political interference with individual liberty may be justified only when an act (or a failure to act), whether it be intended or not, 'concerns others' and then only when it 'harms' others. The sole end of interference with liberty should be self-protection. In those activities which are merely 'self-regarding', i.e., only of concern to the individual, 'independence is, of right, absolute'; for 'over himself, over his own body and mind, the individual is sovereign'.[67]

Mill's principle is, in fact, anything but 'very simple': its meaning and implications remain controversial.[68] For instance, what exactly constitutes 'harm to others'? Does the publication of pornography cause harm? But leaving aside difficulties such as these, it should be noted that in his hands the principle generated a defence of many of the key liberties associated with liberal democratic government. The 'appropriate region of human liberty' became: first, liberty of thought, feeling, discussion and publication; second, liberty of tastes and pursuits ('framing the plan of our life to suit our own character'); and third, liberty of association or combination assuming, of course, it causes no harm to others.[69] The 'only freedom which deserves the name is that of pursuing our own good in our own way, so long as we do not attempt to deprive others of theirs or impede their efforts to obtain it'.[70] Mill contended, moreover, that the current practice of both rulers and citizens was generally opposed to his doctrine and unless a 'strong barrier of moral conviction' can be established against such bad habits, growing infringements on the liberty of citizens can be expected as the centralized bureaucratic state expands to cope with the problems of the modern age. [71]

Liberty and democracy create, according to Mill, the possibility of 'human excellence'. Liberty of thought, discussion and action are necessary conditions for the development of independence of mind and autonomous judgment; they are vital for the formation of human reason or rationality. In turn, the cultivation of reason stimulates and sustains liberty. Representative government is essential for the protection and enhancement of both liberty and reason. Without it arbitrary laws might, for instance, be created which enhance the likelihood of tyranny. Representative democracy is the most suitable mode of government for the enactment of laws consistent with the principle of liberty, as the free exchange of goods in the market place is the most appropriate way of maximizing economic liberty and economic good. [72] A system of representative democracy makes government accountable to the citizenry and creates wiser citizens capable of pursuing the public interest. It is thus both a means to develop self-identity, individuality and social difference – a pluralistic society – and an end in itself, an essential democratic order.

Given that individuals are capable of different kinds of things and only a few have developed their full capacities, would it not be appropriate if some citizens have more sway over government than others? Regrettably for the cogency of Mill's argument he thought as much and recommended a plural system of voting; all adults should have a vote but the wiser and more talented should have more votes than the ignorant and less able. Mill took occupational status as a rough guide to the allocation of votes and adjusted his conception of democracy accordingly: those with the most knowledge and skill – who happened to have most property and privilege – could not be outvoted by those with less, i.e. the working classes. [73] Mill was extremely critical of vast inequalities of income, wealth and power; he recognized that they prevented the full development of most members of the labouring classes and yet he stopped short – far short – of a commitment to political and social equality. The idea that all citizens should have equal weight in the political system remained outside his actual doctrine. Moreover, since he ultimately trusted so little in the judgment of the electorate and the elected, he defended the notion that Parliament should have only a right of veto on legislation proposed and drawn up by a non-elected commission of experts.

It was left by and large to the extensive and often violently repressed struggles of working-class and feminist activists in the nineteenth and twentieth centuries to achieve in some countries genuinely universal suffrage. This achievement was to remain fragile in countries such as Germany, Italy, Spain and was in practice denied to some groups, for instance, many Blacks in the United States before the civil rights movement in the 1950s and 1960s. Through these struggles the idea that 'citizenship rights' should apply to all adults became slowly established;[74] many of the arguments of the liberal democrats could be turned against the *status quo* to reveal the extent to which the principle and aspirations of equal political participation and equal human development remained unfilfilled. It was only with the actual achievement of full citizenship that liberal democracy took on its distinctively modern form:

> a cluster of rules . . . permitting the broadest . . . participation of the majority of citizens in political decisions, i.e. in decisions affecting the whole collectively. The rules are more or less the following: (a) all citizens who have reached legal age, without regard to race, religion, economic status, sex etc. must enjoy political rights, i.e. the right to express their own opinion through their vote and/or to elect those who express it for them; (b) the vote of all citizens must have equal weight; (c) all citizens enjoying political rights must be free to vote according to their own opinion, formed as freely as possible, i.e. in a free contest between organized political groups competing among themselves so as to aggregate demands and transform them into collective deliberations; (d) they must also be free in the sense that they must be in a position of having real alternatives, i.e. of choosing between different solutions; (e) whether for collective deliberations or for the election of representatives, the principle of numerical majority holds – even though different forms of majority rule can be established (relative, absolute, qualified), under certain circumstances established in advance; (f) no decision taken by a majority must limit minority rights, especially the right to become eventually, under normal conditions, a majority.[75]

The idea of democracy remains complex and contested. The development towards the notion of the liberal democratic state in the works of Hobbes, Locke, Bentham and the two Mills comprises a most heterogeneous body of thought. Its enormous influence, especially in the Anglo-American world, has spawned seemingly endless debates and conflicts.[76] However, the whole liberal democratic tradition stands apart from an alternative perspective: the theory of what can be called 'direct' or 'participatory' democracy which had one of its earliest exponents in Rousseau (1712–78). It is worth saying something briefly about Rousseau, not only because of the importance of his thought, but because he had, according to some writers at least, a direct influence on the development of the key counterpoint to liberal democracy – the Marxist tradition.[77]

The idea that the consent of individuals legitimates government and the state system more generally was central to both seventeenth- and eighteenth-century liberals as well as to nineteenth- and twentieth-century liberal democrats. The former regarded the social contract as the original mechanism of individual consent, while the latter focused on the ballot box as the mechanism whereby the citizen periodically conferred authority on government to enact laws and regulate economic and social life. Rousseau was dissatisfied, for reasons I can only briefly allude to, with arguments of both these types. Like Hobbes and Locke, he was concerned with the question whether there is a legitimate and secure principle of government.[78] Like Hobbes and Locke, he offered an account of a state of nature and the social contract. In his classic *Social Contract* (published in 1762), he assumed that although humans were happy in the original state of nature, they were driven from it by a variety of obstacles to their preservation (individual weaknesses, common miseries, natural disasters).[79] Human beings came to realize that the development of their nature, the realization of their capacity for reason, the fullest experience of liberty, could be achieved only by a social contract which established a system of cooperation through a law-making and enforcing body. Thus there is a contract, but it is a contract which creates the possibility of *self*-regulation or *self*-government. In Hobbes's and Locke's versions of the social contract, sovereignty is transferred from the people to the state and its ruler(s) (although for Locke the surrender of the rights of self-government was a conditional affair). By contrast Rousseau was original, as one commentator aptly put it, 'in holding that no such transfer of sovereignty need or should take place: sovereignty not only originates in the people; it ought to stay there'.[80] Accordingly, not only did Rousseau find the political doctrines offered by Hobbes and Locke unacceptable, but those of the type put forward by the liberal democrats as well. In a justly famous passage he wrote:

> Sovereignty cannot be represented, for the same reason that it cannot be alienated . . . the people's deputies are not, and could not be, its representatives; they are merely its agents; and they cannot decide anything finally. Any law which the people has not ratified in person is void; it is not law at all. The English people believes itself to be free; it is gravely mistaken; it is free only during the election of Members of Parliament; as soon as the Members are elected, the people is enslaved; it is nothing.[81]

Rousseau saw individuals as ideally involved in the direct creation of the laws by which their lives are regulated. The sovereign authority is the people making the rules by which they live. Like John Stuart

Mill after him, Rousseau celebrated the notion of an active, involved citizenry in a developing process of government, but he interpreted this in a more radical manner: all citizens should meet together to decide what is best for the community and enact the appropriate laws. The governed, in essence, should be the governors. In Rousseau's account, the idea of self-government is posited as an end in itself; a political order offering opportunities for participation in the arrangement of public affairs should not just be a state, but rather the formation of a type of society – a society in which the affairs of the state are integrated into the affairs of ordinary citizens. [82]

The role of the citizen is the highest to which an individual can aspire. The considered exercise of power by citizens is the only legitimate way in which liberty can be sustained. The citizen must both create and be bound by 'the supreme direction of the general will' – the publicly generated conception of the common good. [83] The people are sovereign only to the extent that they participate actively in articulating the 'general will'. It is important to distinguish the latter from the 'will of all': it is the difference between the sum of judgments about the common good and the mere aggregate of personal fancies and individual desires. [84] Citizens are only obligated to a system of laws and regulations on the grounds of publicly reached agreement, for they can only be genuinely obligated to a law they have prescribed for themselves with the general good in mind. [85] Hence, Rousseau draws a critical distinction between independence and liberty:

> Many have been the attempts to confound independence and liberty: two things so essentially different, that they reciprocally exclude each other. When every one does what he pleases, he will, of course, often do things displeasing to others; and this is not properly called a free state. Liberty consists less in acting according to one's own pleasure, than in not being subject to the will and pleasure of other people. It consists also in our not subjecting the wills of other people to our own. Whoever is the master over others is not himself free, and even to reign is to obey. [86]

Liberty and equality are inextricably linked. For the social contract 'establishes equality among the citizens in that they . . . must all enjoy the same rights'. [87]

Rousseau argued in favour of a political system in which the legislative and executive functions are clearly demarcated. The former belong to the people and the latter to a 'government' or 'prince'. The people form the legislative assembly and constitute the authority of the state; the 'government' or 'prince' (composed of one or more administrators or magistrates) executes the people's laws. [88]

Such a 'government' is necessary on the grounds of expediency: the people require a government to coordinate public meetings, serve as a means of communication, draft laws and enforce the legal system.[89] The government is a result of an agreement among the citizenry and is legitimate only to the extent to which it fulfils 'the instructions of the general will'. Should it fail to so behave it can be revoked and changed.[90]

Rousseau's work had a significant (though ambiguous) influence on the ideas in currency during the French Revolution as well as on traditions of revolutionary thought, from Marxism to anarchism. His conception of self-government has been among the most provocative, challenging at its core some of the critical assumptions of liberal democracy, especially the notion that democracy is the name for a particular kind of state which can only be held accountable to the citizenry once in a while. But Rousseau's ideas do not represent a completely coherent system or recipe for straightforward action. He appreciated some of the problems created by large-scale, complex, densely populated societies, but did not pursue these as far as one must.[91] He too excluded all women from 'the people', i.e. the citizenry, as well as, it seems, the poor. The latter appear to be outcasts because citizenship is made conditional upon a small property qualification (land) and/or upon the absence of dependency on others.[92] Rousseau's primary concern was with what might be thought of as the future of democracy in a non-industrial, agriculturally-based community. As a vision of democracy it was and remains evocative and challenging, but it was not connected to an account of political life in an industrial capitalist society. It was left to Marx, Engels and Lenin, among others, to pursue these connections.

Class, coercion and the Marxist critique

Individuals; individuals in competition with one another; freedom of choice; politics as the arena for the maintenance of individual interests, the protection of 'life, liberty and estate'; the democratic state as the institutional mechanism for the articulation of the general or public interest (as opposed to simple private desires): all these are essential preoccupations of the liberal democratic tradition. While Marx (1818–83) and Engels (1820–95) did not deny that people had unique capacities, desires and an interest in free choice, they attacked relentlessly the idea that the starting point of the analysis of the state can be the individual, and his or her relation to the state. As Marx put it, 'man is not an abstract being squatting outside the world. Man is the human world, the state, society'.[93] Individuals only exist in interaction with and in relation to others; their nature can only be grasped as a social and historical product. It is not the single, isolated individual who is active in historical and political processes, but rather human beings who live in definite relations with others and whose nature is defined through these relations. An individual, or a social activity, or an institution (in fact, any aspect of human life) can only be properly explained in terms of its historically evolving interaction with other social phenomena – a dynamic and changing process of inextricably related elements.

The key to understanding the relations between people is, according to Marx and Engels, class structure.[94] Class divisions are not, they maintain, found in all forms of society: classes are a creation of history, and in the future will disappear. The earliest types of 'tribal' society were classless. This is because, in such types of society, there was no surplus production and no private property; production was based upon communal resources and the fruits of productive activity were distributed through the community as a whole. Class divisions arise only when a surplus is generated, such that it becomes possible for a class of non-producers to live off the productive activity of others. Those who are able to gain control of the means of production form a dominant or ruling class both economically and politically. Class relations for Marx and Engels are thus necessarily exploitative and imply divisions of interest between ruling and subordinate classes. Class divisions are, furthermore, inherently conflictual and frequently give rise to active class struggle. Such struggles form the chief mechanism or 'motor' of historical development.

With the break-up of feudalism and the expansion of market economies, the class system of modern Western capitalist societies became slowly established. The class divisions of these societies are based, above all, Marx and Engels argued, upon one dominant exploitative relationship: that between those with capital and those who only have their labouring capacity to sell. 'Capitalists' own factories and technology while wage-labourers, or 'wage-workers', are propertyless. As capitalism matures, the vast majority of the population become wage-workers, who have to sell their labour-power on the market to secure a living. Societies are capitalist to the extent that they can be characterized as dominated by a mode of production which extracts surplus from wage-workers in the form of 'surplus value' – the value generated by workers in the productive process over and above their wages, and appropriated by the owners of capital.[95] This relationship between capital and wage-labour designates, in Marx's and Engel's account, the essential social and political structure of the modern epoch.

How then can the nature of the state be understood? What is the role of the state in the context of a class society? Central to the liberal and liberal democratic traditions is the idea that the state can claim to represent the community or public interest, in contrast to individuals' private aims and concerns. But, according to Marx and Engels, the opposition between interests that are public and general, and those that are private and particular is, to a large extent, illusory.[96] The state defends the 'public' or the 'community' as if: classes did not exist; the relationship between classes was not exploitative; classes did not have fundamental differences of interest; these differences of interest did not define economic and political life. In treating everyone in the same way, according to principles which protect the freedom of individuals and defend their right to property, the state may act 'neutrally' while generating effects which are partial – sustaining the privileges of those with property. Moreover, the very claim that there is a clear distinction between the private and the public, the world of civil society and the political, is dubious. The key source of contemporary power – private ownership of the means of production – is ostensibly *depoliticized*, that is, treated as if it were not a proper subject of politics. The economy is regarded as non-political, in that the massive division between those who own and control the means of production, and those who must live by wage-labour, is regarded as the outcome of free private contracts, not a matter for the state. But by defending private property the state already has taken a side. The state, then, is not an independent structure or set of institutions above society, i.e. a 'public power' acting for 'the public'. On the contrary, it is deeply embedded in socio-economic relations and linked to particular interests.

There are at least two strands in Marx's account of the relation between classes and the state; while they are by no means explicitly distinguished by Marx himself, it is illuminating to disentangle them.[97] The first, henceforth referred to as position (1), stresses that the state generally, and bureaucratic institutions in particular, may take a variety of forms and constitute a source of power which need not be directly linked to the interests, or be under the unambiguous control of, the dominant class in the short term. By this account, the state retains a degree of power independent of this class: its institutional forms and operational dynamics cannot be inferred directly from the configuration of class forces – they are 'relatively autonomous'. The second strand, position (2), is without doubt the dominant one in his writings: the state and its bureaucracy are class instruments which emerged to coordinate a divided society in the interests of the ruling class. Position (1) is certainly a more complex and subtle vision. Both positions are elaborated below. I shall begin with position (1) for it is expressed most clearly in Marx's early writings and highlights the degree to which the second view involves a narrowing down of the terms of reference of Marx's analysis of the state.

Marx's engagement with the theoretical problems posed by state power developed from an early confrontation with Hegel (1770–1831), a central figure in German idealist philosophy and a crucial intellectual influence on his life. In the *Philosophy of Right*, Hegel portrayed the Prussian state as divided into three substantive divisions – the legislature, the executive and the crown – which together express 'universal insight and will'.[98] For him, the most important institution of the state is the bureaucracy, an organization in which particular interests are subordinated to a system of hierarchy, specialization, expertise and coordination on the one hand, and internal and external pressures for competence and impartiality on the other. According to Marx, in the *Critique of Hegel's Philosophy of Right*, Hegel failed to challenge the self-image of the state and, in particular, of the bureaucracy.[99]

The bureaucracy is the 'state's consciousness'. Marx describes the bureaucracy, by which he means the corps of state officials, as 'a particular closed society within the state', which extends its power or capacity through secrecy and mystery.[100] The individual bureaucrat is initiated into this closed society through 'a bureaucratic confession of faith' – the examination system – and the caprice of the politically dominant group. Subsequently the bureaucrat's career becomes everything, passive obedience to those in higher authority becomes a necessity and 'the state's interest becomes a particular private aim'. But the state's aims are not thereby achieved, nor is competence guaranteed.[101] For, as Marx wrote,

> The bureaucracy asserts itself to be the final end of the state . . . The aims of the state are transformed into aims of bureaus, or the aims of bureaus into the aims of the state. The bureaucracy is a circle from which no one can escape. Its hierarchy is a hierarchy of knowledge. The highest point entrusts the understanding of the particulars to the lower echelons, whereas these, on the other hand, credit the highest with an understanding in regard to the universal [the general interest]; and thus they deceive one another.[102]

Marx's critique of Hegel involves several points, but one in particular is crucial: in the sphere of what Hegel referred to as 'the absolutely universal interest of the state proper' there is, in Marx's view, nothing but 'bureaucratic officialdom' and 'unresolved conflict'.[103] Marx's emphasis on the structure and corporate nature of bureaucracies is significant because it throws into relief the 'relative autonomy' of these organizations and foreshadows the arguments elaborated in what may be his most interesting work on the state, *The Eighteenth Brumaire of Louis Bonaparte*.

The Eighteenth Brumaire is an eloquent analysis of the rise to power between 1848 and 1852 of Louis Napoleon Bonaparte and of the way power accumulated in the hands of the executive at the expense of, in the first instance, both civil society and the political representatives of the capitalist class, the bourgeoisie. The study highlights Marx's distance from any view of the state as an 'instrument of universal insight' or 'ethical community' for he emphasized that the state apparatus is simultaneously a 'parasitic body' on civil society and an autonomous source of political action. Thus, in describing Bonaparte's regime, he wrote:

> This executive power, with its enormous bureaucratic and military organization, with its ingenious state machinery, embracing wide strata, with a host of officials numbering half a million, beside an army of another half million, this appalling parasitic body . . . enmeshes the body of French society like a net and chokes all its pores.[104]

The state is portrayed as an immense set of institutions, with the capacity to shape civil society and even to curtail the bourgeoisie's capacity to control the state.[105] Marx granted the state a certain autonomy from society: political outcomes are the result of the interlock between complex coalitions and constitutional arrangements.

The analysis offered in *The Eighteenth Brumaire*, like that in the *Critique*, suggests that the agents of the state do not simply coordinate political life in the interests of the dominant class of civil society. The executive, under particular circumstances – for example, when there is a relative balance of social forces – has the capacity to promote change as well as to coordinate it. But Marx's focus, even when discussing this idea, was essentially on the state as a conservative force. He emphasized the importance of its information network as a mechanism for surveillance, and the way in which the state's political autonomy is interlocked with its capacity to undermine social movements threatening to the *status quo*. Moreover, the repressive dimension of the state is complemented by its capacity to sustain belief in the inviolability of existing arrangements. Far then from being the basis for the articulation of the general interest, the state, Marx argued, transforms 'universal aims into another form of private interest'.

There were ultimate constraints on the initiatives Bonaparte could take, however, without throwing society into a major crisis, as there are on any legislative or executive branch of the state. For the state in a capitalist society, Marx concluded from his study of the Bonapartist regime, cannot escape its dependence upon that society and, above all, upon those who own and control the productive process. Its dependence is revealed whenever the economy is beset by crises; for economic organizations of all kinds create the material resources on which the state apparatus survives. The state's overall policies have to be compatible in the long run with the objectives of manufacturers and traders, otherwise civil society and the stability of the state itself are jeopardized. Hence, though Bonaparte usurped the political power of the bourgeoisie's representatives, he protected the 'material power' of the bourgeoisie itself − a vital source of loans and revenue. Accordingly, Bonaparte could not help but sustain the long-term economic interests of the bourgeoisie and lay the foundation for the regeneration of its direct political power in the future, whatever else he chose to do while in office. [106]

Marx attacked the claim that the distribution of property lies outside the constitution of political power. This attack is, of course, a central aspect of Marx's legacy and of what I am calling position (2). Throughout his political essays and especially in his more polemical pamphlets such as the *Communist Manifesto*, Marx (and indeed Engels) insisted on the direct dependence of the state on the economic, social and political power of the dominant class. The state is a 'superstructure' which develops on the 'foundation' of economic and social relations. [107] The state, in this formulation, serves directly the interest of the economically dominant class: the notion of the state as a site of autonomous political action is supplanted by an emphasis upon class power, an emphasis illustrated by the famous slogan of the *Communist Manifesto*: 'The executive of the modern state is but a committee for managing the common affairs of the whole bourgeoisie'. This formula does not imply that the state is dominated by the bourgeoisie as a whole: it may be independent of sections of the bourgeois class. [108] The state, nevertheless, is characterized as essentially dependent upon society and upon those who dominate the economy: 'independence' is exercised only to the extent that conflicts must be settled between different sections of capital (industrialists and financiers, for example), and between 'domestic capitalism' and pressures generated by international capitalist markets. The state maintains the overall interests of the bourgeoisie in the name of the public or general interest.

There are, then, two (often interconnected) strands in Marx's account of the relation between classes and the state: the first conceives the state with a degree of power independent of class forces; the second upholds the view that the state is merely a 'superstructure' serving the interests of the dominant class. On the basis of position (1) it is possible to think of the state as a potential arena of struggle which can become a key force for socialist change. The social democratic tradition, as developed by people like Eduard Bernstein (1850–1932), elaborated this notion: through the ballot box the heights of state power could be scaled and used against the most privileged, while one by one institutions of the state could be progressively turned against the interests of capital.[109] In contradistinction, revolutionary socialist traditions developed from position (2). Following Marx's analysis, Lenin insisted that the eradication of capitalist relations of production must be accompanied by the destruction of the capitalist state apparatus: the state, as a class instrument, had to be destroyed and direct democracy – as imagined in part by Rousseau – installed.[110]

Position (1) has been emphasized above because it is generally downplayed in the secondary literature on Marx.[111] Marx's work on the state remained incomplete. Position (1) left several important questions insufficiently explored. What is the basis of state power? How do state bureaucracies function? What precise interest do political officials develop? Position (2) is even more problematic: it postulates a capitalist-specific (or, as it has been called more recently, 'capital logic') organization of the state and takes for granted a simple causal relation between the facts of class domination and the vicissitudes of political life. But Marx's combined writings do indicate that he regards the state as central to the integration and control of class divided societies. Furthermore, his work suggests important limits to state intervention within capitalist societies. If intervention undermines the process of capital accumulation, it simultaneously undermines the material basis of the state; hence, state policies must be consistent with capitalist relations of production. Accordingly, a dominant economic class can rule without directly governing, that is, it can exert determinate political influence without even having representatives in government. This idea retains a vital place in contemporary debates among Marxists, liberal democratic theorists and others.

On the whole, Lenin (1870–1924) followed the tenets of Marx's position (2). His views are stated succinctly in *State and Revolution*

(1917), where he listed his first task as the 'resuscitation of the real teaching of Marx on the state'.[112] Lenin conceived of the state as a 'machine for the oppression of one class by another'. The modern representative state was 'the instrument for the exploitation of wage-labour by capital' – 'a special repressive force'.[113] Thus, the distinguishing feature of the state, apart from its grouping of people on a territorial basis, is its dependence on force, exercised through specialized bodies such as the army, police and prison service. Many of the routine activities of the state, from taxation to legislation concerned with the protection of officials, exist essentially to ensure the survival of these repressive institutions.

The ruling classes maintain their grip on the state through alliances with government – alliances created both by government dependence on the stock exchange and by the corruption of ministers and officials. The vital business of the state takes place, not in representative assemblies, but in the state bureaucracies, where alliances can be established out of public view. Further, even democratic rights such as freedom of association, freedom of the press, or freedom of assembly, are a major benefit to the dominant classes. They can claim these institutions are 'open' while controlling them 'through ownership of the media, control over meeting places, money, and other resources'.[114]

Although *State and Revolution* reiterates what I have called Marx's position (2), Lenin made more than Marx did of one central point: the crystallization of class power within the organs of state administration. For the Lenin of *State and Revolution*, 'so long as the state exists, there is no freedom. When freedom exists, there will be no state'. Strong central control would be necessary after the Revolution, but a precondition of revolutionary success is the destruction of the 'old state machine': 'The bureaucracy and the standing army, direct products of class oppression, have to be smashed. The army would be replaced by armed workers and the bureaucrats by elected officials subject to recall'.[115] There would be 'immediate introduction of control and supervision by *all*, so that *all* may become "bureaucrats" for a time and that, therefore, nobody may be able to become a "bureaucrat"'. Officials and soldiers would be necessary but they would not become 'privileged persons divorced from the people and standing *above* the people'. Lenin never doubted that discipline was essential in political organizations, but he argued that this does not entail the creation of an elite of functionaries.[116] Following the lessons which Marx and Engels drew from the Paris Commune – lessons interpreted to some degree in the spirit of Rousseau's vision of direct democracy – Lenin maintained that the new socialist order must and could replace 'the government of persons' by 'the administration of things'.[117]

The survival of bureaucracy in the early days of post-Revolutionary Russia was frequently explained by Lenin in terms of the lingering influence of capitalism and the old regime. He continually affirmed a causal relation between forms of state organization and classes, even in his famous 'last testament' where problems concerning central administration and the bureaucratization of the party and the state were sources of great anxiety.[118] This position had dire consequences: it led, in part, to the widespread belief among Bolsheviks that, with the abolition of capitalist property relations (and the expansion of forces of production), problems of organization, control and coordination could be easily resolved.

There are many tensions in Lenin's treatment of the state and political organization. He thought that the work of the new socialist order could be conducted by workers organized in a framework of direct democracy (soviets), yet he defended the authority of the party in nearly all spheres. His argument that state bureaucracies need not entail fixed positions of power and privilege is suggestive, but it remains, especially in light of the massive problems of organization faced during and after the Revolution, a very incomplete statement. Lenin failed to examine the degree to which state organizations are influenced by diverse interests, political compromises and complex circumstances which do not merely reflect 'class antagonisms which must be reconciled from above'. To this extent his views on the state do not represent an advance on Marx's position (1).

In the last 20 years there has been a massive revival of interest in the analysis of state power among contemporary Marxist writers.[119] Marx left an ambiguous heritage, never fully reconciling his understanding of the state as an instrument of class domination with his acknowledgment that the state might also have significant political independence. Lenin's emphasis on the oppressive nature of capitalist state institutions certainly did not resolve this ambiguity; and his writings seem even less compelling after Stalin's purges and the massive growth of the Soviet state itself. Since the deaths of Marx and Engels, many Marxist writers have made contributions of decisive importance to the analysis of politics (for instance, Lukács, Korsch and Gramsci explored the many complex and subtle ways dominant classes sustain power), but not until recently has the relation between state and society been fully re-examined in Marxist circles.

Ralph Miliband provided a stimulus with the publication of *The State in Capitalist Society* in 1969.[120] Noting the increasingly central position of the state in Western societies, he sought to re-assess the relationship Marx posited between class and state on the one hand, and, on the other, to evaluate the reigning liberal democratic view of state – society relations, a view which posited the state as the referee adjudicating between competing interests in society. (This latter view involved a pluralist model of society, which I shall discuss later.) Against those who held that the state is a neutral arbiter among social interests, he argued: (a) that in contemporary Western societies there is a dominant or ruling class which owns and controls the means of production; (b) that the dominant class has close links to powerful institutions, political parties, the military, universities, the media, etc; and (c) that it has disproportionate representation at all levels of the state apparatus, especially in the 'command positions'. The capitalist class, Miliband contended, is highly cohesive and constitutes a formidable constraint on Western governments and state institutions, ensuring that they remain 'instruments for the domination of society'. However, he insisted – defending what I called Marx's position (1) – that in order to be politically effective, the state must be able to separate itself routinely from ruling-class factions. Government policy may even be directed against the short-run interest of the capitalist class. He was also quick to point out that under exceptional circumstances the state can achieve a high order of independence from class interests, for example, in national crises and war.

Nicos Poulantzas challenged Miliband's views in a debate which has received much attention.[121] In so doing, he sought to clarify further Marx's position (1). He rejected what he considered Miliband's 'subjectivist' approach – his attempt to explore the relation among classes, bureaucracy and the state through 'interpersonal relations' (for Miliband, the social background of state officials and links between them and members of powerful institutions). Although Poulantzas exaggerated the differences between his position and Miliband's, his starting point was radically different. He did not ask: Who influences important decisions and determines policy? What is the social background of those who occupy key administrative positions? The 'class affiliation' of those in the state apparatus is not, according to Poulantzas, crucial to its 'concrete functioning'.[122] Much more important for Poulantzas are the structural components of the capitalist state which lead it to protect the long-term framework of capitalist production even if this means severe conflict with some segments of the capitalist class.

In order to grasp these structural components, it is essential, Poulantzas argued, to understand that the state is the unifying element in capitalism. More specifically, the state must function to ensure (a) the 'political organization' of the dominant classes which, because of competitive pressures and differences of immediate interest, are continually broken up into 'class fractions'; (b) the 'political disorganization' of the working classes which, because of the concentration of production, among other things, can threaten the hegemony of the dominant classes. [123] Since the dominant classes are vulnerable to fragmentation, their long-term interests require protection by the state. The state can sustain this function only if it is 'relatively autonomous' from the particular interests of diverse fractions. What is more, the state itself, Poulantzas stressed, is not a monolithic bloc; it is an arena of conflict and schism (the 'condensation of class forces'). [124] The degree of autonomy actual states acquire depends on the relations among classes and class fractions and on the intensity of social struggles. Relative autonomy 'devolves' on the state 'in the power relations of the class struggle'. Thus, the centralized modern state is both a necessary result of 'the anarchic competition in civil society' and a force in the reproduction of such competition and division. [125]

Poulantzas's views have by no means met with universal approval among Marxists. Foremost amongst those who reject his perspective are Claus Offe and Jürgen Habermas, who belong to a quite different 'tradition' of Marxist thought. [126] Among their criticisms is the charge that Poulantzas (and Miliband) regard capitalist states only from a 'negative' perspective; that is to say, the state is treated only from the point of view of how far it stabilizes capitalist economic enterprise, or prevents the development of potentially revolutionary influences. This results in a peculiar de-emphasis, which Offe and Habermas seek to avoid, of the capacity of the working classes to influence the course and organization of state administration. [127] Further, Poulantzas's emphasis on the state as the 'condensation of class forces' means that his account of the state is drawn without sufficient internal definition or institutional differentiation. How institutions operate and the manner in which the relationship among élites, government officials, and parliamentarians evolves, are neglected. In contrast, Offe and Habermas examine how the state sustains the institutional order in which capitalistic mechanisms occupy a prime place and how it mediates (expresses and changes) class antagonisms. Attention is focused on the way social conflicts and severe economic problems are 'displaced' onto the state, initiating an erosion of mass loyalty to the *status quo*, i.e. a legitimation crisis.

Contemporary Marxism is in a state of flux. There are now as many differences between Marxists as between liberals or liberal democrats. Moreover, the reconsideration of the classical Marxist account of the state – in part stimulated by the state's growth in

Western and Eastern Europe during recent decades – has led to a reappraisal by some Marxists of the liberal democratic tradition with its emphasis on the importance of individual liberties and rights, i.e. citizenship.[128] The significance of 'citizenship rights' as a limit to the extension of state power has been more fully appreciated. At the same time, some liberal democrats have come to understand the limitations placed on political life by, among other things, massive concentrations of economic ownership and control.[129] But exactly how one reconciles some of the most important insights of these fundamentally competing traditions of thought remains an open question.

Bureaucracy, parliaments and the nation-state

The notion that the state, and bureaucratic organization in particular, constitute 'parasitic' entities is a position Marx and many other Marxists have espoused. Max Weber (1864–1920), a founder of sociology, a champion of European liberalism and of the German nation-state, contested this view. Although he drew extensively upon Marx's writings, he did so critically and nowhere more critically perhaps than with reference to the modern state. In contrast to Marx, Engels and Lenin, Weber resisted all suggestion that forms of state organization were 'parasitic' and a direct product of the activities of classes. He stressed the similarities between private and public organizations as well as their independent dynamics. Moreover, the idea that institutions of the modern state should be 'smashed' in a revolutionary process of transformation was, according to him, at best a foolhardy view.

Centralized administration may be inescapable. Weber's consideration of this issue makes his work especially important. He dismissed the feasibility of direct democracy,

> . . . where the group grows beyond a certain size or where the administrative function becomes too difficult to be satisfactorily taken care of by anyone whom rotation, the lot, or election may happen to designate. The conditions of administration of mass structures are radically different from those obtaining in small associations resting upon neighborly or personal relationships . . . The growing complexity of the administrative task and the sheer expansion of their scope increasingly result in the technical superiority of those who have had training and experience, and will thus inevitably favor the continuity of at least some of the functionaries. Hence, there always exists the probability of the rise of a special, perennial structure for administrative purposes, which of necessity means for the exercise of rule.[130]

The question of the class nature of the state is, Weber maintained, distinct from the question of whether a centralized bureaucratic administration is a necessary feature of political and social organization. It is simply misleading to conflate problems concerning the nature of administration in itself with problems concerning the control of the state apparatus. [131] In Weber's opinion, Lenin's commitment to the 'smashing' of the state was based on his failure to see these as two distinct issues.

Weber developed one of the most significant definitions of the modern state, placing emphasis upon two distinctive elements of its history: territoriality and violence. The modern state, unlike its predecessors which were troubled by constantly warring factions, has a capability of monopolizing the legitimate use of violence within a given territory; it is a nation-state in embattled relations with other nation-states rather than with armed segments of its own population. 'Of course,' Weber emphasized,

> . . . force is certainly not the normal or only means of the state – nobody says that – but force is a means specific to the state . . . the state is a relation of men dominating men [and generally – one should add – men dominating women], a relation supported by means of legitimate (i.e. considered to be legitimate) violence. [132]

The state maintains compliance or order within a given territory; in individual capitalist societies this involves crucially the defence of the order of property and the enhancement of domestic economic interests overseas, although by no means all the problems of order can be reduced to these. The state's web of agencies and institutions finds its ultimate sanction in the claim to the monopoly of coercion, and a political order is only, in the last instance, vulnerable to crises when this monopoly erodes.

However, there is a third key term in Weber's definition of the state: legitimacy. The state is based on a monopoly of physical coercion which is legitimized (that is, sustained) by a belief in the justifiability and/or legality of this monopoly. Today, Weber argued, people no longer comply with the authority claimed by the powers that be merely on the grounds, as was common once, of habit and tradition or the charisma and personal appeal of individual leaders. Rather, there is general obedience by 'virtue of "legality", by virtue of the belief in the validity of legal statute and functional "competence" based on rationally created *rules*'. [133] The legitimacy of the modern state is founded predominantly on 'legal authority', i.e. commitment to a 'code of legal regulations'.

Foremost among the state's institutions are the administrative apparatuses – a vast network of organizations run by appointed officials. Although such organizations have been essential to states at many times and places in history, 'only the Occident', on Weber's account, 'knows the state in its modern scale, with a professional administration, specialized officialdom, and law based on the concept of citizenship'. These institutions had 'beginnings in antiquity and the Orient', but there they 'were never able to develop'.[134]

The modern state is not, Weber contended, an effect of capitalism; it preceded and helped promote capitalist development.[135] Capitalism, however, provided an enormous impetus to the expansion of rational administration, that is, the type of bureaucracy founded on legal authority. Weber extended the meaning of the concept of bureaucracy: when Marx and Lenin wrote about it, they had in mind the civil service, the bureaucratic apparatus of the state, but Weber applied the concept much more broadly, as characterizing all forms of large-scale organization (the civil service, political parties, industrial enterprises, universities, etc.). In the contemporary world, he believed, private and public administration are becoming more and more bureaucratized.[136] That is to say, there is a growth of office hierarchy; administration is based upon written documents; specialist training is presupposed and candidates are appointed according to qualification; formal responsibilities demand the full working capacities of officials; officials are 'separated from ownership of the means of administration'.[137]

Under practically every imaginable circumstance, bureaucracy is, according to Weber, 'completely indispensable'.[138] The choice is only 'between bureaucracy and dilettantism in the field of administration'. Weber explained the spread of bureaucracy in the following terms:

> The decisive reason for the advance of bureaucratic organization has always been its purely *technical* superiority over any other form of organization. The fully developed bureaucratic apparatus compares with the non-mechanical modes of production. Precision, speed, unambiguity, knowledge of the files, continuity, discretion, unity, strict subordination, reduction of friction and of material and personal costs – these are raised to the optimum point in the strictly bureaucratic administration, and especially in its monocratic form.[139]

As economic life becomes more complex and differentiated, bureaucratic administration becomes more essential.

While rule by officials is not inevitable, considerable power accrues to bureaucrats through their expertise, information and access to secrets. This power can become, Weber says, 'over-towering'. Politicians and political actors of all kinds can find themselves dependent on the bureaucracy. A central question – if not preoccupation – for Weber was, how can 'bureaucratic power' be checked? He was convinced that, in the absence of checks, public organization would fall prey to powerful private interests (among others, organized capitalists and major landholders) who would not have the nation-state as their prime concern; moreover, in times of national emergency, there would be ineffective leadership. Bureaucrats, unlike politicians, cannot take a passionate stand. They do not have the training – and bureaucracies are not structurally designed – for the consideration of political, alongside technical or economic, criteria. However, Weber's solution to the problem of unlimited bureaucratization was not one that depended merely on the capacity of individual politicians for innovation. Writing about Germany, he advocated a strong parliament which would create a competitive training ground for strong leadership and serve as a balance to public and private bureaucracy.[140] In so arguing, Weber was taking 'national power and prestige' as his prime concern. As one commentator aptly noted, 'Weber's enthusiasm for the representative system owed more to his conviction that national greatness depended on finding able leaders than to any concern for democratic values'.[141]

Weber's position on the relationship between social structure, bureaucracy and the state can be clarified further by examining his assessment of socialism. He believed that the abolition of private capitalism 'would simply mean that . . . the *top management* of the nationalized or socialized enterprises would become bureaucratic'.[142] Reliance upon those who control resources would be enhanced, for the abolition of the market would be the abolition of a key countervailing power to the state. The market generates change and social mobility: it is the very source of capitalist dynamism.

> State bureaucracy would rule alone if private capitalism were eliminated. The private and public bureaucracies, which now work next to, and potentially against, each other and hence check one another to a degree, would be merged into a single hierarchy. This would be similar to the situation in ancient Egypt, but it would occur in a much more rational – and hence unbreakable – form.[143]

While Weber argued that 'progress' toward the bureaucratic state is given an enormous impetus by capitalist development, he believed that this very development itself, coupled with parliamentary government and the party system, provided the best obstacle to the usurpation of state power by officials.

Weber accepted that intense class struggles have occurred in various phases of history and that the relationship between capital and wage-labour is of considerable importance in explaining many of the features of industrial capitalism. However, he dissented strongly from the view that the analysis of power could be assimilated to the analysis of classes. For Weber, classes cannot be reduced to economic relations, and they constitute in themselves only one aspect of the distribution of and struggle for power. What Weber calls 'status groups', political parties and nation-states are at least as significant.[144] The fervour created by sentiments of group solidarity, or of ethnic community, or of power prestige, or of nationalism generally, is a vital part of the creation and mobilization of political power in the modern age. But of all these the most important for Weber was the struggle between nation-states – a decisive feature of the modern world which promised to keep history open to 'human will' and the 'competition of values' in an ever more rationalized, bureaucratic world.[145]

Weber's attempt to analyse the internal workings of public (and private) organizations and his observations about trends in bureaucratization constitute a major contribution to understanding the state. His work provides a counterbalance to the Marxist and particularly Leninist emphasis on the intimate connection between state activities, forms of organization and class relations.[146] The argument that private and public administrations are similarly structured – as opposed to causally determined by class power – is important and provocative.

But Weber's analysis also has severe limits. His assumption that the development of bureaucracy leads to increased power for those at the highest levels of administration leads him to neglect the ways in which those in subordinate positions may increase their power.[147] In modern bureaucratic systems there appear to be considerable 'openings' for those in 'formally subordinate positions to acquire or regain control over their organizational tasks' (for example, by hindering or blocking the collection of vital information for centralized decision making).[148] Bureaucracies may enhance the potential for disruption from 'below' and increase the spaces for circumventing hierarchical control. Weber did not characterize adequately internal organizational processes and their significance for developments in other political spheres. In addition, one can search his writings in vain for a satisfactory explanation of the precise character of the relation between the growing bureaucratic centralization of the state and modern capitalism.[149] In his historical account of patterns of bureaucratization in diverse societies, he did not isolate the degree to which certain bureaucratic processes may be specific to, or influenced by, capitalist development *per se*. He failed to disentangle the 'impact of cultural, economic and technological forces' on the growth of bureaucracy, and to say to what extent these were independent of capitalist development. In the end, the particular connection between the state, bureaucratization and capitalism is left obscure. Further, although Weber's stress on the conflicts between nation-states captures an important aspect of the international context of states, it is also left clouded by a variety of intriguing but incomplete reflections on the nature of such states and by a dubious patriotic fervour.

Weber's writings have had an enormous influence on the development of sociology and political science in the Anglo-American world. They have stimulated a rich variety of developments, two of which deserve some attention here: 'pluralism' or empirical democratic theory (which takes as a starting point Weberian ideas about the multi-dimensionality of power) and 'geopolitical' conceptions of politics (which focus on the state at the intersection of national and international conditions and pressures). While neither of these bodies of work has grown out of Weber's work alone, his writings have certainly had a notable impact on both.

A variety of pluralist theories have been expounded, but I shall focus initially on what may be regarded as the 'classical version' of pluralism developed in the writings of Laswell, Truman and Dahl, among others.[150] This version had a pervasive influence in the 1950s and 1960s. Relatively few political and social theorists would accept it in unmodified form today, though many politicians, journalists and others in the mass media still appear to do so. Dahl and his colleagues deployed Weberian ideas as part of their effort to challenge fundamental Marxian axioms about class as the central structural determinant of the state and political outcomes. In the process they totally recast the connections between state, bureaucratic organizations and classes, and shifted the attention of political sociology and political science to those institutional arrangements designed to ensure a responsiveness by political leaders to citizens – in particular, the competition for electoral support and the activities of social groups or organized interests in relation to government.[151]

The essence of the classical pluralist position stems from the view that there are many determinants of the distribution of power other than class and, therefore, many power centres. But this idea is taken much further than Weber took it himself. In the pluralist account, power is non-hierarchically and competitively arranged. It is an inextricable part of an 'endless process of bargaining' between numerous groups representing different interests, eg. business organizations, trade unions, parties, ethnic groups, students, prison officers,

women's institutes, religious groups.[152] Clearly there are many inequalities in society (of schooling, health, income, wealth, etc.) and
not all groups have equal access to equal resources. However, nearly
every 'interest group' has some advantage which can be utilized in the
democratic process to make an impact. Hence the determination of
political decisions at either a local or national level cannot reflect a
'majestic march' of 'the public' united upon matters of basic policy –
as imagined, albeit in quite different ways, by Locke, Bentham and
Rousseau.[153] Political outcomes are, rather, the result of governments
and, ultimately, the executive trying to mediate and adjudicate
between competing demands. In this process the state becomes almost
indistinguishable from the ebb and flow of bargaining, the competitive pressure of interests. Indeed, individual government departments
are sometimes conceived as just another kind of interest group.

This situation is not regarded as a bad thing; for competition
among social groups, in the context of the open contest for government – the rules of democratic procedure – ensures that the competition is fair and creates government by multiple groups or multiple
minorities which, in turn, secures the democratic character of a
regime. Dahl calls this 'polyarchy' or rule by the many or 'minorities
government'.[154] It is, in his view, both a desirable state of affairs and
one to which most liberal democracies approximate.

The position can be criticized on many grounds – grounds which
many 'pluralists', among them Dahl, would now accept.[155] The
existence of many power centres hardly guarantees that government
will (a) listen to them all equally; (b) do anything other than com-
municate with leaders of such groups; (c) be susceptible to influence
by anybody other than those in powerful positions; (d) do anything
about the issues under discussion, and so on.[156] Additionally, it is
patently clear that not only do many groups not have the resources to
compete in the national political arena with the clout of, say, multinational corporations, but many people do not even have access to the
minimum resources for political mobilization. Moreover, the very
capacity of governments to act in ways that interest groups may desire
is constrained, as many Marxists have argued and as 'neo-pluralists'
like Charles E. Lindblom now accept. The constraints on Western
governments and state institutions – constraints imposed by the
requirements of private accumulation – systematically limit policy
options. The system of private investment, private property, etc,
creates objective exigencies which must be met if economic growth
and stable development are to be sustained. If these arrangements are
threatened, economic chaos quickly ensues and the legitimacy of
governments can be undermined. As Lindblom put it, 'depression,

inflation, or other economic disasters can bring down a government. A major function of government, therefore, is to see to it that businessmen perform their tasks'.[157] The state must follow a political agenda which is at least favourable to, i.e. biased towards, the development of the system of private enterprise and corporate power. Of course, 'neo-pluralists' retain some of the essential tenets of 'classical pluralism' including the account of the way liberal democracy generates a variety of interest groups and provides a crucial obstacle to the development of a monolithic unresponsive state.

One of the most severe deficiencies of existing theories of the state is their tendency to concentrate on, for example, group bargaining within *a* nation-state (pluralism), or on the citizen and his or her relation to *the* state (liberal democracy), or on the relation between classes, the economy and the state in *a* capitalist country albeit with imperialist ambitions (Marxism). It is important to relate 'the state' to the context of international conditions and pressures. For instance, the capitalist world was created in dependence on an international market – the 'European world economy' – which generated multiple interconnections between nation-states that were beyond the control of any one such state.[158] Weber's work has had a notable impact on the development of ideas such as these, emphasizing how the very nature of the state crystallizes at the intersection of international and national conditions and pressures.

Among social scientists who have pursued this perspective today is Theda Skocpol.[159] Her work bears the mark of Weber as well as other closely related figures, including the historian Otto Hintze (1861–1940).[160] Hintze sought to show how two phenomena, above all, condition the real organization of the state. 'These are, first, the structure of social classes, and second, the external ordering of . . . states – their position relative to each other, and their overall position in the world.'[161] Struggles among social classes at home and conflicts among nations have a dramatic impact on the organization and power of states. The 'shape' of a state – its size, external configuration, military structure, ethnic composition and relations, labour composition, among other things – is deeply rooted in the history of external events and conditions.[162] The state is, as Skocpol put it, 'Janus-faced, with an intrinsically dual anchorage in class-divided socio-economic structures and an international system of states'.[163]

Skocpol rejects 'society-centred' approaches to the explanation of the state and governmental activities because their explanatory strategies involve conceiving of the state simply as an 'arena' for the struggle of groups, movements and/or classes contending for advantage, or as merely a 'functional entity' responding to the 'imperatives' or 'needs' of civil society or the capitalist economy. Either way the focus is on societal 'inputs' and 'outputs' to and from the state and the state itself *qua* specific kinds of organizations, resources and relations is blocked from view.[164] There are intrinsic limits to all theories, whether pluralist or Marxist, which adopt such approaches: they cannot provide an adequate focus on states 'as distinctive structures with their own specific histories'.[165]

If class relations as well as complex international circumstances provide the context of the state, how should the state itself be conceptualized? In Skocpol's account,

> The state properly conceived . . . is a set of administrative, policing, and military organizations headed, and more or less well coordinated by, an executive authority. Any state first and fundamentally extracts resources from society and deploys those to create and support coercive and administrative organizations . . . Of course . . . political systems . . . also may contain institutions through which social interests are represented in state policy making as well as institutions through which non-state actors are mobilised to participate in policy implementation. Nevertheless, the administrative and coercive organizations are the basis of state power . . . [166]

Such a perspective helps illuminate: the way state organizations themselves vary; how the capacities of state organizations change in relation to the organization and interest of socio-economic groups and the 'transnational' environment; how state personnel develop interests in internal security, policy formulation and competition with other nation-states which may be at variance with the interests of other social groups or classes. It allows, Skocpol argues, the distinctiveness and histories of particular state agencies to be unpacked, thus 'bringing the state back in' to the abstract theory of the state.[167]

These reflections were developed by Skocpol in relation to the theory of revolutions, but on their own it is clear that they constitute less a theory and more a framework for analysis of the state – a useful framework, nonetheless, to the extent that it offsets some of the limitations of 'society-centred' theories.[168] At the same time, however, it may fail, as Wallerstein's work implies, to stress adequately the way the sovereignty of nation-states has been, and is ever more, compromised by the international interconnections of the world economy.[169] Further, while it is indeed important to examine the 'corporate identity' of state organizations and the interests state personnel develop, it is critical not to overstate this; for among the most valuable contributions of both Marxists and pluralists are insights into how social struggle is 'inscribed' into the organization, administration and policies of the state – the extent, for example, to which parliamentary forms themselves are the outcome of conflicts over the old powers of the monarchy, landed nobility and bourgeoisie. Moreover, the economic and electoral constraints on state activities mean that state autonomy from societal relations will almost always, at least in Western capitalist societies, be compromised, with the exception perhaps of phases of military adventure and war – although, it must be admitted, this exception begins to look ever more significant as the means of waging war become more menacing.[170]

Concluding remarks

There are many conceptual problems in surveying over four hundred years of writing on 'the modern state'. Even if writers since the late sixteenth century have taken the state to mean all the institutions and relations associated with 'government', these terms of reference have been profoundly altered. Most of the writers dealt with have taken different positions on what the state could, and indeed should, do; and in the case of figures like Bentham, Marx and Weber, it is clear that their analyses actually refer to disparate political phenomena. In concluding this essay, it may be useful to highlight some of the problems and disagreements.

Among the developments in the theory of the state since the sixteenth century, two notable innovations stand out: the concept of the state as an impersonal or 'anonymous' structure of power, and the problem of reconciling authority and liberty through a fundamentally new view of the 'rights, obligations and duties' of subjects. While Hobbes marks an intermediate point between absolutism and liberalism, liberal political theory since Locke clearly affirms the state as an impersonal (legally circumscribed) structure, and connects this idea to an institutional theory of political power, such as the division between legislatures and executives. The central problem facing liberal and liberal democratic theory concerned the relationship between the state, as an independent authority with supreme right to declare and administer law over a given territory, and the individual, with a right and interest to determine the nature and limits of the state's authority. In short, the question was: how should the 'sovereign state' be related to the 'sovereign people' who were in principle the source of its powers?

Modern liberal and liberal democratic theory has constantly sought to justify the sovereign power of the state while at the same time justifying limits upon that power. The history of this attempt since Machiavelli and Hobbes is the history of arguments to balance might and right, power and law, duties and rights. On the one hand, the state must have a monopoly of coercive power in order to provide a secure basis upon which trade, commerce and family life can prosper. On the other hand, by granting the state a regulatory and coercive capability, liberal political theorists were aware that they had accepted a force which could (and frequently did) deprive citizens of political and social freedoms.

It was the liberal democrats who provided the key institutional innovation to try to overcome this dilemma – representative democracy. The liberal concern with reason, law and freedom of choice could only be upheld properly by recognizing the political equality of mature individuals. Such equality would ensure not only a secure social environment in which people would be free to pursue their private activities and interests, but also that the state's personnel would do what was best in the general or public interest, eg. pursue the greatest happiness of the greatest number. Thus, the democratic constitutional state, linked to the free market, resolved, the liberal democrats argued, the problems of ensuring both authority and liberty.

The struggle of liberalism against tyranny and the struggle by liberal democrats for political equality represented, according to Marx and Engels, a major step forward in the history of human emancipation. But for them the great universal ideals of 'liberty, equality and justice' could not be realized simply by the 'free' struggle for votes in the political system and by the 'free' struggle for profit in the market place. The advocates of the democratic state and the market economy present them as the only institutions under which liberty can be sustained and inequalities minimized. However, by virtue of its internal dynamics, the capitalist economy inevitably produces systematic inequality and hence massive restrictions on real freedom. While each step towards formal political equality is an advance, its liberating potential is severely curtailed by inequalities of class. As Marx wryly put it: 'Just as Christians are equal in heaven yet unequal on earth, so the individual members of a people are equal in the heaven of their political world yet unequal in the earthly existence of society'.[171]

In class societies, Marx and Engels maintained, the state cannot become the vehicle for the pursuit of the 'common good' or 'public interest'. Far from the state playing the role of emancipator, protective knight, umpire or judge in the face of disorder, the agencies of the state are enmeshed in the struggles of civil society. Marxists conceive of the state as an extension of civil society, reinforcing the social order for the enhancement of particular interests – in capitalist society, the long-run interests of the capitalist class. It is not the state, as Marx put it in his early writings, which underlies the social order, but the social order which underlies the state. Marx did not deny the desirability of liberty and equality – far from it. His argument is that political emancipation is only a step toward human emancipation, i.e. the *complete* democratization of society as well as the state. In his view, liberal democratic society fails when judged by its own principles; and to take these principles seriously is to become a socialist. 'True democracy' can only be established with the destruction of social classes and ultimately the abolition of the state itself: the state must 'wither away' leaving a system of self-government linked to collectively shared duties and work.

The history of Marxism, and of socialism more generally, since Marx has been distinguished by deep conflicts about how to define appropriate political goals and about how to develop political strategy in historical conditions often quite different from those envisaged by Marx himself. A preoccupation with actually taking power shifted attention, at least in much of the work of Lenin and his followers, to questions about the role of the Party, Party organization and the nature of the transition to socialism. In the process, consideration of the problem of state power was regarded as of secondary importance to the practical exigencies of making revolution.

Weber believed that the Bolsheviks' political ambitions were premissed on a deficient understanding of the nature of the modern state and the complexity of political life. In his account, the history of the state and the history of political struggle could not in any way (even 'in the last instance') be reduced to class relations: the origins and tasks of the modern state suggested it was far more than a 'superstructure' on an economic 'base'. Moreover, even if class relations were transformed, institutions of direct democracy could not replace the state; for there would be a massive problem of coordination and regulation which would inevitably be 'resolved' by bureaucracy, and by bureaucracy alone, unless other institutions were nourished to check its power. The problems posed in the liberal pursuit of a balance between might and right, power and law, are, Weber thought, inescapable elements of modernity.

Weber feared that political life in West and East would be ever more ensnared by a rationalized, bureaucratic system of administration – a 'steel-hard cage', as he wrote. Against this he championed the countervailing power of private capital, the competitive party system and strong political leadership to secure national power and prestige; all of which could prevent the domination of politics by state officials. In so arguing, the limitations of his political thought become apparent: some of the key insights and principles of both Marxist and liberal political theory seem to have been set aside. The significance of massive inequalities of political and class power are played down because of the priority of power, i.e. interstate, politics; and this priority leaves the balance between might and right in the end to the judgment of 'charismatic' political leaders locked into the competition between state and economic bureaucracies – a situation which comes perilously close to accepting that even the tenets of traditional liberalism can no longer be upheld in the modern age.

The difficulties of coming to a judgment about the modern state are compounded when one examines it in relation to the system of nation-states and the international interconnections of the world economy. The more one explores this context, the more tenuous appears the abstract idea of 'the state'. Historical and geographical variation in the relations between states, as well as in the nature of the states themselves, force us to ask whether the search for a theory of 'the state' is misplaced. Yet while we must be sensitive to the existence of 'states' and 'societies', we recognize a continuity through states in their modern guise – a peculiar mix of force and right that constrains and shapes the lives of generations. This presence compels us to pursue seriously – and ever more urgently in the face of the global struggle for resources and the escalating capacity for mass destruction – the issues of might and right, liberty and equality, class power and domination, violence and the nation-state.

Notes and References

1.   I have benefited enormously from the comments and advice of many people on earlier drafts of this essay. I would like to thank in particular: David Beetham, John Dunn, Anthony Giddens, Bram Gieben, Stuart Hall, Joel Krieger, John Keane, Paul Lewis, Noel Parker, Michelle Stanworth, John Thompson, Tony Walton and Adam Westoby. This essay was originally printed in David Held *et.al.* (eds), *States and Societies*, Oxford, Martin Robertson, 1983.

2.   See Quentin Skinner, *The Foundations of Modern Political Thought*, 2 Vols, Cambridge, Cambridge University Press, 1978. Cf. Franz Neumann, *The Democratic and the Authoritarian State*, New York, Free Press, 1964.

3.   See, for example, Gianfranco Poggi, *The Development of the Modern State*, London, Hutchinson, 1978; Charles Tilly, 'Reflections on the History of European State-making', in C. Tilly (ed.) *The Formation of National States in Western Europe*, Princeton, Princeton University Press, 1975; Theda Skocpol, *States and Social Revolutions: A Comparative Analysis of France, Russia and China*, Cambridge, Cambridge University Press,

1979; Reinhard Bendix, *Kings or People*, Berkeley, University of California Press, 1980; S.I. Benn and R.S. Peters, *Social Principles and the Democratic State*, London, Allen & Unwin, 1959; and John Keane, *Public Life and Late Capitalism*, Cambridge, Cambridge University Press, 1984, Essay 6.

4.   Quoted in Skinner, *The Foundations of Modern Political Thought*, Vol. 2, p. 349.

5   *Ibid*, p. 353, and see his concluding remarks on this idea, pp. 349–58.

6   See Jürgen Habermas, *Strukturwandel der Öffentlichteit*, Neuwied, Luchterhand, 1962; Carole Pateman, *The Problem of Political Obligation*, Chichester, John Wiley and Sons, 1979; and John Keane, *Public Life and Late Capitalism*.

7.   See C.B. Macpherson, *The Real World of Democracy*, Oxford, Oxford University Press, 1965, Ch. 1. Cf. Anthony Giddens, *A Contemporary Critique of Historical Materialism*, London, Macmillan, 1981, Chs 8 and 9.

8.   For an interesting discussion see John Dunn, *Western Political Theory in the Face of the Future*. Cambridge, Cambridge University Press, 1979, Ch. 2.

9.   Macpherson, *The Real World of Democracy*, p. 6.

10. Hobbes, *Leviathan*, edited by C.B. Macpherson, Harmondsworth, Penguin, 1968, p. 81. For an interesting reflection on this idea see Kenneth Dyson, *The State Tradition in Western Europe*, Oxford, Martin Robertson, 1980, Ch. 7.

11. For a helpful introductory account see John Plamenatz, *Man and Society*, Vol. 1, London, Longman, 1963, pp. 116–54.

12. See Dunn, *Western Political Theory in the Face of the Future*, pp. 23, 42–3, 50. Cf. Quentin Skinner, 'The Ideological Context of Hobbes's Political Thought', *The Historical Journal*, IX, 3, 1966, pp. 286–317.

13. Hobbes, *De Cive* in *The English Works of Thomas Hobbes*, edited by Sir William Molesworth, London, 1839–44, Vol. 2, p. 109 and quoted in Steven Lukes, *Individualism*, New York, Harper and Row, 1973, p. 77.

14. Cf. C.B. Macpherson, 'Introduction' to Hobbes, *Leviathan*. For a fuller account see his *The Political Theory of Possessive Individualism*, Oxford, Clarendon Press, 1962.

15. Hobbes, *Leviathan*, p. 161.

16. See R.S. Peters, *Hobbes*, Harmondsworth, Penguin, 1956, Ch. 9, or his concise statement in *The Encyclopedia of Philosophy*, Vol. 4, New York, Macmillan, 1967, pp. 41–3.

17. See *Leviathan*, Part 1, chs 13–15.

18. *Ibid*, ch. 13.

19. See Plamenatz, *Man and Society*, Vol. 1, pp. 122–32, for a clear discussion of these ideas.

20. See *Leviathan*, Chs 14 and 15.

21. An interesting discussion of this idea of sovereignty in relation to other conceptions can be found in S.I. Benn, 'The Uses of Sovereignty', *Political Studies*, 3, 1955, pp. 109–22.

22. See *Leviathan*, Ch. 14.

23. *Ibid*, p. 223.

24. *Ibid*, pp. 227–8.

25. *Ibid*, p. 220.

26. Cf. R.S. Peters, *Hobbes*, Ch. 9.

27. C.B. Macpherson, 'Introduction' to Hobbes, *Leviathan*, p. 45. Cf. *Leviathan*, p. 728.

28. *Leviathan*, pp. 376, 382–3.
29. Ibid, Ch. 21.
30. See, for example, Milton Friedman, *Capitalism and Freedom*, Chicago, University of Chicago Press, 1962.
31. Locke, *Two Treatises of Government*, a critical edition with an 'Introduction' by Peter Laslett, Cambridge, Cambridge University Press, 1963, p. 372. See Laslett's comment in note 36 on the same page.
32. Ibid, p. 371.
33. See John Dunn, *The Political Thought of John Locke*, Cambridge, Cambridge University Press, 1969, Part 3.
34. Cf. Plamenatz, *Man and Society*, Ch. 6 and Dunn, 'Consent in the Political Theory of John Locke', in *Political Obligation in its Historical Context*, Cambridge, Cambridge University Press, 1980, pp. 29–52.
35. See Laslett, 'Introduction' to Locke, *Two Treatises of Government*, pp. 130–5.
36. Locke, *Two Treatises of Government*, p. 309.
37. Ibid, p. 311.
38. Ibid, p. 395, para. 123.
39. Ibid, pp. 327–44. Interesting and contrasting accounts of Locke on property can be found in Macpherson, *The Political Theory of Possessive Individualism*, Plamenatz, *Man and Society* and Dunn, *The Political Thought of John Locke*.
40. See, for example, *Two Treatises of Government*, pp. 316–17, para. 13.
41. Ibid, p. 308, para. 3 and pp. 395–6, para. 124.
42. Ibid, pp. 372–6, paras 94–7. See Laslett, 'Introduction' to this work, pp. 127–8, whose account of these agreements I have followed.
43. Ibid, for example, pp. 402–3, para. 135 and pp. 412–13, para. 149.
44. Ibid, p. 410. Cf. Plamenatz, *Man and Society*, pp. 218, 228–9.
45. Cf. Dunn, *The Political Thought of John Locke*, Ch. 10 and Julian H. Franklin, *John Locke and the Theory of Sovereignty*, Cambridge, Cambridge University Press, 1978.
46. See Plamenatz, *Man and Society*, p. 228.
47. Lukes, *Individualism*, pp. 80–1.
48. See Dunn, 'Consent in the Political Theory of John Locke', pp. 36–7.
49. Dunn, *Western Political Theory in the Face of the Future*, p. 39 (my emphasis).
50. Cf. Laslett, 'Introduction', pp. 134–5.
51. Ibid, p. 123.
52. Plamenatz, pp. 231, 251–2.
53. One must guard against exaggerating this claim. See Dunn, 'The Politics of Locke in England and America in the Eighteenth century', in *Political Obligation in its Historical Context*, pp. 53–77.
54. Bentham, *Constitutional Code*, Bk. 1, ch. 9 in *The Works of Jeremy Bentham*, Vol. IX, edited by Bowring, p. 47, quoted in C.B. Macpherson, *The Life and Times of Liberal Democracy*, Oxford, Oxford University Press, 1977, p. 36.
55. See Macpherson, *The Life and Times of Liberal Democracy*, Ch. 2, which provides an account of Bentham and James Mill to which I am indebted.
56. Cf. Bentham, *Fragment on Government*, in W. Harrison (ed.), Oxford, Blackwell, 1960 and James Mill, *An Essay on Government*, Cambridge, Cambridge University Press, 1937.
57. Cf. the extracts from Bentham, *Fragment on Government*, in Part 1, 'Classical Conceptions of the State', of Held *et.al.* (eds) *States and Societies*, Oxford, Martin Robertson, 1983.

58. See Bentham, *Principles of the Civil Code*, in *Works*, Vol. I.
59. See James Mill, 'Prisons and Prison Discipline', in *Essays on Government*, London, J. Innis, 1828, pp. 1–24.
60. Cf. Michel Foucault, *Discipline and Punish*, London, Allen Lane, 1977, Part 3, and Michael Ignatieff, *A Just Measure of Pain*, London, Macmillan, 1978, Ch. 6. I am grateful to John Keane for comments on this issue.
61. Macpherson, *The Life and Times of Liberal Democracy*, pp. 42–3.
62. Cf. Carole Pateman, *Participation and Democratic Theory*, Cambridge, Cambridge University Press, 1970, Ch. 1.
63. See John Stuart Mill, *Representative Government* in *Utilitarianism, Liberty, and Representative Government*, London, Dent and Sons, 1951 and, in particular, the extracts from this work in Part 1, 'Classical Conceptions of the State', of Held et.al. (eds), *States and Societies*. See also Mill, *On Liberty*, Harmondsworth, Penguin, 1982.
64. Cf. Macpherson, *The Life and Times of Liberal Democracy*, Ch. 3 and Dunn, *Western Political Theory in the Face of the Future*, pp. 51–3.
65. J.S. Mill, *On Liberty*, p. 59.
66. Ibid, p. 68.
67. Ibid, p. 69.
68. See Alan Ryan, *The Philosophy of John Stuart Mill*, London, Macmillan, 1970.
69. *On Liberty*, pp. 71–2.
70. Ibid, p. 72.
71. Ibid, Ch. 5.
72. Mill was committed to *laissez-faire* in economic policy in his early works, but he later modified his views. See Pateman, *Participation and Democratic Theory*, Ch. 2.
73. See Macpherson, *The Life and Times of Liberal Democracy*, pp. 57–64 for a discussion of the complexity of Mill's reflections on voting.
74. For a fuller account of 'citizenship rights' and some of the struggles concerning them, see the extracts by Marshall and Therborn in Part 3 of Held et.al. (eds), *States and Societies*.
75. Noberto Bobbio, 'Are there Alternatives to Representative Democracy?' *Telos*, 35, Spring 1978, p. 17.
76. In Britain and the United States a variety of theories of the liberal democratic state have developed in recent times including various theories of pluralism elaborated by, among others, Schumpeter, Laswell, Truman and Dahl, and 'liberal anarchist' or 'libertarian' views expounded by, for example, Hayek and Nozick.
77. See, for example, Lucio Colletti, *From Rousseau to Lenin*, London, New Left Books, 1972.
78. Rousseau, *The Social Contract*, Harmondsworth, Penguin, 1968, p. 49.
79. Ibid, p. 59.
80. Maurice Cranston, 'Introduction', *The Social Contract*, p. 30.
81. *The Social Contract*, p. 141.
82. Caution is required about the use of the term democracy in relation to Rousseau's writings. He refers to the political system under discussion as 'republicanism'. See ibid, pp. 114 and 82, and for a general account, Bk. 3, Chs 1–5.
83. Ibid, pp. 60–1.
84. Ibid, pp. 72–3, 75.

85. Ibid, p. 65. cf. p. 82.
86. '*Lettres écrites de la montagne*', 2, letter 8, in J.J. Rousseau, *Oeuvres Complètes de J.J. Rousseau*, Paris, 1911, 3, p. 227, quoted in Keane, *Public Life and Late Capitalism*, Essay 6.
87. *The Social Contract*, p. 76. cf. p. 46.
88. Ibid, Bk. 3, Chs 1, pp. 11–14, 18. There are additional institutional positions set out by Rousseau, for instance, that of 'the Lawgiver', which cannot be elaborated here. See ibid, pp. 83–8, 95–6.
89. Ibid, p. 102.
90. Ibid, pp. 136–9, 148.
91. Ibid, for example, Bk. 3, Ch. 4.
92. Cf. William Connolly, *Appearance and Reality*, Cambridge, Cambridge University Press, 1981, Ch. 7, for an interesting discussion.
93. Marx, *The Critique of Hegel's Philosophy of Right*, Cambridge, Cambridge University Press, 1970, p. 131 (modified translation).
94. For an overview of Marx's and Engels's account of class see Anthony Giddens and David Held (eds), *Classes, Power and Conflict*, Part 1, London, Macmillan, 1982, pp. 12–39.
95. Ibid, pp. 28–35.
96. See John Maguire, *Marx's Theory of Politics*, Cambridge, Cambridge University Press, 1978, Ch. 1.
97. This discussion draws heavily on my paper with Joel Krieger, 'Theories of the State: Some Competing Claims' in S. Bornstein *et al.* (eds) *The State in Capitalist Europe*, London, Allen & Unwin, 1984, as do some remaining parts of this chapter. However, the arguments have been modified and developed in several respects.
98. G.W.F. Hegel, *The Philosophy of Right*, trans. T.M. Knox, Oxford, Oxford University Press, 1967. See M. Perez-Diaz, *State, Bureaucracy and Civil Society*, London, Macmillan, 1978 for a clear and helpful discussion of Marx's relation to Hegel. The view of Hegel I have briefly presented here is very much Marx's view – a view which is challengeable in many respects. Cf. Gillian Rose, *Hegel Contra Sociology*, London, Athlone, 1981, especially Ch. 7.
99. Marx, *The Critique of Hegel's Philosophy of Right*, pp. 41–54.
100. Ibid, p. 46.
101. Ibid, pp. 48, 51.
102. Ibid, pp. 46–7.
103. Ibid, p. 54.
104. Marx, *The Eighteenth Brumaire of Louis Bonaparte*, New York, International Publishers, 1963, p. 121.
105. See Maguire, *Marx's Theory of Politics* and M.E. Spencer, 'Marx on the State', *Theory and Society*, 7, 1–2, pp. 167–98.
106. See *The Eighteenth Brumaire of Louis Bonaparte*, pp. 118 ff.
107. See, for instance, Marx and Engels, *The Communist Manifesto*, New York, International Publishers, 1948, and Marx, 'Preface' to *A Contribution to the Critique of Political Economy*, London, Lawrence and Wishart, 1971.
108. Cf. Ralph Miliband, 'Marx and the state', *Socialist Register, 1965*, London, Merlin Press, 1965.
109. Edüard Bernstein, *Evolutionary Socialism*, New York, Schocken Books, 1961.
110. See Lenin, *State and Revolution*, New York, International Publishers, 1971.
111. Some important exceptions are Maguire, *Marx's Theory of Politics*; Perez-

Diaz, *State, Bureaucracy and Civil Society*; and Hal Draper, *Karl Marx's Theory of Revolution*, Vol. 1, New York, Monthly Review Press, 1977.

112. *State and Revolution*, p. 7. For an account which is sensitive to the complexities of the development of Lenin's thought, see Neil Harding, *Lenin's Political Thought*, 2 Vols, London, Macmillan, 1977 and 1981.

113. *State and Revolution*, p. 17.

114. Ibid, pp. 72–3.

115. Ibid, pp. 35–9.

116. Lenin was far from consistent on these matters. For a useful discussion see R. Brown *et al, Bureaucracy*, Port Melbourne, Edward Arnold, 1979, pp. 72–87.

117. *State and Revolution*, p. 16.

118. See M. Lewin, *Lenin's Last Struggle*, London, Pluto Press, 1975.

119. For surveys of this material see Bob Jessop, 'Recent Theories of the Capitalist State', *Cambridge Journal of Economics*, 1, 1977, pp. 343–73, and D.A. Gold *et al*, 'Recent Developments in Marxist Theories of the Capitalist State', *Monthly Review*, 27, 5–6, 1975.

120. See Miliband, *The State in Capitalist Society*, London, Weidenfeld & Nicolson, 1969. Cf. his 'The Capitalist State – Reply to Nicos Poulantzas', in R. Blackburn (ed.) *Ideology in Social Science*, London, Fontana, 1972, and *Marxism and Politics*, Oxford, Oxford University Press, 1977.

121. See Poulantzas, 'The Problem of the Capitalist State', in R. Blackburn (ed.) *Ideology in Social Science*.

122. Poulantzas, *Political Power and Social Classes*, London, New Left Books, 1973, pp. 331–40.

123. Ibid, pp. 287–8.

124. See Poulantzas, *Classes in Contemporary Capitalism*, London, New Left Books, 1975.

125. See Poulantzas, *State, Power, Socialism*, London, Verso and New Left Books, 1980, for his most interesting elaboration of these ideas.

126. For an introduction to this tradition see David Held, *Introduction to Critical Theory*, London, Hutchinson, 1980.

127. Cf. Giddens, *A Contemporary Critique of Historical Materialism*, Ch. 9, and Boris Frankel, 'The State of the State after Leninism', *Theory and Society*, 7 1/2, 1979.

128. See, for example, Giddens, 'Class Division, Class Conflict and Citizenship Rights', in *Profiles and Critiques in Social Theory*, London, Macmillan, 1983.

129. For example, Charles E. Lindblom, *Politics and Markets*, New York, Basic Books, 1977, whose work is discussed briefly in the following section.

130. Weber, *Economy and Society*, Vol. 2, Berkeley, University of California Press, 1978, pp. 951–2.

131. See Martin Albrow, *Bureaucracy*, London, Pall Mall, 1970, pp. 37–49.

132. Weber, 'Politics as a Vocation', in H.H. Gerth and C.W. Mills (eds) *From Max Weber*, New York, Oxford University Press, 1972, p. 78.

133. Ibid, p. 79, and see the extracts from Weber's work in 'Classical Conceptions of the State', Held *et al* (eds) *States and Societies*.

134. Weber, *General Economic History*, London, Allen & Unwin, 1923, p. 232.

135. *Economy and Society*, Vol. 2, pp. 1381 ff.

136. Ibid, p. 1465.

137. *Economy and Society*, Vol. 1, pp. 220–1.

138. Ibid, p. 223.

139. *Economy and Society*, Vol. 2, p. 973.

140. See Wolfgang J. Mommsen, *The Age of Bureaucracy*, Oxford, Basil Blackwell, 1974.

141. Albrow, *Bureaucracy*, p. 48 and see Mommsen, ibid, last chapter.

142. *Economy and Society*, Vol. 2, p. 1402.
143. Ibid, p. 143.
144. See the Weber extracts in *Classes, Power and Conflict*, edited by Giddens and Held, pp. 60–86.
145. See Guenther Roth and Wolfgang Schluchter, *Max Weber's Vision of History*, Berkeley, University of California Press, 1979.
146. Cf. Erik Olin Wright *Class, Crisis and the State*, London, New Left Books, 1978, Ch. 4.
147. Giddens, *Central Problems in Social Theory: Action, Structure and Contradiction in Social Analysis*, London, Macmillan, 1979, Ch. 4.
148. Ibid, pp. 147–8.
149. See Joel Krieger, *Undermining Capitalism*, Princeton, Princeton University Press, 1983, for an interesting and important discussion of Weber's concept of bureaucracy.
150. Cf, for example, D.B. Truman, *The Governmental Process*, New York, Knopf, 1951; and Robert A. Dahl, *A Preface to Democratic Theory*, Chicago, University of Chicago Press, 1956, *Polyarchy: Participation and Opposition*, New Haven, Yale University Press, 1971, and *Who Governs? Democracy and Power in an American City*, New Haven and London, Yale University Press, 1975.
151. See Pateman, *Participation and Democratic Theory*, Ch. 1.
152. See the extract from Dahl in Part 1, 'Classical Conceptions of the State', of Held et al, (eds) *States and Societies*.
153. Dahl, *A Preface to Democratic Theory*, p. 146.
154. Ibid, p. 133.
155. See Dahl, 'Pluralism revisited', *Comparative Politics*, 10, 1978, pp. 191–204.
156. See Jack Lively, *Democracy*, Oxford, Basil Blackwell, 1975, pp. 20–4, 54–6, 71–2, 141–5, for a discussion of these points. Cf. Steven Lukes, *Power*, London, Macmillan, 1977.
157. Lindblom, *Politics and Markets*, pp. 122–3.
158. See Immanuel Wallerstein, *The Modern World-System*, New York, Academic Press, 1974.
159. See Skocpol, *States and Revolutions*, Cf. her chapter, as well as those by Anderson and Nairn, in Part 2 of Held et al (eds.) *States and Societies*.
160. *States and Revolutions*, p. 307, n. 77. Cf. Otto Hintze in Felix Gilbert (ed.) *Historical Essays*, New York, Oxford University Press, 1975, Chs 4–6, 11.
161. Hintze, *Historical Essays*, p. 183.
162. For some of the theoretical background to these ideas see Dyson, *The State Tradition in Western Europe*.
163. Skocpol, *States and Revolutions*, p. 32.
164. Ibid, pp. 25–33.
165. See Jonathan Zeitlin, 'Shop Floor Bargaining and the State: a Contradictory Relationship', p. 24, to be published in S. Tolliday and J. Zeitlin (eds), *Shop Floor Bargaining and The State: Historical and Contemporary Perspectives* (forthcoming, 1984).
166. *States and Revolutions*, p. 29.
167. See Skocpol, 'Bringing the State Back In', *Items* (SSRC) 36, 1/2, June 1982, pp. 1–8.
168. Cf. Zeitlin, 'Shop Floor Bargaining and the State', pp. 24–6.
169. Cf. Wallerstein, *The Modern World-System*, and 'The Rise and Future Demise of the World Capitalist System', *Comparative Studies in Society and History*, 16, 4, 1974, pp. 387–415.
170. Cf. Giddens, *A Contemporary Critique of Historical Materialism*, Ch. 10.
171. Marx, *The Critique of Hegel's Philosophy of Right*, p. 80.

CHAPTER 3

Capitalist state or democratic polity? Recent developments in Marxist and pluralist theory

Gregor McLennan

1. Introduction: Two Traditions of State-Theory

Students of social theory and state-theory are confronted today with a difficult problem. The main post-war perspectives in social science – Marxism and pluralism – seem to have subdivided into several offshoots, each having distinctive characteristics. The rival parent paradigms are increasingly blurred at the edges and debates between one variant of a theory and another appear to be as consuming as the clash of the broad traditions themselves. This eclectic and nuanced state of play raises the question of whether, for example, the Marxist tradition retains any overall coherence such as to decisively mark it off from critical brands of pluralism.

Also, the *political* significance of the intellectual or academic debates is less clear-cut than in previous eras. In the 1950s, or perhaps even in the early 1970s the real-life implications of Marxism and pluralism as theories of society were more obvious than is now the case. If you wanted a class-based perspective and a revolutionary socialist politics, then Marxism was for you. If you were happy with affluent, white, parliamentary democracy, pluralism fitted the bill. The normative character of the respective analyses was fairly plain to see. Today it is at least questionable whether there can be a timeless stability in the very terms 'pluralism' and 'Marxism'. Not only are there several varieties of each species, but in each tradition the ties between the analytical-explanatory dimension and the normative-political aspect have weakened. Moreover, the resurgence of a radical brand of conservatism in which theory and practice are coherently linked significantly affects the relationship between the other paradigms. As theory and practice, neo-liberalism – discussed in other parts of this book – is based on a critique of pluralist democracy. The latter is held to lead to an overloaded state, creeping socialism and a turbulent people, despite its intention to preserve both *representative* democracy and the capitalist mode of production. Of course, the neo-liberal resistance to participatory democracy, and its commitment to free market capitalism place it quite against the Marxist tradition. A critical space opens up, therefore, for some kind of dialogue between pluralists who reject neo-liberalism and Marxists who seek to overcome the constraints of a rigid demarcation between revolutionary theory and reformist politics.

The purpose of this chapter is to provide one kind of mapping of these theoretical shifts. I will try as clearly as I can to outline problems *within* each camp, and to assess the nature of their current opposition to one another. The focus is more on the sociological and methodological *analysis* of the state in western capitalist society rather than political *prescriptions*, which are discussed at length in Chapter 9. However, I will be making the connection between politics and theory, first by describing the social context of theory-change, and later by indicating the particular aspects of the general 'debate' between Marxism and pluralism which strike me as importantly open-ended.

We can begin by noticing, almost tautologously, that without a state there would be no theory of the state. Such an elementary reminder is, however, essential in locating the emergence of rival traditions of state-theory. Theories emerge as multi-layered responses to concrete social developments, and they evolve according to *changes* in social processes. The *way* in which theories evolve is of course to do with intellectual reasoning about their assumptions, structure, and implications, and this aspect might be termed their 'intrinsic' histories. But there are also primary or 'extrinsic' reasons as to why theories change, and these are to be found not simply in ideas but in social reality. Since I will mainly be concerned with 'intrinsic' questions, it is as well to remind ourselves of the material inescapability of the 'extrinsic'. For example, both Marxism and pluralism are responses to the historical process in which the democratic state has emerged as part of an industrial capitalist society. Pluralism is a means of coming to terms with the fact that the democratic ideal has been only imperfectly realized in capitalist societies. Whether due to the complexities of industrial civilization itself or to the economic injustices of capitalism, pluralists a) aim accurately to describe the workings of imperfect democracy and b) have tended to praise the political sphere in capitalist societies as securing at least some valuable elements of democracy in an imperfect world. Marxists turn this logic around and attempt to explain how in a world of manifest exploitation and class struggle, the people have come to accept their limited and essentially *formal* leverage on political power. And Marxists have politically encouraged workers to see that their real interests cannot be satisfied by merely *political* democratic concessions.

2. Pluralism

Let us, then, consider the internal logic of our principal traditions in greater detail. Contrary to assumption, what might be termed 'classical' democratic theory never did provide a utopian scenario in which equal citizens actively, knowledgeably and collectively decide upon the rational course of action for their society. In *practice*, Athenian democracy – the great exemplar – was restricted to propertied men and citizenship was forbidden to the slaves upon whose exploitation Athens depended. And a majority of political thinkers since Plato have despised even this kind of limited attempt to evade the necessity of government by *oligarchy*. Amongst advocates of the rule of the common masses – the *demos* – democracy inevitably had to be accepted as something less than direct rule. In Rousseau's conception, for example, 'representation' was an unworthy perversion of the idea of the people's will. Yet he was resigned to the fact that where the people were less than gods their government could not be perfect (Ryan, 1983, p. 40–1). So the state as something over and above the popular will is inscribed from the first as a problem for self-government, and the keynote of classical democratic theory – popular participation – requires to be expressed in terms of imperfect representative democracy accompanied by guarantees of political freedom.

Pluralism arises on the back of the failure, or the unreality, not only of the classical democratic ideal, but even of representative government as developed by theorists such as J.S. Mill. Individual citizens – as individuals – have virtually no influence on the political process; representatives are opinion-formers and office seekers rather than delegates; the people are less active and less informed than classical theory describes – this kind of empirical fact about modern democracy leaves the classical picture merely speculative. Pluralism gets off the ground by claiming to be first of all an empirical theory about the reality of democratic politics. From this point of view, classical theory needed not so much updating as replacement.

There are several key notions in the pluralist perspective. Western society, for one thing, is not made up of homogeneous citizens. Rather, we have a number of interest groups, coming together voluntarily or organizationally in order to assert their social identity and political demands. These interest groups may be structured around economic or cultural 'cleavages' such as social class or religion; but they may also be single-issue affairs about schooling or local concerns about leisure and the environment. Moreover, such a constellation of forces would tend to crystallize, then dissolve, over time. In this pluralist conception, the state itself is equated with the 'political system' and as such becomes the main focus of democratic political pressure. If society comprises a whole series of interest groups more or less in competition with one another for economic resources and access to power, then the state's role is to balance these pressure-group claims in order to secure political and social stability. The state is thus a kind of switchboard which separate interests plug into, are connected together, and whose message is received. Another metaphor – one which gives the state a more realistic degree of autonomy – is that the state arbitrates as between the rival demands, achieving as fair a result as possible. Not all interests need be fully satisfied in this model.

The analytical strand in pluralism, then, was intended to demonstrate with hard-nosed realism that democracy was imperfect. Social inequalities rather than ideal citizenship sullied the purity of the democratic vision, and the role of politicians could be accepted as more or less cynical. Joseph Schumpeter (1942) portrayed democratic politics as the process by which elite teams secured popular endorsement – by fair means or foul. Anthony Downs (1957) argued that democratic parties were akin to economic firms in search of a lucrative market: policy choices were calculations for victory or re-election as much as expressions of ideological belief. A series of large-scale voting studies (eg. Campbell, 1960) revealed the American electorate to be in the main hostile to politics, apathetic about voting, and uninformed about issues.

For all that, the normative aspects of pluralism were no secret. After all, the demise of classical democracy could not be a matter for regret if it was utopian and impossible. At least the people had the chance to vote, the freedom to organize, and the opportunity to have pressure group demands considered and possibly satisfied. Social inequalities might exist, but in the pluralist view these could be resolved with optimism. In S.M. Lipset's account, social conflict becomes a civilized exchange, 'a fight without ideologies, without red flags, without May Day parades' (Lipset 1960, p. 408). Even in the realistic model, the state was still equated with an open political process, that is to say, an arena or neutral mechanism finely tuned to the achievement of societal equilibrium. One gets in pluralism little sense of the active, coercive, non-democratic aspects of state power over and above the everyday channels of access. Power is essentially conceived as being dispersed *throughout* society, as a plurality of locations of decision-making, policy-formulating, and 'counter-vailing' institutions. Whilst in some respects participation might be thought low, the effective distribution of power seemed nevertheless to secure a widespread consensus about the ability of the western system to deliver the goods. Both in terms of post-war economic growth (the 'age of affluence') and in terms of the limited but significant civic consensus, imperfect democracy or 'polyarchy' (Dahl 1971) was nevertheless to be considered a major achievement. Pluralism served as a source of justification for the brasher side of 'democracy – American style' (Margolis, 1983, p. 116):

> America has been and continues to be one of the world's most demo-cratic nations. Here, far more than elsewhere, the public is allowed to participate widely in the making of social and political policy. The public is not unaware of its power and the ordinary American tends to be rather arrogant about his right and competence to participate . . . The people think they know what they want and are in no mood to be led to greener pastures. (Hacker 1967, p. 68 quoted by Margolis 1983, p. 117)

Pluralist empirical democratic theory became the orthodoxy in political thinking through the 1950s and 1960s. Its demise was due in no small part to the 'extrinsic' history of the society in which it arose. Towards the later 1960s the by-now familiar catalogue of events requires only a cursory mention to reveal the false complacency of normative pluralism. In the context of the overarching trend to economic recession (capitalist crisis, some would argue) in the advanced societies, the major cities of the US erupted in racial and social violence. Poverty remained endemic and increasing, running to many millions of US citizens. Students questioned the supposed moral superiority of consensus politics. In the later 1960s, battered by this social dissent and by disaffection stemming from the politically ruin-ous Vietnam War, middle-America turned to the openly more discip-linary politics of the Nixon era. Yet the supposedly trusted and open power structure was increasingly revealed as a tissue of lies and corruption, from Lyndon Johnson's deception on the bombing of North Vietnam to the Watergate 'bugging' scandal of 1973–4.

As a result, *theoretical* pluralism has dissolved into a series of competing schools and tendencies. I want to pick out the main concerns of the revised pluralist camp and in order to do so it is important to make some conceptual distinctions. This is necessary because in the absence of a recognized consensus about pluralism itself, there is a danger that the term is becoming so broad as to be meaningless. In that context, the kind of pluralism in question, and the methodological level at which it operates, must be clarified for debate to progress. I would emphasize three sorts of pluralism, which we can dub 'sociological', 'methodological', and 'idealist'.

By 'sociological pluralism' I mean the kind of critical theory which makes an analysis of exactly *which* pressure groups make demands on the state and how they are differentially rewarded. In this conception, the interest groups are not necessarily equal in political strength or economic muscle, nor can the state any longer be seen as a neutral arbiter or switchboard. In particular, critical pluralists of this sort have argued that the business corporation wields disproportionate influence over the state. In a sense this is a structural necessity as long as western democracies are based upon capitalist economies. For the state to operate in conditions of stability – and therefore of political 'equilibrium' – business needs must first be met (Lindblom 1977, p. 122–3). Yet it seems unlikely that, given this, the state could avoid having an active policy to enhance business interests and of necessity to ignore or downplay claims from rival interest groups. Moreover, the state's less accountable sectors – above all the *military* machine – inevitably sponsor and promote contracts with the big corporations. Political democracy, then, is not a reflection of equally-encouraged interest groups. Rather it is one potential popular channel by means of which other groups can try, against the odds, to check the privileged voice of big business in the state. Instead of 'polyarchy' the critical pluralist idea is of a 'pluto-democracy' comprising two *contradictory* impulses: 'political decisions are made within an arena in which the two principle forces are the voters and the rich capitalists' (Duverger 1974, p. 5). This bias is secured as much through state *inaction* or 'non-decision making' on some crucial social issues (for example, poverty) as it is through decisions unequivocally favourable to the business class.

In sociological pluralism, therefore, the number of key social groups and the quality of their access to the state is critically examined and revised. Indeed, the focus on *capitalist* interests in this perspective suggests affinity with Marxist critiques of the bourgeois state. Yet this affinity falls short of an *identity*, since these writers reaffirm the standard pluralist view that economic cleavages and political processes remain to an important degree separate from one another, and that through vigilant democratic pressure in the electoral sphere, the power of business can be stalled without overturning the free enterprise system as such.

'Methodological pluralism' denotes something quite different from, and not strictly comparable to, any particular theory of social interest groups. The idea can be conveyed by considering a contradiction in pluralism. On the one hand, naive pluralism conceives the state as neutral or at least as an open *arena* in which competing social claims are swapped. But pluralism also seeks to respect the diversity of social movements and individual action. In this latter sense pluralism stands in contrast to 'monocausal' approaches to power-relations which might affirm that, ultimately, politics rigidly reflects a particular kind of social relation (the class structure, for example). Rather, for pluralists there are many sources of discontent and in any case a political consensus can be achieved which *transcends* particular demands and which highlights the virtues of the political system itself. This line of thought is indeterminist, and seems to go against the first pluralist idea of the state reflecting society.

Since there are many ways of being a pluralist – it is pointless to give the term one precise meaning – we need not dwell on this contradiction *per se*. But for an analysis of the *state* it is a damaging impasse. Sociological pluralism denies any autonomy to the state, whilst consensus pluralism erects a transcendent moral virtue where the real structures of the state should be. That at least is the charge of one advocate of 'the autonomy of the democratic state' (Nordlinger 1981). Nordlinger objects to any theory which seeks to underplay the specific interests and tasks of the state personnel. Don't state officials themselves constitute a powerful – indeed uniquely placed – interest group? Isn't it the case that many vital state decisions are not about satisfying social interests but about regulating and extending the very activities of the state itself? This trenchant line of questioning is, as one might expect, directed against Marxist views. But it also counters the reductionist side of pluralism: the state *itself* constructs political alliances and re-defines the very issues of democratic politics. State actions can dampen or mobilize pressure groups, reflect or endorse specific demands. Even where the state seems most obviously to 'take on board' the interests of a specific constituency, it may be doing so *for reasons of its own*. In other words, our whole conception of a complex state structure which has diverse and often deliberate effects must recognize without qualification its autonomy from civil society. And once the idea that states have no invariable functions or preferences is granted, then logically there can be no return to a political science methodology (Marxist or pluralist) which conceives the state as merely an 'arena'.

The methodological perspective of state autonomy therefore lays incisive charges against classical pluralism. Yet in a sense it is also part of the logic of pluralism. The state is occupied after all by knowledge-able and self-interested people – a premise of pluralism inherited from the liberal democratic tradition. The state is thus an identifiable interest in its own right: indeed *several* distinct interest groups if the state is conceived as a complex of separate institutions. And whilst *economic* interest may be an important factor in political life, the concern for power, efficiency, bureaucracy, order and ideals cannot be relegated under one specific kind of motive. The autonomy of the state view is consequently one of the most explicit forms of pluralism at the methodological level. The number of groups and the causes of action are many.

The third development of pluralism I mentioned concerned its 'idealist' tendencies. The concern with stability and equilibrium, I argued, moved pluralist theorists to become moral philosophers as well as empirical observers. As the objective conditions for the harmonious social interaction of 1950s pluralism have become unfavourable, so the *prospect* of a return to consensus has become the overriding value and goal of some influential pluralist writers. This is evident, for example, in the work of Samuel Beer. In a now-classic text (Beer 1969), Beer upheld British politics as something of a pluralist model. Certainly, there was class conflict to cope with. Yet the very strength of the classes seemed to ensure a stability and tradition from which a mixed economy and 'collectivist' polity could draw strength. In what amounts to a sequel to *Modern British Politics*, Beer (1982) confesses himself to be rather disillusioned with the turn of events which finds *Britain Against Itself*. Of course, it is hard to deny that Britain's experience of social change and economic crisis have not a part to play in any explanation. In Beer's terms, the 'social foundation' of British stability have been eroded as the class structure has become more amorphous. Similarly, in the polity, the parties have witnessed and exacerbated a 'pluralist stagnation' where destructively swift and agressive changes of ideology reflect an increasing social 'scramble' for benefits, subsidies, and pay. In all these ways, the movement of pluralist democracy has been from stability to chaos.

Yet Beer acknowledges that something of all this was inherent even in the 'golden' era of post-war Britain. In effect, the decisive factor in Beer's account – decisive for stability then and chaos now – lies in cultural *attitudes* (Beer 1982, p. 5). For all the 'contradictions' in social and political life, the virtues of British democracy – as Beer sees them – lie in the delicate and mutual sense of public morality and, on the part of the majority of the electorate, social *deference* to the governing elite. This follows in the footsteps of a number of pluralist writers who sought to identify the basis of the virtuous 'civic culture' of the western democracies (eg. Almond and Verba 1963). Amongst the current array of fragmentation and self-interest, Beer sees the main hope in the recovery of a cultural consensus which spans class divisions and vying antagonistic ideologies, a consensus which now rides on the fortunes of the Social Democratic Party.

We can see here, I think, how some of the normative preferences of pluralism have to an extent invaded and replaced a concern merely to be realistic. Analytically, Beer gives causal priority to subjective attitudes over political strategies or economic contradictions. And the analytical privilege focuses on one factor – the prevalence of deference – as the original cause of both pluralist ideal and actual pluralist stagnation. Substantively, this refers to another recurrent pluralist theme: the desirability of a politics in which interests are never pressed *too* far, and where stability depends on a respectful and passive political population and a responsive governing elite. The type of pluralism represented by Beer is consequently an *idealist* type. Causal primacy is given to attitudes rather than material reality, and this very priority invests even the most insightful analytical description with a degree of wishful thinking.

3. Marxism

In Chapter 2, David Held noted that Marx himself left no detailed unambiguous theory of the state. Certainly, Marx wrote about the general connection between politics and economic classes in a range of societies, and he wrote in detail on the capitalist economic structure. Yet a body of Marxist theory about the state in capitalist society is a relatively recent development. If there is a 'classical' Marxist theory of the state, it is probably to be found in Lenin's short polemic *State and Revolution*. Yet for all its clarity and drive, this text can hardly be asked to stand in for a Marxist tradition which has long challenged and at times puzzled over the political structures of democratic capitalist states.

Nevertheless, I would say, the following three propositions would have to form the 'core' of any recognizably Marxist approach to the state. The first point is that modern western societies are based upon capitalist economies. The real ownership and control of economic and human resources in these societies is concentrated in the hands of a small minority of the population. The majority are wage-earners whose productive labour realizes the surplus which enables production to continue and which is the source of the significantly unequal distribution of personal and corporate wealth. Capitalist production therefore generates class divisions and is based upon economic exploitation. It is true that a sizeable 'public sector' has grown up, and this has led to the widespread term the 'mixed economy'. However, this is misleading in so far as it suggests a rough balance of 'public' and 'private' economic forms. From a Marxist position, *both* spheres operate by the criterion of profitability rather than social need. Even where the state sector is large, the logic of its operations remains capitalist.

The second 'core' point would be that the state's role is to ensure the stability of capitalist society. Economically, this entails that public sector money is used to bolster ailing capitalist firms or to take over unprofitable areas in the economy. This buoys up the general level of capitalist enterprise. But more than this, the state's budgetary, research, and regulation facilities are profoundly geared to the advancement of a strong market economy. Politically, the state ensures – by coercion if necessary – the smooth running of social life to the benefit of profitable economic production. As we will see, there is a further argument between Marxists as to whether this role of the state is relatively uncomplicated and deliberate or complex and contingent, but as a schematic description of the *general outcome* of state policy, Marxists are committed to this point.

The third aspect of Marxist theory concerns the democratic process. Marxists would not deny that democracy has given working people a 'voice' – a voice which in principle can be expressed in majority *opposition* to capitalism. However two things qualify the importance of democracy 'as we know it'. In the first place, democracy (like all political arrangements) has been historically connected to the rise and struggles of particular social classes. Democracy was revived and utilized as the political form by which, at first, the bourgeoisie challenged the rule of the landed aristocracy, and subsequently by which the proletariat has in turn sought to gain a foothold on political power, this time against the dominance of the bourgeoisie itself. That democratic reforms are achieved by classes or class fractions can be shown on a broad empirical canvas over the last few centuries (Therborn 1977). That they periodically involve serious social conflict is evident to most analysts who are not (Marxists would say) blinkered by the illusory restriction of the meaning of democracy to merely parliamentary debate. Secondly, Marxists would wish to assert that the very separation of political freedoms and economic unfreedom serves to deflect the potential mounting of a popular challenge to the source of exploitation and inequality – the capitalist mode of production itself. This is because workplace relations and the cultural communities are *collective* phenomena: they derive by and large from people's common class identity. The process of political democracy, when restricted in meaning to the act of periodic voting, casts people in the role of atomised individuals who, as individuals, make decisions which have political effects. But there is a discrepancy between that limited individual effect on the endorsement or replacement of *government*, and the need for democracy to become a much more active, frequent and multi-layered process embracing industrial and community power structures as well as those of parliaments. This tangible extension of democracy would certainly heighten tension between popular aspirations and the state as a whole. The coercive, undemocratic aspect of the state and its role as stabiliser for capitalist production would be correspondingly contested. It is no mere accident, therefore, that the political establishment, the press magnates and the state media make a virtue out of trying to confine the very term 'democracy' to the individualized moment of electoral politics.

If this picture amounts to a core Marxist perspective, and one which certainly distinguishes it from more pluralist positions, it is essential to indicate why, in extrinsic terms, 'classical Marxist' theory is nowadays difficult to sustain. For one thing, the state has grown enormously since Marx's time. In terms of the sheer weight of forces, of powers which permeate the entire fabric of society, and of formidable technological resources, the idea that the aroused proletariat can (with effort) knock over existing state apparatuses to inaugurate a democratic workers commonwealth seems increasingly hopeful rather than probable. Neither Marx in his writings on the Paris Commune nor Lenin in *State and Revolution* were naive about the depth and strength of the state. But they tended to see it as an instrument of capitalism which might be taken over by the organized insurgent workers themselves, who in turn would be adequately representative of the people as a whole.

This instrumentalist view of the state was not the only one in Marx or the Marxist tradition, but in the Bolshevik and Communist experience it has come to raise serious problems of Marxists, problems which are tangibly real as well as theoretical. In the Soviet Union – especially under Stalin – the state which in theory was meant to 'wither away' became massively strengthened in the name of the 'dictatorship of the proletariat' (itself exercised by the party). The use of unprecedented coercion in the building of an industrial base for socialist society, whatever the adverse international conditions, has left few socialists in any doubt that the state, democracy, and freedom are issues which go alongside *but beyond* their embodiment in particular sorts of economic relations. And this salutory lesson applies whether or not Marxists feel able to describe the countries of 'actually existing socialism' as 'genuinely' socialist, or even on the road to genuine socialism. That, of course, is a hotly disputed political question, but the conflict between self-declared socialist states (USSR against China, Vietnam against China, Kampuchea against Vietnam) should suffice to make it plain that Marxists cannot deflect questions of state organization and accountability by reference only to how the economy is nominally classified.

In the west, the class structures of advanced capitalism have arguably become more complex, the inroads of 'reformist' labour movements significant, and the real popularity of formal freedoms undeniable. The prospect of a concerted revolutionary offensive against the capitalist class and state is to contemporary Marxists more of a talisman than a political strategy. However, the terms of political discourse exert a spell of their own, and socialist politics has witnessed a number of divisions according to just how the changes in capitalism should be addressed and confronted. In the 1970s, some of the major European Communist Parties openly accepted the need to re-think the problem of the state in capitalist society. In this movement – termed 'Eurocommunism' – the notion of the dictatorship of the proletariat was dropped, and the relationship of several CPs to the traditional head of the international communist movement, the USSR, became distant and critical (Carillo 1977). Internally, these parties gave unprecedented priority to national issues of popular democracy and adopted more open inner-party structures. This broader approach spurred a greater effort to appeal to *current* ideologies, to construct a series of political 'alliances' which cut across economic class divisions (with middle strata professionals, women's movements and ethnic groups, for instance), and required a declared intent to work against the capitalist state from 'within' the procedures of parliamentary democracy. All in all, this strategy accepted the reality of modern politics whilst at the same time questioning some of the basic Marxist positions. Yet by combining a realistic analysis of trends with which Marx was familiar but which had become intensified, with a concern to identify qualitatively *new* phenomena in advanced capitalism, Eurocommunism could claim to be a 'creative' Marxism suited to contemporary conditions. Despite notable political advances in the mid-1970s, Eurocommunism did not fare well thereafter. The Italian CP's impressive presence in social and electoral life remains unequalled, but has slipped gradually; the Spanish party has crumbled under internal polemic, and almost every other CP world-wide (including the dramatically sliding French) became by the early 1980s riven with divisions along 'Leninist v. Eurocommunist' lines. Both the insurrectionism of Lenin and the reformism of Eurocommunism tends to be severely caricatured in these debates, but there are genuine and deep differences as to how to apply the Marxist conception of the state to pluralist democracy *in practice*.

In this context, it is possible to pick out three broad clusters of Marxist perspectives on the state. I will designate these positions 'reductionism', 'relative autonomy', and 'idealism'. Even less than in the case of the three varieties of pluralism I described, are these divisions within Marxism entirely satisfactory. For example, as in the case of my pluralist discussion, the focus is as much on the *method* of analysis as the substantive content of a particular theoretical variant. Thus the 'state-monopoly capitalist' school and the 'capital-logic' perspectives (described below) are classified together here in spite of several differences between their accounts of capitalism (cf. Jessop 1982, Chs. 3 and 4). However, a line has to be drawn somewhere, and I consider the schema adopted to be as fruitful as an initial way of characterizing the debates as any other.

'Reductionist' Marxism denotes the tendency to reduce the state to its capitalist essence in spite of the many other organizational and social functions it possesses. Two Trotskyist writers thus maintain that the 'continued rule of the bourgeoisie in some "democratic" capitalist states' and 'the bureaucratic distortions of the workers' states' are in truth forms of appearance of the death agony of capitalism and the unresolved crisis of revolutionary leadership of the working class (Dragstedt and Slaughter 1981, p. 24).

In this proposition, the political effects of the political sphere (democracy or distorted bureaucracy) are held to be superficial effects of capitalist economic crisis. This is what is meant by economic reductionism, where the 'crisis' is assumed to be a semi-permanent and single economic essence, whilst the political substance of democracy or bureaucracy is 'merely' superficial. But there is also a note of historical inevitability in the statement: the working class is now ready to seize state power, and indeed will eventually do so, once it has overcome the disorganization imposed upon it by the lack of clear revolutionary leadership. This conception is of a relatively simple struggle as to which class – bourgeoisie or proletariat – wields state power as 'an instrument of class oppression' (Dragstedt and Slaughter 1981, p. 25).

So reductionist variants of Marxism can take a 'class' or an 'economic' form and may often combine the two. On the 'economic' side, it has been maintained that the economy goes through certain historic phases from laissez-faire through the dominance of big monopolies to a stage of 'state-monopoly capitalism'. This latter phase (the current one) entails the large-scale intervention of the state to provide credit and conditions of expansion for especially manufacturing or productive capital. Now this is not simply an 'economic' state of affairs, for in state-monopoly capitalism an entire socialization of techniques, skills, and resources takes place. Thus the state has to ensure programmes of education, welfare, housing, and so on. So 'reductionism' need not be considered an inevitably one-dimensional method which necessarily ignores events in the political sphere. Yet amongst these theories there is a tendency to assume that the economic motor of capital accumulation inexorably produces its required effect at the level of state intervention. Thus the 'political' is determined by the 'economic'.

Of course, Marx himself considered the 'superstructure' to follow – maybe with time-lags and awkward fits – the logic of the economic structure or 'base'. Some Marxist economists have tried to get by without this metaphor as a way of escaping the reductionism of state-monopoly capital theory. The so-called capital-logic school thus try to derive the political forms in capitalist society from the fact that capitalism is not simply an economy, but a general *social* relationship embracing political relations too. For example, the economy is mediated by legal regulations, social reproduction, and popular legitimacy, and none of these factors can be described as purely economic. So, again, a certain kind of capital-logic analysis might seek to avoid reductionism altogether. However, the very term 'capital-logic' implies that there is an objective set of needs (social or economic) which are met to ensure capitalist reproduction, and it is these which explain the specific forms of politics and cultural experiences which develop historically in capitalist societies. Indeed, laws, welfare, education, electoral democracy are part of the logic of capital itself in its expanded phase of socialization. In an attempt to overcome the mechanical separation of base and superstructure, this perspective has posited a seamless web of social phenomena whose centre is the circuit of capital. Despite the more organic cast of the theorizing, capital-logic, like state-monopoly capitalism, tends to distil or reduce a range of cultural contradictions into the surface forms of the essence of capitalism.

The second batch of Marxist approaches I termed 'relative autonomy'. In fact, these need not be radically different from the more fundamentalist scenarios, since the autonomy of the state is always *relative*, never 'absolute'. Marx himself allowed the state considerable independent powers, whilst making sense of political regimes by at least trying to connect them to the functional needs of the economic system. Similarly, today's Marxists attempt to balance the real effects of the state *per se* against its ultimate basis in the structures of capitalist production. For example, the 'structuralist' position of Louis Althusser (1972) and Nicos Poulantzas (1973) asserts that only by being autonomous from explicit capitalist direction can the state succeed in managing society to the benefit of capital *in general*. According to this argument classes do not operate as whole entities or occupy in person the positions of power. The intrinsic complexity of the state institutions would make this unlikely, divisions within the ruling class would tend to hamper any 'instrumentalist' conception even amongst the dominant capitalists, and class struggle would ensure that the political sphere is a contested arena. Yet the structuralists have also maintained that whilst the activities of the capitalist state are inescapably *political*, it is only because of this 'displacement' from the economy that the state adequately secures the social cohesion necessary for capitalism to prosper. By being removed from direct capitalist control and thus being open to class struggle 'from below', the state actually succeeds more comprehensively to serve capital in general.

The 'relative autonomy' view – in its structuralist version – cannot quite evade the problem of appearing to resort to a cast-iron 'functionalist' guarantee. It is a paradox which others share. Ralph Miliband, for example, was criticized by Poulantzas for paying too much attention to *who* ruled in the interests of capital as against analysing the objective structures of the capitalist state (Miliband 1983, part 1). Yet Miliband's more empirical, sociological approach has not escaped the structuralist dilemma. Miliband suggests in attractive terms that whilst the police, courts, media and so on are not *simply* to be seen as the agencies of capitalist propaganda, this is not to say that they are not *also* that (Miliband 1982, p. 84). The state does not work at the *behest* of the capitalist class; but it does work on its *behalf*. Non-structuralist Marxists such as Miliband thus share the problem of a certain reductionist analysis creeping in by the back door. The state's relative autonomy and subjection to class struggle is said to be crucial, but 'the state's purpose has always been unambiguous, namely to help capitalist enterprise to prosper' (Miliband 1982, p. 95).

Marxists who have taken up the work of the Italian Communist Antonio Gramsci (Gramsci 1971) are less equivocal about relative autonomy. Gramsci's own contribution emphasized the way in which political forces achieve 'hegemony' (intellectual, moral and political leadership, not merely economic domination). For the capitalist power bloc of forces – again, classes do not rule 'nakedly' here – the state is a central *educative* channel. Capitalism is sustained not just in terms of economic requirements being fulfilled, but by the active cultivation of a widespread popular endorsement of the 'civilization' it represents. Incarcerated in a fascist jail from the age of 35 until his death, Gramsci needed no reminding of the 'iron fist' of the state. Yet he was concerned to emphasize the interweaving of coercion and consent as components of a hegemonic political strategy. And it is clear from his work that the latter is never based either on pure economic motives to the exclusion of cultural influence in everyday life, or on the actions of single social classes outside of alliances with other social forces.

Gramsci's work has been the subject of intense debate. His legacy has been claimed as the basis of Eurocommunism and this has been resisted by those who see clear affinities with Lenin's emphasis on the power of political will. Despite a strong antipathy to the organic, 'culturalist' cast of the Italian tradition, erstwhile structuralists such as Poulantzas have been significantly influenced by Gramsci. A flour-ishing research programme in Marxist studies of the police, media, education, and the family have drawn on the Gramscian approach to the state, and in particular its emphasis on the shifting balance of economy and ideology, or coercion and consent. Still, it is also clear that the neo-Gramscian positions can result in extremely flexible and even fuzzy theoretical formulae about the state's relative autonomy. Gramsci's own condensed and allusive prison writings cannot be applied directly to contemporary politics, nor are they unambiguous. The demarcation between state and society is a shifting, overlapping one in Gramsci, and 'hegemony' in capitalist society extends beyond the state as such. Gramsci and his followers are rightly interested in cultural formations and ideological arenas in connection with the role of the state, but there is no warrant for thinking that Gramsci would deny the ultimately class-based causes and outcomes of political events. It may be true that

> Gramsci's theory of civil society and its complex relations with the state provide a perspective for the transition from capitalism to socialism (Simon 1982, p. 79).

It would nevertheless be a mistake to think that this perspective is a fully developed, coherent or directive one. 'Relative autonomy' in

Gramscian analysis becomes a rich and multidimensional phenomenon; but it is not a logically tight or politically explicit one.

The Marxist views I have been discussing retain the core propositions I outlined before. But it is a growing worry amongst some
contemporary Marxists that the core itself intrinsically contains the
risk of reductionism. As we have seen, the latter can be openly
adopted or avoided by qualifications either in principle or in application. But is it possible to be a Marxist whilst dropping part of the
core itself? This is an important issue which has major repercussions
for even how we *define* 'Marxism'. It is implicit, for example, that the
'core' Marxist propositions see the economic contradictions of
capitalism as explanatorily primary – whether in the first or last
instance. What if that idea was not merely qualified but rejected?

Arguments as to the indissolubility of economic and political
processes need not follow the 'economistic' path of the capital-logic
school. If economic constraints and political processes are part of the
same complex reality of class struggle or strategy, who is to say which
'ultimately' determines the other? Arguments of this sort within
Marxism have become fashionable. One approach is to criticize the
conception of a structural economic base which underlies and determines politics. Since this base refers to the calculations of firms and
governments, then it cannot exist outside specific strategies or the
discourses of groups of agents within those processes. Similarly, the
socialist conception of economic prosperity and a better society does
not exist in some metaphysical realm separate from debates and
organizations amongst people who address those issues. It follows
that there can be no persuasive case for thinking that the economy
prescribes the content of political affairs. The state is not 'given' by a
capitalist economy, nor is a suitable 'class' perspective leading to
socialism magically endowed upon people who happen to be workers.
What happens at the political level, the argument runs, cannot be
assessed independently of specifically *political* mechanisms: parties,
elections, campaigns and so on.

This is a cogent and destructive critique of classical Marxism from
within. Some who pursue this view show little concern that virtually
nothing is left of the 'core' position of Marxism (cf. Cutler *et al* 1977,
Hindess 1983). They are prepared to accept the consequence that
Marxist categories, like any others, have no necessary privilege
stemming from the character of capitalist societies themselves, that is,
from reality. Marxist terms of reference *may* be used, however, as
long as these are recognized to be discursive only. In other words, all
politics – and thus the state too – is a matter of specific concepts,
agencies and political programmes. I call this view an idealist view

because the superiority of any analysis or programme is said to come, not from its adequacy to social reality, but from its place in a preferred discourse. The view is not idealist in the sense of being simply about ideas or attitudes: it began as a concern to focus Marxist attention on the real effect of political *practices* and *organizations* rather than abstract doctrine. But it is idealist in 'bracketing off' the idea of a world outside discourse – a device which takes this critical perspective outside the ambit of the 'classical' Marxist tradition altogether.

Other commentators influenced by such a philosophical critique (for that is really what it boils down to) are less confident about taking that step over the borders of Marxism. Ironically their views are the weaker for the understandable hesitancy. The American political scientist Adam Przeworski, for example, argues that 'class' itself as a concept cannot be arrived at through economic analysis alone. Indeed the idea of an 'objective' class position is a product of proletarian class struggle, not a pre-existing datum. In this sense, political struggle and ideological projects *constitute* class itself (Przeworski 1977, p. 368). This is an idealist position because 'consciousness' predetermines 'objective' social relations. The point of Przeworski's analysis is especially relevant to the minority situation of proletarians in the USA as measured by strict Marxist criteria. Such a classification offers little hope to socialists who have no option but to accept an electoral system of majority vote as the only means of challenging state power. Przeworski's idea is that by emphasizing the possibilities of social struggle in the arena of the democratic state, the working class might be appropriately re-constituted or re-formed. The socialist optimism of the outlook thus expressed does not, however, square up to the materialism of the Marxist method. To focus on the centrality of popular but cross-class ideas, ideologies and discourses seems very important. Yet in spite of their unrelenting critique of reductionism, theorists who take this angle (eg. Laclau 1980, Laclau and Mouffe 1981) continue – paradoxically – to think that ultimately a *class* identity prevails on the elements of political discourse. This is an extremely damaging paradox because they root Marxist analysis and social hope in a category they have asserted to be a purely *discursive* construct. That being so, however, there is no necessity whatever in giving either discursive or practical priority to class. In the best detailed recent survey of Marxist ideas on the state the idealist position just examined is praised as being among the most 'advanced' (Jessop 1982, p. 203). I think we can see, though, that as long as this view remains an avowedly Marxist one, its sense of complexity about the state and politics has led 'advanced' Marxism into a serious and unresolvable impasse. Of course, this might not matter if all 'discourses' were self-referential! But ultimately, Marxism's credibility depends on its explanatory appeal, some part of which must be avowedly empirical.

4. Beyond the Debate?

General comparisons

So far I have outlined the developments within the theoretical frameworks (or 'problematics') of pluralism and Marxism. It should be apparent that the very existence of a number of rival conceptions – some of which may seem 'heretical' – make the idea of a grand clash between pluralism and Marxism somewhat anachronistic. Such grand clashes do occur at the political and theoretical levels between particular variants of each problematic, and between the neo-liberal framework and anything from pluralism leftwards. But the nature of the debate between Marxism and pluralism has become more nuanced and less strident. The purpose of this part is to describe the parallels and sketch the remaining bones of contention. This is done firstly by a general theoretical account in the manner of part one, then by briefly considering whether two more delimited questions in state-theory (corporatism and democracy) take us 'beyond' a simple opposition between Marxism and pluralism.

In my discussion of pluralism, I concluded that that tradition as a unified theory and as a *justification* of advanced capitalist democracy had collapsed. Certainly, some pluralists (particularly the 'idealists') will hanker after another phase of cross-class consensus. And this view is quite incompatible with the Marxist idea that class struggle and exploitation constantly undercut the basis of harmony and equilibrium.

Critical pluralists however can accept that critique. Their reservations about Marxism concern not the pertinence of class division but its effect and extent. Analytically, all pluralists would be less confident than Marxists about giving definitive causal accounts of the social structure. Substantively, pluralists deny the privilege Marxists assign to class, to the economy, and to social 'contradictions' in general. And the writings of all Marxists, including 'revisionist' Marxists, continue to show the pervasive influence of those concepts. In that sense, there can be no question of a smooth 'convergence' between Marxism and pluralism, since disagreements over causality and social structure are the most basic in social science. Here Marxism has made impressive inroads into 'bourgeois' social science and the theory of the state.

However, it would be quite wrong to conclude from this general philosophical contrast that there have not been significant moves towards a synthesis between Marxism and pluralism, at least in its critical variety. Since I hold no brief for consensus theory I do not invest the term 'synthesis' with any particular moral or scholarly relish! But it would be unusual if no strands of convergence came out of the dislocation of the classical paradigms, and some of these strands may be important in the development of a broad-based 'critical' social theory of the state. One thing to bear in mind, for example, is that there is now a whole range of critical commentators on state and society who would consider themselves to be neither Marxists nor pluralists (other than perhaps in the methodological sense I have been at pains to emphasize). And today it seems no contradiction for some Marxists (as defined by the 'core' propositions) to have both a pluralistic conception of democracy (including socialist democracy), and an analysis of the state which recognizes the multi-dimensional constraints on state power and state action.

'Pluralistic' Marxists and 'critical' pluralists thus have a common ground of analysis and politics. Bob Jessop, for example, has persuasively argued that the search for any general theory of the state within Marxism must be relinquished (Jessop 1982, p. 211). In other words, there are no inevitable or logical economic functions which the state comes into existence to serve. This entails, firstly, that the idea of *all* states being solely instruments of class oppression must be doubted; and, secondly, that the role of the *capitalist* state is not simply one of facilitating capitalist interests. These are contingent questions to be decided by historical analysis not philosophical assumption.

Two further consequences are inherent in this kind of pluralist Marxism. The state itself is no longer seen as a single, purposeful entity. Rather 'the state comprises a plurality of institutions' (Jessop 1982, p. 222). This enables Marxists happily to accept a) the possibility of *contradictions* between branches of the state and b) that the state is often concerned with the 'reproduction of the state apparatus itself as a system of domination' (Jessop 1982, p. 231). This last point is a surprising endorsement of Nordlinger's claim that whether or not class interests are involved, the state is always concerned to protect and extend its own specific privileges. A more general concession offered by the 'pluralist' Marxist state-theorists is the abandonment of the very notion of objective class interests. The state itself is accepted as being present at the *onset* of class society: so it does not *derive* from class division. (Poulantzas 1980, p. 39). And one of the central tasks of the state has been to mediate between dominant and subordinate classes (Therborn 1980, p. 181). This operation cannot be achieved in terms restricted to those of class interest, which in any case is always a matter of debate and strategy rather than objective fact.

In the light of these 'concessions', Marxism moves closer to a more open-ended perspective on the state. To characterize the state institutionally, contingently, and free from an all-pervasive 'task' to secure class interests allows greater flexibility in historical and contemporary analysis. There seems no reason for Marxists to deny the claim of a self-declared critic of historical materialism that 'it is dangerously misleading to speak of "the" capitalist state, rather than the more accurate designation "capitalist states"' (Giddens 1981, p. 210). And in terms of *historical* analyses, a Marxist concern to discover class interests can be replaced by research into the more complicated dynamics of class struggle *plus* state autonomy in the study of political upheavals such as the French and Russian revolutions (cf. Skocpol 1979).

This kind of more open-ended Marxism will naturally be frowned upon by those intent on protecting the 'core' at all costs. And since the price to pay for flexibility is a less compelling general theory of society, the protest is not without point. Yet in itself, this general convergence of perspectives does not represent an advantage to pluralism as such, and certainly not to classical pluralism – which could muster no such sophisticated historical research agenda. This is because the best critics of dogmatic Marxism continue to base their accounts on the concepts of capitalism, exploitation, inequality, and social conflict: concepts developed and defended above all in the Marxist tradition.

Corporatism

Corporatism refers to the widespread tendency across the advanced capitalist countries for industrial relations between employers and trade union organizations to be resolved and institutionalized at the level of the state itself. In fact, the progress of corporatism has been effectively stalled in a number of countries due to the resurgence of free market conservatism. Yet it will continue to stand as the principle alternative to the latter. This political significance is reflected in theoretical discussions about corporatism, in which a number of different Marxist and pluralist considerations are in play.

Initially, 'corporatism' analysis sought to go beyond classical pluralism. Instead of the latter's picture of many power centres based upon voluntary groups, corporatist theory reflected the increasing *centralization* of *organized* interest groups (especially capital and labour) (Schmitter 1979). Moreover, corporatism witnessed the special role of the state itself in constructing a framework for both economic and political affairs. The classical conception of parliamentary or territorial representation had to be recognized as an inadequate way of understanding the centrality of functional representation and corporate power (the unions and the big monopolies). Corporatism thus reflects the transgression of the division between state and society as previously assumed in the pluralist and liberal democratic traditions. Two questions arise here, despite some clear advances beyond classical pluralism. One is, how does neo-corporatist theory *explain* corporatism? The other is, does neo-corporatism transcend the broader division in political theory between pluralism and Marxism? Actually, the answer to the first question supplies much of the reply to the second. This is because neo-corporatist theory gives a number of *different* accounts of the characteristics of corporatism, and the explanatory content of the term is unclear. As a descriptive term, corporatism refers to such phenomenon as incomes policies, national plans, 'tripartite' negotiations, and a state-run public sector. Some theorists require that corporatism proper is only achieved when interest groups have an institutionalized place in the state apparatus which survives particular changes of government (as in the case of the Austrian post-war 'social partnership'). Others are happy to classify as corporatist – albeit 'weak' corporatism – the British Labour governments' efforts to secure 'social contracts' with the unions. So as a *description*, corporatism seems to refer only to a range of 'interest group negotiations' receiving some kind of state sponsorship.

As to *explanations* of the corporatist phenomena, neo-corporatist theory similarly lacks a common focus. Some argue that the state's control of industry and political representation is qualitatively new, constituting a new form of economy altogether (Pahl and Winkler 1974). This line of approach recalls the fact that 'corporatism' was widely used to characterize Mussolini's fascist economy in the 1920s and 1930s. However, in the advanced capitalist democracies, this seems exaggerated. The Marxist argument that the state remains constrained by the need to secure, and operate in terms of, the conditions of profitability of private capital remains persuasive. And politically, whilst corporatism knocks holes through parts of the received idea of western democracy (Middlemas 1979, p. 381), there is little indication that functional representation has *replaced* parliament as a means of policy-formation and of securing general state legitimacy.

So the non-Marxist accounts of corporatism flounder somewhat on the rocks of explanation. This lack of a coherent causal story was said earlier to be a characteristic trait of all pluralist analysis. In other senses too, neo-corporatism remains tied to pluralist ideas. The state is by no means invisible, but in several versions of the theory, it continues to be seen as a 'broker' for independently vying social constituencies. Moreover, neo-corporatist writers persist in treating the relationship between interest groups as that of equal partners. Trade unions, employers, the state: each is conceived as a counter-balance to the other. This residual pluralist notion sits uneasily with the frequent – but frequently off-hand – acknowledgement in the literature that corporatism is a means of stabilizing *capitalist* economic relations. But historically it seems clear that not only are the forces of capital normally stronger than those of labour, they are on the whole bolstered by the state, which is seldom a neutral broker or even-handed umpire between interest groups.

A proportion of the work on corporatism, then, remains caught in unsatisfactory pluralist assumptions about interest group power, the state as an 'arena', and tends to share its analytical evasiveness. The Marxist critique of neo-corporatism is correspondingly strong. But we can also ask whether Marxist accounts of corporatism are adequate in themselves. Here we find, again, an array of Marxist approaches somewhat at odds with one another. A 'reductionist' Marxist view is that corporatism is straightforwardly a form of class collaboration. The unions are duped into a false sense of social recognition and are 'incorporated' into the logic of capitalist economic restraint. Corporatism is thus a state strategy operating directly on behalf of the capitalist class. This type of approach is rarely unqualified in Marxist work on corporatism, but it does exert a distinct influence in some of the prominent texts on the issue (eg. Panitch 1980). These reductionist connotations suffer from the same faults of *a priori* schematism mentioned earlier in connection with economistic Marxism in general.

Insofar as the literature on corporatism as a whole represents a critical effort to come to terms with a novel aspect of state-society relations, Marxists cannot dismiss it out of hand. For one thing, it is obvious in the 1980s that capitalism has no 'need' to resort to corporatism as its main source of survival: the logic of the market and the strong arm of the state will do equally well. Indeed it could be argued that in corporatism it is above all the long term struggle of *labour* which is recognized, negotiated, and (possibly) furthered. There is a growing school of neo-Marxist commentators who insist that welfare states and high standards are *won* from capitalism, even if in an apparently concessionary way. And in several countries, above all perhaps Sweden, a form of corporatism has enabled the working class to become entrenched in economic and political life to the extent that from such a basis, a peaceful transition to socialism can be launched over the medium term (eg. Stephens 1979, Korpi 1983).

This perspective seems too optimistic to serve as a justification for corporatism; but it draws attention to the weaknesses of a reductionist analysis. From a position akin to the 'idealist' variant of Marxism, it has been claimed that the whole idea of corporatism is a vulgarization of a process in which economic interests are *politically* constructed and open to a variety of challenges. Corporatism does not 'reflect' any pre-given social interests, whether those of capital or labour. Rather, political mechanisms have their *own* conditions, effects, and sites of conflict (Tomlinson 1981).

A somewhat less revisionist Marxist perspective would be to assume that the ways in which corporatism represents an advance or setback for capitalism is a matter for empirical investigation and careful distinction. And even where, 'in general' the corporatist pattern favours capital over labour, there may be institutional differences within and across capitalist states. Moreover, there are politically interesting questions about corporatism as a form of political representation which do not pertain to economic interest alone (Jessop 1979). This more circumspect Marxist approach coincides to an extent with some pluralist concerns to emphasize the international *diversity* in state strength and organization (Birnbaum 1982), and to maintain, whilst accepting the capitalist character of the economy, that a more empirical attitude to its 'needs' is required (cf. Crouch 1979).

Democracy and Power

There is no space here to enter into a lengthy account of the political sphere in capitalist society (for an introduction see McLennan 1984). But we can begin to map out current issues by saying a word about the customary complaint against Marxism that it conceives the processes of political democracy to be a 'sham', imposed in order to deflect the workers from overthrowing the system. In fact, this is a serious and harmful caricature, which has probably never been accurate. Nevertheless the logic of reductionism has led some Marxists to underestimate the strength and depth of electoral democracy in advanced capitalism, and to overstate the revolutionary potential which is thought to reside in the economic experience of the working class. Today, though, this tendency would be kept in check by Marxists. Their emphasis is placed not on the 'sham' of elections as such, but on the de-mobilizing consequences of *restricting* the scope and meaning of democracy to the electoral process. Most Marxists have entered the arena of party competition either by joining social democratic parties or by standing for election as specifically Marxist parties. So the electoral realm may be *limited*, but it cannot be discounted without inconsistency. Similarly the short-term interests and beliefs which surface in electoral issues may be compromises on long-term socialist goals, but they have a real basis in people's lives. 'Fundamental' or long-term interests which are seldom recognized as such are at best possibilities. They are not objective forces. To persist in this view poses real difficulties for parties committed – as Marxists are – to rational as well as passionate political argument.

One of the consequences of entering the arena of electoral politics is that Marxists have come to accept and embrace issues – including forms of social inequality and oppression – which are not reducible to class. Electoral democracy in capitalist societies (and perhaps in any society) brings together voters mainly as *individuals*, and covers a range of 'national–popular' issues. These will undoubtedly have a class-related content – housing, transport, leisure facilities and so on. But often they will not. Questions of gender inequality, environment, international relations, law, and trade-regulation are other questions which in various ways go beyond class *per se*. And inevitably, personal and local concerns, the quality of candidates, and party performance all add to the complicated determinants of representative politics. For these reasons too, class can never be the sole analytical factor in accounting for electoral trends. This is why some Marxists have tried to avoid the sociological reductionism which consists of explaining the electoral decline of the Labour Party for example as a straightforward function of changing class composition.

None of this means that Marxist, or class analysis generally, do not make an important contribution to electoral analysis. But at the specific level of electoral trends, their claims cannot be to the exclusion of other factors prized by pluralist and other non-Marxist commentators. At the level of the state as a whole (which is considerably wider than electoral politics) the Marxist argument about the limitations of electoralism is in many ways confirmed. The state personnel are seldom accountable, parliament itself is not much more than the vehicle for government decisions, and the increasingly heterogeneous and sceptical electorate can be at any time subject to the interference and surveillance of an entire machinery of coercion and regulation. Without strenuous collective effort, individuals are poorly placed to challenge this form of state power. One of the key roles of this state apparatus is to defend the capitalist system and to 'atomize' popular movements. In that sense, Marxists are quite right to say that overall, the political weight of ordinary working people is kept to a minimum, and that the existence of electoral democracy is small consolation.

This argument, though, is not only a point about class oppression. For the growth of the strong state is guided by its own logic as well as a capitalist rationale; and of course the coercive nature of state intervention in Eastern European countries which claim to be post-capitalist is empirically obvious to all but apologists. So again, democracy, in its fullest sense of popular participation and freedom, offers common ground for Marxists and critical pluralists to build upon both analytically and politically. The basis of this re-alignment is (analytically) the idea of *power* and the normative charge is that effective democracy should be extended beyond what is officially sanctioned as the public sphere.

The core of the Marxist analysis of power has always been *exploitation*: it is by virtue of control of economic resources and the appropriation of surplus labour that ruling classes have ensured their *political* domination. The traditional force of this proposition is not annulled by 'new' conflicts. Modern Marxists point out cogently that the major non-class forms of oppression – of women, of ethnic and cultural groups, of children – are also, centrally, linked to the intensified exploitation (in the classical Marxist sense) to which these groups can be subjected. However, notions of exploitation, domination, oppression and coercion form a family of related conditions, none of which is quite the same as any other. And of course Marxist historians are perfectly familiar with the fact that forms of economic exploitation (in feudalism for example) can themselves be dependent upon 'extra-economic' relations of power such as law, ideology, and armed might.

Indeed, in recent years critical theorists of many sorts have returned to the fairly stark perception that all forms of power begin and end with bodily fear and submission. For example, in many countries of the world failure to work (however cheaply) results in near-starvation. In all countries, women's social and economic inferiority to men is predicated upon the ultimate sanction of physical violence in the home and family. And the classical definition of the state is that it wields a monopoly of legitimate violence over the popular masses of a given territory. In each of these examples it is obvious – to me at any rate – that economic benefit will be a crucial stake in these various strategies of power. Perhaps *the* stake. Yet the modalities of power are at once elementally physical and psychologically complex. Relations of power – state against people, men against women, employer against employee, young against old – have a specific dynamic of their own. In that sense, there are indeed a *plurality* of social 'contradictions'.

It is partly in accordance with these considerations that some radical writers have chosen to regard Marxism as no longer the dominant 'paradigm' in social analysis. Indeed, some appear to have challenged the idea that the state itself is a privileged locus and source of power. In the view of Michel Foucault for example (Foucault 1979, 1981), power is inherent in innumerable social relationships, each 'pole' of domination generating its own corresponding pole of resistance. This critique of the idea that power is a property of unique sovereign entities (be it the state, the government, or the ruling class) is interesting and novel. It is nevertheless difficult to assess and to accept mainly because it seems to prohibit the assertion of a *hierarchy* of determinate power relations. Above all, it is impossible to grant the tangible concentration of resources in the state if (as appears in Foucault's conception) power is qualitatively spread over innumerable 'micro-situations' and 'strategic discourses'. From a revised Marxist perspective, itself pessimistically sensitive to the extension of state power beyond class, Nicos Poulantzas has plausibly likened this Nietzsche-influenced vision of dispersed power precisely to the classical pluralist conception of politics (Poulantzas 1980, p. 44).

There is good reason then to continue to regard – and to fear – the state as the supreme location of power even though its power is not always or directly class-based. It is in the state, by and large, that policies governing the family, women's control of their own fertility, worker's organizations, civil rights, economic equality and access to state information are carried through or baulked. Each of these contradictions requires due attention if the power of the state is to be democratically prized open and returned to the people in a more substantial way than currently exists. At this level the terminological opposition between Marxism and pluralism can be regarded as overconstrictive on the range of democratic alternatives to a weakened parliamentary system and strong state. The feminist movement has made a stringent critique of Marxism's tendency (which it is said to share with orthodox political theory) to operate an artificial distinction between the public sphere of political activism and the supposedly 'private' sphere of personal relationships. (cf. Siltanen and Stanworth 1984, Pateman 1983). Moreover, the Marxist emphasis on *production* can be challenged when it is asserted to the detriment of issues around consumption, community, and leisure: issues which seem set to become more important as capitalist industry is restructured. Within political theory a current of 'radical democratic' thought (cf. Duncan 1983) has sought to reintroduce aspects of the classical democratic ideal of direct popular participation in the polity. Despite a certain academic vagueness about political programmes and the 'potential' of the ordinary voter, this kind of approach at least resurrects a broad-based optimism about the future of democracy which can be both shared and occupied by Marxists and others in their own way.

The critiques of the state stemming from Marxism, feminism, and radical democratic theory are not equivalent. Each draws upon a different aspect of social domination, aspects which nevertheless do overlap with one another. Similarly, each has a conception of what a fully democratic order should look like, and these will surely overlap too. But the building of a democratic society – its precise mechanisms of collective decision making – are of necessity less easy to arrive at. Some serious contradictions between groups of equals, and between localities seem certain to exist in a post-capitalist democratic society. This is the central political issue behind even the more abstract analytical terms of the Marxism–pluralism debate. My own conclusion would be this: Marxism has gained in breadth in recent years to its own enhancement. Critical pluralism is a rather less coherent tendency arising from the ruins of clasical pluralism. Despite the arguments *within* Marxism, and thus despite a certain loss of identity, the tradition of Marxist work has proved more impressive than pluralism – where the latter is conceived mainly as a 'school of thought'. But Marxism cannot be revised indefinitely: its 'core' position is a necessary restriction on what can be said in its name. It follows that social analysis, like politics, cannot simply be a matter of asking Marxism to 'cover' yet another type of social contradiction. The strength of the Marxist perspective is thus bought at a price, for it cannot be expected to say everything about gender, power, or culture. As these latter issues are perceived to be increasingly important, it is arguable that Marxist categories must take their place as an important part – but only a part – of an overlapping series of critical concepts in social thought. In that sense we are already 'beyond' the debate between Marxism and pluralism.

References

Almond, G. and Verba, S. (1963). *The Civic Culture*. Princeton University Press.
Althusser, L. (1972). 'Ideology and Ideological State Apparatuses', in *Lenin and Philosophy*, London, New Left Books.
Beer, S.H. (1969). *Modern British Politics*. London, Faber.
Beer, S.H. (1982). *Britain Against Itself*. London, Faber.
Birnbaum, P. (1982). 'The state versus corporatism', *Politics and Society* Vol. 11 No. 4.
Campbell, A. (*et al*). (1960). *The American Voter*. New York, John Wiley.
Carillo, S. (1977). *Eurocommunism and the State*. London, Lawrence and Wishart.

Crouch, C. (1979). 'The State, Capitalism, and Liberal Democracy' in C. Crouch (ed.), *State and Economy in Contemporary Capitalism*. London, Croom Helm.

Cutler, A. (*et al*) (1977). *Marx's Capital and Capitalism Today* Vol. 1. London, Routledge and Kegan Paul.

Dahl, R. (1971). *Polyarchy*. Yale University Press.

Downs, A. (1957). *An Economic Theory of Democracy*. New York, Harper and Row.

Dragstedt, A. and Slaughter, C. (1981). *State, Power and Bureaucracy*. London, New Park Publications.

Duncan, G. (ed.) (1983). *Democratic Theory and Practice*, Cambridge, Cambridge University Press.

Duverger, M. (1974). *Modern Democracies: Economic Power versus Political Power*. Illinois, The Dryden Press.

Foucault, M. (1979). *Discipline and Punish*. Harmondsworth, Peregrine.

Foucault, M. (1981). *The History of Sexuality*. Vol. 1., Harmondsworth, Pelican.

Giddens, A. (1981). *A Contemporary Critique of Historical Materialism*. London, Macmillan.

Gramsci, A. (1971). *Selections from the Prison Notebooks*. London, Lawrence and Wishart.

Hacker, A. (1967). 'Power to Do What?' in W. Connolly (ed.) *The Bias of Pluralism*, Chicago, Atherton.

Hindess, B. (1983). *Parliamentary Democracy and Socialist Politics*. London, Routledge and Kegan Paul.

Jessop, B. (1979). 'Corporatism, Parliament and Social Democracy' in Lehmbruch and Schmitter (1979).

Jessop, B. (1982). *The Capitalist State: Marxist Theories and Methods*. Oxford, Martin Robertson.

Korpi, W. (1983). *The Democratic Class Struggle*. London, Routledge and Kegan Paul.

Laclau, E. (1980). 'Populist Rupture and Discourse', *Screen Education* 34.

Laclau, E. and Mouffe, C. (1981). 'Socialist Strategy – Where Next?' *Marxism Today*, January.

Lehmbruch, G. and Schmitter, P. (1979). *Trends Towards Corporatist Intermediation*. London, Sage.

Lenin, V.I. (1917). *The State and Revolution*. Vol. 5 of Lenin, *Collected Works*. Moscow, Progress.

Lindblom, C.E. (1977). *Politics and Markets*. New York, Basic Books.

Lipset, S.M. (1960). *Political Man*. London, Heinemann.

Margolis, M. (1983). 'Democracy: American Style' in Duncan (ed.) 1983.

Marx, K. (1969). *The Civil War in France* in Marx and Engels, *Selected Works*. London, Lawrence and Wishart.

McLennan, G. (1984). 'The Contours of British Politics: Representative Democracy and Social Class' in McLennan *et al* (eds) *State and Society in Contemporary Britain*. Cambridge, Polity Press.

Miliband, R. (1982). *Capitalist Democracy in Britain*. Oxford, Oxford University Press.

Miliband, R. (1983). *Class Power and State Power*. London, Verso/NLB.

Middlemas, K. (1979). *Politics in Industrial Society: the Experience of the British System since 1911*. London, Andre Deutsch.

Nordlinger, E.A. (1981). *On the Autonomy of the Democratic State*. Cambridge, Mass., Harvard University Press.

Pahl, R.E. and Winckler, J.T. (1974). 'The Coming Corporatism', *New Society*, October.

Panitch, L. (1980). 'Recent Theorizations of Corporatism', *British Journal of Sociology*, Vol. XXXI No. 2.

Pateman, C. (1983). 'Feminism and Democracy' in Duncan (ed.) (1983).

Poulantzas, N. (1973). *Political Power and Social Classes*. London, New Left Books.

Poulantzas, N. (1980). *State, Power, Socialism*. London, Verso/NLB.

Przeworski, A. (1977). 'Proletarians into Class', *Politics and Society* Vol. 7 No. 4.

Ryan, A. (1983). 'Mill and Rousseau: utility and rights', in Duncan (ed.) 1983.

Schmitter, P. (1979). 'Still the Century of Corporatism?' in Lehmbruch and Schmitter (eds) 1979.

Schumpeter, J. (1942). *Capitalism, Socialism, and Democracy*. New York, Harper and Row.

Simon, R. (1982). *Gramsci's Political Thought*. London, Lawrence and Wishart.

Siltanen, J. and Stanworth, M. (1984). 'The Politics of Private Woman and Public Man' in Siltanen and Stanworth (eds) *Women and the Public Sphere*. London, Hutchinson.

Skocpol, T. (1979). *States and Social Revolutions*. Cambridge, Cambridge University Press.

Stephens, J.D. (1979). *The Transition from Capitalism to Socialism*. London, Macmillan.

Therborn, G. (1977). 'The Rule of Capital and the Rise of Democracy', *New Left Review* No. 103.

Therborn, G. (1980). *What Does the Ruling Class Do When it Rules?* London, Verso/NLB.

Tomlinson, J. (1981). 'Corporatism: a Further Sociologisation of Marxism', *Politics and Power*, 4.

CHAPTER 4

Justifying the welfare state

Tony Walton

1. Introduction: freedom, rights and equality

Opponents of the welfare state hold that the only justifiable mechanism for allocating resources is the market. On this view individuals are free only when they are not prevented by the state from disposing of their resources as they choose. Priority is placed on the autonomy of civil society and the domain of negative freedom.

Critics of the laissez-faire, market-dominated conception of the state have rejoined that the notion of freedom involved is inadequate, that it ignores the importance of social equality, and that it is inadequate in respect of the demands of, to use T.H. Marshall's term, full citizenship (Held, *et al*, 1983, pp. 248–60). There has been considerable debate over these issues at both the theoretical and political levels. At the turn of the century the questions involved took on a certain urgency as laissez-faire was called into question and the extent of state activity increased. Since that time the issue of how far the state should be allowed to intervene in society has remained central to political debate, especially in the post-1945 era with the development of the welfare state, and more latterly when Conservative governments have attempted to achieve the 'rolling back' of the state.

Much of the debate has hinged upon the question of whether the state should intervene to secure reasonable social equality through a fully comprehensive welfare state and the redistribution of wealth. Revisionist liberals such as T.H. Green (1836–1882) and ardent socialists like R.H. Tawney (1880–1962) associated laissez-faire with inequality and injustice. Their thought suggested an enlarged conception of freedom which made reference to the positive power and capacity of individuals to exercise their freedom. The merely negative freedom of being left alone was insufficient. And Marshall's conception of citizenship extended the notion of equality beyond the civil and political domains to the area of social equality. Entailed in the notion of citizenship, argued Marshall, was the equal enjoyment of social rights.

This enlarged conception of freedom, rights, and citizenship involved, however, deep and controversial issues. Marshall himself identified the importance of individual civil rights, and the requirement that there should be a sphere of activity which ought not to be interfered with by the state. Theorists from John Locke (1632–1704) to Robert Nozick have stressed the strong moral claim which individuals have in respect of their private rights. On their view there is no warrant for interfering with the inviolable private domain unless to do so is necessary for safeguarding private rights. In Robert Nozick's Anarchy, State, and Utopia (1974) the concept of individual rights has been developed as the basis for a vigorous attack on the welfare state, and involves the claim that individual rights have priority over other principles such as equality. For Nozick, liberty and equality are necessarily in tension with one another, the former having a prior moral claim over the latter.

Whether Nozick is correct or not in specifying the priority of liberty over equality is questionable. Can the meaning of freedom be exhausted by reference to its negative aspects alone? Clearly the idea of negative freedom is important, and is in certain respects indispensable. Freedom involves, at least partly, the protection of private rights, free scope to choose for oneself, and guarantees against excessive encroachment by the state. However, a fully comprehensive conception of freedom requires both negative and positive aspects. Anti-state theorists can be criticized for reducing the concept of freedom to its negative component, thus failing to account for those areas where freedom can be genuinely enlarged, in the positive sense, through the activities of the state. It remains, of course, a moot point how, precisely, negative and positive freedoms should be combined, especially in instances where there is conflict between the two, for example, when the provision of additional welfare services requires greater bureaucratic control. Nevertheless, the problematic nature of the relationship between the two types of freedom does not undermine their status, but merely suggests the need to give detailed attention to how best they can be combined, and how the increasing size of the state apparatus can be subject to genuine democratic control.

The outstanding question, however, is whether the conceptual apparatus supplied by individualism is adequate for settling disputes over the scope of distributive justice and the role of the state. Nozick draws on individualist arguments in support of a theory of the minimal state. Rawls justifies the welfare state on individualist assumptions. In the final section of this chapter I will argue that there are severe limits to individualist political theory, in both its Nozickean and Rawlsian forms, and will suggest that questions concerning the character and role of the state must make reference to non-individualist categories such as the *common good* and *community*.

2. John Rawls: Equality and the difference principle

The preceding remarks indicated the importance of equality as a substantive social principle. The difficulty, though, with much egalitarian thought is its vagueness. What, exactly, are the grounds of equality? People are not obviously equal in some descriptive sense; they have unequal capacities and make unequal contributions to society. Ought they then to be treated unequally, and do they not *deserve* differential levels of reward? These are some of the objections levelled against egalitarianism.

To *assert* the moral importance of equality is not to supply a *theory* defending it. It is such a theory that Rawls attempts to provide by constructing arguments which are an ingenious blend of concepts drawn from Kant's practical philosophy and modern social choice theory.

John Rawls is a contemporary American philosopher, and his book *A Theory of Justice* (1972) is one of the most widely discussed and disputed books in modern political theory. It is an attempt systematically to lay out principles for the distribution of resources within society, and it is a liberal defence of the welfare state. It treats the issue of equality as central to questions of justice, and supplies critical leverage on conservative attitudes towards redistribution and state intervention.

The key concept for Rawls is what he calls the *difference principle*. (The difference principle is not exhaustive of Rawls's entire theory of justice in which figures his *first principle* which is concerned with citizens' equal right to basic liberties such as the right to vote, freedom of conscience, and so on (Rawls, 1972, p. 61). In this chapter we will, however, only be concerned with the difference principle which figures in Rawls *second principle* of justice, and is concerned with redistribution.)

The point of departure for Rawls's account of the difference principle is a critique of negative (or what he calls 'natural') liberty, and of the market when it is taken to be the appropriate distributive mechanism.

> The system of [negative] liberty asserts, then, that a basic structure . . . in which positions are open to those able and willing to strive for them will lead to a just distribution. Assigning rights and duties in this way is thought to give a scheme which allocates wealth and income, authority and responsibility, in a fair way whatever this allocation turns out to be.
> (Rawls, 1972, p. 66)

What Rawls means here is that on the negative view of freedom people should be free to use their skills and talents in whatever way they choose. Personal negative liberty is the ultimately prior principle, and whatever is the outcome of the activities of negatively free individuals acting in the free market is the just outcome. What is important is *how* people derive their wealth, not *what* wealth they have. The distribution is just so long as it is acquired under conditions where all people are (negatively) free to use their skills and talents; that is, when they are not interfered with by the state.

Rawls's objection to natural (or negative) liberty is the following. People derive benefits from the market in accordance with their skills and abilities, and it is said that they *deserve* reward in proportion to those skills. But it is Rawls's contention that from a moral point of view the possession of skills is irrelevant. People have skills in virtue of naturally or socially acquired advantages. In Rawls's view it is arbitrary to reward people in proportion to contingently acquired talents. The state ought to intervene and correct for the inequalities produced by the market on the basis of the *difference principle*.

According to the difference principle 'the higher expectations of those better situated are just if and only if they work as part of a scheme which improves the expectations of the least advantaged members of society' (Rawls, 1972, p. 75). Inequalities are only justified if the 'better expectations allowed to entrepreneurs encourages them to do things which raise the long term prospects of the labouring class. Their better prospects act as incentives so that the economic process is the more efficient, innovation proceeds at a faster pace, and so on' (Rawls, 1972, p. 78).

There are two points involved in the difference principle. First, all persons must be thought of as possessing rights and freedoms, and if their enjoyment is differentially distributed that is an injustice. Equality is, thus, not antithetical to freedom and rights, but rather essential to them. Thus, Rawls's view amounts to the following. It is as absurd to suppose that freedom and rights are adequately enjoyed in the context of differential advantages as it would be to suppose that people properly have the right to vote when additional votes could be bought at a price by those with the necessary purchasing power. The idea of political rights *entails* the equal enjoyment of them, and injustice follows on their unequal distribution. So, too, with wealth and access to health and welfare.

Second, Rawls invokes the idea of entrepreneurial incentives, and does so in quite a standard way. But it is important to note that this is an empirical argument about what is likely to ensure greater productivity and thus be for *everyone's* benefit. It is not an argument claiming that those with the greatest skills *deserve* to be rewarded. 'The assertion that a man deserves the superior character that enables him to make the effort to cultivate his abilities is . . . problematic for his character depends in large part upon fortunate family circumstances for which he can claim no credit' (Rawls, 1972, p. 104). For Rawls the only inequalities that are justified are those likely to lead to *everyone* being better off because they lead to an increase in the overall size of the cake.

Let us now look more closely at the grounds for Rawls's account of the need for equality. He takes the view that a person cannot be thought of as the privileged possessor of his or her skills and the advantages that accrue from them. On Rawls's view the person capable of amassing more wealth than others because of the possession of special talents has no automatic right to retention. On the contrary, he regards people's skills and advantages as *common assets* which ought to be distributed on the basis of just principles. 'We see that the difference principle represents, in effect, an agreement to regard the distribution of natural talents as a common asset and to share in the benefits of this distribution whatever it turns out to be' (Rawls, 1972, p. 101). Rawls, as we have seen, disputes that we have any special right to the fruits of contingently acquired advantages. Revealing the deep influence of Kant upon his thought, Rawls's 'deontological' liberalism disputes the possessive individualist claim that persons' possessions are constitutive of their identity. The identity of a person is antecedent to any contingent ends or capacities the person may have (see Sandel, 1982, Ch. I). Consequently, there are no claims which can be made in respect of any special rights to the advantages accruing from the possession of personal capacities. On the contrary, the freedom and identity of a person can be realized only by reference to just principles which are not, as the identity of the person is not, tied to contingent empirical factors.

It is interesting to see how the above argument provides leverage on the issue of the relationship between the public and private spheres, state and civil society. Extreme liberal individualists, such as Nozick, make strong claims on behalf of the sanctity of the private domain. Rawls, too, writes within the broadly individualist tradition, but his approach weakens the rigid distinction between the spheres of the public and the private.

On Rawls's view, what appears to be exclusively private, namely the fruits of one's skills and resources, turns out to have a wider public significance encapsulated in the notion of common assets. Moreover, it is publicly applicable principles which then accord to individuals just distributive shares. Thus for Rawls what we are and what we have as private persons have a wider public significance, and cannot be settled by reference to the private rights of individuals residing in an exclusively private domain. Moreover, it falls to the state to reconstitute the relationship between state and society through the application of principles of distributive justice.

There are, however, large questions remaining regarding what kind of a relationship between the individual and the state is established by Rawls's principles of distributive justice. Rawls takes the typically liberal individualist view that the social and political universe is inherently harmonious, and that the state consequently stands in a neutral relation to the various interests constituting civil society. For instance, Rawls supposes that the difference principle secures genuine reciprocity (Rawls, 1972, p. 104); there may be inequalities, but they work to everyone's advantage so long as the difference principle is applied. The difference principle is an ultimate principle of right which is universal and impartial, and to be contrasted with any particular interest. Thus, the state, so long as it is guided by the difference principle, acts impartially in relation to particular interests.

Why is Rawls not successful in demonstrating the coherence of the political universe and the impartiality of the state? Let us take his argument against desert. If we say that a person *deserves* to be rewarded more highly than others we are claiming that it is the possession of certain skills and capacities that warrants greater reward. Rawls's general argument against desert, namely that it is arbitrary to reward a person for contingently acquired skills and capacities derived from, say, class position is a good one. But it is not clear that it applies in all cases. Suppose, for instance, that there are two people with equal skills and similar social backgrounds, and suppose that one is industrious and the other chooses not to be industrious. Rawls's argument is that people's disposition to work hard is determined by social circumstances, and there is a great deal to that. But to hold to it uncompromisingly would be to subscribe to a dubiously deterministic position on individual responsibility. People do *choose* to work hard or not, and on occasions may be held responsible for their laziness and perhaps be less well rewarded.

There appears, then, to be a conflict between the principles of desert and common assets, which leaves the state's position ambiguous. Which principle should be favoured and on what grounds? To favour one principle as opposed to the other is to favour one set of interests over another, perhaps even one class over another. If this is so, the typically liberal notion of the neutral state is seriously weakened, and the political universe should be characterized less in terms of coherence and harmony, and rather in terms of disharmony and conflict.

The most vigorous attack on the notion of the neutral liberal state comes from Marxism. Rawls supposed that it was possible to construct principles of justice applicable to a capitalist society (which he favours) which are to everyone's advantage. Remember the second part of the difference principle to the effect that inequalities are justified if they are to the advantage of the least well off. The Marxist objection (see Macpherson, 1973 and Miller in Daniels, 1975) is that this rests on a mistaken account of the character of capitalism. If it is the case, as Marxist theory suggests, that inequalities under capitalism signify modes of domination and exploitation, claims about mutual advantage and the impartiality of the principles of justice (and hence also of the state) look very thin. Capitalist entrepreneurs, on this view, are not a means to the general advantage; they are a ruling class with its own particular interests which are privileged and protected by the capitalist state. As one critic has put it, Rawls's 'line of reasoning is inadequate to establish the tolerability of commitment to the difference principle, if the best off are a *ruling class* in an exploitative society' (Miller in Daniels, 1975, p. 215).

These objections are powerful ones if the propositions on which they rest are true: that there is a ruling class and that society is fundamentally exploitative. These are contentious claims and in order to assess them it would be necessary to consider (as Chapter 3 does) the relative merits of Marxist as opposed to, say, liberal pluralist theory. If the latter supplies an adequate explanation of the modern capitalist state, then Rawls's theory has a strong foundation. However, even independent of the merits of the Marxist case for the existence of a ruling exploitative class, there are strong grounds for questioning liberal pluralist theory, principally because of its failure adequately to address questions of structural privilege and their bearing on the distribution and exercise of power. Rawls attacks the market for privileging some people over others, but he assumes that a suitably organized state is sufficient to rectify the inequalities produced by the market. If, on the other hand, it is argued that the problems of the market are structural in the deepest sense, then the role of the state must be that of transformation rather than alleviation. Whether this would require the total transformation of the market and the development of common ownership remains a moot point. Nevertheless, at the least it involves a degree of reconstitution of the operation of the market beyond that envisaged by Rawls.

Questions about the operation of the market are raised by Nozick's theory of the minimal state, and it is to that theory that we now turn.

3. Robert Nozick: Patterns and entitlements

Nozick is a supporter of the minimal non-interventionist state and his book *Anarchy, State and Utopia* (1974) has been, like Rawls's *A Theory of Justice*, widely discussed. He summarizes his views in the following way:

> Our main conclusions about the state are that a minimal state, limited to the narrow functions of protection against force, theft, fraud, enforcement of contracts, and so on, is justified; and that the minimal state is inspiring as well as right. Two noteworthy implications are that the state may not use its coercive apparatus for the purpose of getting some citizens to aid others, or in order to prohibit activities to people for their *own* good or protection.
> (Nozick, 1974, p. ix)

The implications of the above quotation for the welfare state are clear. A common argument *for* health provision, for instance, is that people *need* it. The fact that they need it is considered to be the only relevant criterion to be considered when providing it – not whether people have the money to purchase it (or whether they are black or white, Jew or Gentile, or whatever). Not addressing himself to the question of whether the possession of money is any less contingent than possessing a black or a white skin, Nozick says 'Presumably, then, the only criterion for the distribution of barbering services is barbering need . . . In what way does the situation of a doctor differ? Why must his activities be allocated via the internal goals of medical care?' (Nozick, 1974, p. 234). The rejoinder, presumably, is that there is something particularly fundamental about health care, and that making something so fundamental dependent upon selling and purchasing power is equivalent in all relevant respects to making it dependent upon the colour of a person's skin (or height, weight, colour of eyes, or whatever).

It could also be argued that since doctors' activities are only relevant and socially meaningful in the context of their relationship with their patients and their needs, there are grounds for supposing that their activities should be based upon meeting those needs irrespective of purchasing power. But on Nozick's view, the doctors' skills and resources are their own, and they have the right to use them as they wish. Skills are not, to use Rawls's term, *common assets*. The doctor's skills are peculiarly his in the strongest possessive sense. Thus, Nozick's position is different in respect of the conditions of personal identity. Rawls, it will be recalled, regards the identity of a person as prior to his or her possessions and skills. For Nozick, on the other hand, to take away a person's possessions is to rob him or her of the conditions of identity, and to take away what is essential to being a free subject.

Nozick recognizes that there are difficulties in saying that doctors *deserve* the fruits of their assets, but he does claim that they are *entitled* to them. 'Whether or not people's natural assets are arbitrary from a moral point of view, they are entitled to them, and to what flows from them' (Nozick, 1974, p. 226). Thus, according to the 'entitlement conception of justice in holdings, one *cannot* decide whether the state must do something to alter the situation merely by looking at a distributional profile or at facts such as these' (Nozick, 1974, p. 232).

Nozick considers that he has displayed the absurdity of Rawls's position. 'An application of the principle at maximizing the position of those worst off might well involve forceable, redistribution of bodily parts . . .' (Nozick, 1974, p. 206). This 'hysterical' (to use Nozick's own description) example clearly gets into the obvious difficulty that there are significant differences between redistributing wealth and redistributing bodily parts. However, the analogy does forcefully convey the sense of the entitlement theory. Surely, it might be argued, if people have special skills they are *entitled* to use them to their own advantage as far as they can. What right have others to prevent them from doing so? And so long as people do not acquire what they have through force or fraud, why should they not be entitled to keep it and to use it in whatever way they see fit? Why, in Rawlsian terms, should people's acquisitions be thought of as *common* assets? If they cannot be thought of as common, then the grounds for a further process of redistribution look thin. Nozick pursues this line of thought through an uncompromising individualism which attempts both to establish the rights of individuals over their assets and to show that the notion of common assets in unintelligible.

The key to Nozick's position is his claim that according to theories of the welfare state 'it is *society* that, somehow, is to arrange things so that the doctor, in pursuing his own goals, allocates according to need . . .' (Nozick, 1974, p. 234). Nozick's objection is that it is society which takes on the task of allocating resources, and this is illegitimate because it invokes the notion of something which, in reality, does not exist except in the minimal sense of being an aggregate of individuals. 'There are only individual people with their own individual lives' (Nozick, 1974, p. 33). If there is nothing 'beyond' individuals, if society is no more than the sum of its individual components, there is no warrant for invoking more general principles said to pertain to society *as a whole*. Thus for Nozick, Rawls is not individualistic enough, and fails to follow to their logical conclusion the implications of his own professed commitment to individualism. He therefore justifies a more extensive state than *can* be justified on individualist grounds, and he can only do so by departing from the individualist assumptions he claims to be at the heart of his theory.

According to Nozick, Rawls's account of the role of the state expresses a *patterned* conception of justice. A patterned conception of justice is one which, literally, imposes a pattern which is not the 'natural' outcome of the multiplicity of free negotiations and bargains which take place in the market, and which have no fixed outcome. The only 'pattern' that is admissable is the one which is the contingent historical outcome of whatever exchanges happen to have taken place between free individuals who are sovereign over their own possessions. The Rawlsian attempt to ensure equality through the state is the arbitrary imposition of a pattern. Nozick therefore turns the tables on Rawls since in his view it is not the market which is arbitrary, but rather the attempt to impose a pattern which is at variance with the principle of absolute freedom and autonomy.

The implications of Nozick's argument for the role of the state locates him in a tradition of theory which is basically anti-state and which values, above all, the independence of citizens. Thus, Nozick, like many others, detects in state intervention the threat of the Orwellian nightmare, of increasing bureaucracy, and the steady diminution of freedom. Thus, no 'distributional patterned principle of justice can be continuously realized without continuous interference in people's lives' (Nozick, 1974, p. 163).

The spectre of the state taking over our lives looms large in Nozick's image of the interventionist state.

Seizing the results of someone's labor is equivalent to seizing hours from him and directing him to carry on various activities. If people

force you to do certain work, or unrewarded work, for a certain period
of time, they decide what you are to do and what purposes your work is
to serve apart from your decisions. This process whereby they take this
decision from you makes them a *part-owner* of you; it gives them a
property right in you.
(Nozick, 1974, p. 172)

On this view, state intervention is appropriation, of both one's
resources and one's self; it is a fundamental attack on the sovereignty
of the individual. It is, however, worth noting that while the kinds of
arguments used by Nozick lead to an attack on intervention to
provide a welfare state, they are, however, compatible with extensive
intervention for the purposes of peace and order. States committed to
restricting welfare are sometimes simultaneously committed to
increasing the strength of the state in respect of its police and security
functions.

As an account of the state is Nozick's market-dominated conception of state and society compelling? When Nozick says that the
processes of allocation ought not to be patterned he is assuming that
there is some ideal condition under which they are *not* patterned.
However, perhaps a more adequate explanation of the market is that
it is in fact patterned, albeit not necessarily deliberately. This view
was the basis of Marshall's claim that the state needs to be used to
correct the inequalities of the class structure. For Marxists, Marshall,
and many others, the market privileges some groups over others in
virtue of their structural position within the system of production and
exchange. If that is so, the idea of the free and sovereign individual
choosing what to do with his or her resources has to be seen as a myth.
The difficulty is that Nozick's theory ignores the processes by which
some groups are privileged over others through the operation of the
market: he assumes the free and sovereign individual. However, with
that mistake much of the basis for his theory disappears since the only
possible justification for tolerating the inequalities of the market
could be that they were the outcome of the free interactions and
exchanges of sovereign individuals who, potentially, could seek to
bring about changes in the distributional pattern through their own
efforts. If, on the other hand, people's resources are to a large extent
determined by structural factors beyond their control, little foundation is left for the theory.

One factor, for instance, which Nozick's view does not take into
account is that the distribution of disease is to some extent socially
'patterned', and was certainly very much so before the welfare state. If
the distribution of disease reflects the structure of the class and
occupation system, the grounds for supposing that there should be

intervention to ameliorate this are very strong indeed; and leaving people alone will be a means to perpetuating the social division of illness.

The above issues raise once again the question of the neutrality of the state and the impartiality of the principles guiding it. We have already examined this issue in relation to Rawls, and Nozick shares with Rawls the view that the state can and should stand in a neutral relation to individual interests and aspirations. However, the above comments on the character of the market and structural privilege cast grave empirical doubt on Nozick's claims about the neutrality of the state. The minimal state favours the 'free' market. But if the market structurally privileges some interests over others, the state will not be the neutral state Nozick supposes it to be.

There is a further reason for questioning the neutrality of Nozick's state and this bears on the connection between the public and the private. We have been looking at whether the distinction between the public and the private really holds, and at whether what is apparently exclusively private has, in fact, a public aspect.

Following in the tradition of John Locke, Nozick speaks of the prior and inalienable rights of the individual, possessed independently of society. Rights are a property of individuals *qua* individuals, and the state arises as a response to the need to secure the prior rights of the individual. Thus, Locke spoke of 'natural' rights. The case for 'natural' rights has been greatly disputed and one line of attack has been to argue that rights are not *natural* and *prior* to society and the state, but are constructed by them. A feature of the modern state is that it has recognized a range of individual rights which were not recognized by, for example, ancient Greek or medieval society, and which would have been unintelligible in those societies to the extent that it would be odd to criticize the rulers of those periods for not giving scope to individual rights. If it is true that rights are socially and historically constituted, then it is the case that the rights which Nozick defends as natural and prior are actually those of the historically specific market; and these are defined and constituted by, and within, the context of capitalist property relations. They cannot be claimed to be 'natural', and consequently, claims for the priority and exclusiveness of the private domain are weakened. It does not derive its status from unalterable 'natural' facts about human beings. On the contrary, its status is defined and given by a social and political context which is historically produced. It appears, then, that in order adequately to explain the character of society and the rights which it accords to individuals it is necessary to relax individualist assumptions and make reference to the constituting social context. The following section will follow up some of the implications of arguing from non-individualist premises.

4. The state and the common good: reformism

Marshall and Rawls both stand in a tradition of thought which rejects laissez-faire and the dominance of the market, and with the emphasis they place on equality they are part of the *reformist* tradition. Reformism had its origins in the late nineteenth-century rejection of laissez-faire individualism, and saw its most rapid application in the period following the 1939–45 war with the growth of the welfare state. However, Marshall and Rawls occupy only part of the theoretical and political terrain of reformism. Reformism historically has been a blend of individualist and collectivist ideas, a compromise between liberalism and socialism. Marshall and Rawls share with reformism a commitment to equality, but do not markedly draw on the collectivism of much reformist thinking. In this part of the chapter I shall examine certain features of collectivism and consider their bearing on questions of justice and the state.

All schools of reformist thought shared a commitment to representative democracy, the rights and freedoms of citizens, and can be sharply distinguished from the crushing collectivism of, say, the Webbs (Gutmann, 1980, p. 83). However, collectivist reformism was especially critical of an exclusively self-interested pursuit after personal interest encouraged by laissez-faire and classical liberalism. It advocated state intervention in order to regulate the market if it threatened to disrupt social life, generate inequalities, and produce social atomism and fragmentation.

Collectivist reformism identified the foundation for arguments about welfare in the idea of the common good. It did not, in Rawlsian fashion, derive the basis of welfare in an individualistic conception of rights. All classes and interests ought to be united in the common concern to provide a decent and humane society in which all persons shared equally. It was in the common good that this should be so.

T.H. Green's (1836–1882) reformist liberalism was individualist to the extent that it was deeply concerned with individual freedom. Nevertheless, it fundamentally revised the conception of the individual; and in particular it revised the individualist account of how individuals come to have rights. Green stressed the extent to which individuals were *social beings*, and how they come to acquire their capacities by being implicated in a larger social whole. This was not just a straightforward sociological claim, but also an ethical claim about the extent to which individuals are bound up with a larger *common good*. To be a free, rational and moral person is to live in accordance with the common good which also supplies a criterion of the individual's rights (Sabine, 1963, p. 732). For Green, rights could not be explained in terms of an individual's 'natural' freedom and autonomy, or by reference to a pre-social individual autonomy held to be the property of the individual *qua* individual. On the contrary, the extent of a person's rights is sanctioned and recognized by the common good which is their source and foundation. On this view the demand that the disadvantaged should be helped is derived from the common good; it is for the common good that we should live in the kind of society which distributes basic resources reasonably equally. Only such a society is consistent with our essentially *social* self. Moreover, to recognize the importance of one's social self is to be committed to a particular way of life which is valued, not because it is a means to individual satisfaction, but because it is shared and held to be intrinsically worthwhile.

Several points follow from the above arguments. First, the state is not conceived, as it is by many liberals such as Rawls, as embodying abstract principles which are value-neutral and independent of any particular account of the good. For Rawls, society is construed as a plurality of individuals each pursuing their own good in their own way, the state expressing an impartial framework of principles of right within which individual goods can be pursued. For Green, on the other hand, there is a good, a *common* good, which the state should pursue. The state is thus given a role in constituting the kind of society in which we live.

Secondly, Green's theory breaks down the traditional liberal distinction between state and civil society, and more particularly between the state and the economy (Sabine, 1963, p. 735). The market was seen as a social institution rather than as a natural fact of human life, and should therefore be regulated for social purposes if necessary.

Thirdly, it is worth noting that it was only with the development of ideas such as Green's that the word 'state' came into regular English usage. Previously the term 'government' had been more usual (Sabine, 1963, p. 738). This change was important because it conveyed the sense of society as fundamentally constituted and organized by the political authority. The term 'state' was unusual in England because of the dominance of liberal individualism, whereas on the continent with its very different legal and political traditions, it was in common usage, and more powerfully conveyed the importance of the state in the constitution of society.

R.H. Tawney (1880–1962) developed collectivist ideas within the socialist tradition, and in ways which have affected the labour movement's conception of itself. Tawney was a sharp critic of the acquisitive society of liberal capitalism. He observed the power which money and wealth held over people, and vigorously criticized the unequal relations generated by capitalism (Gutmann, 1980, p. 81). Moreover, competition and inequality undermined human fellowship and community, and made the realization of a common good impossible. Precisely what Tawney meant by the common good is not clear, but he did regard it as a principle of distribution (Gutmann, 1980, p. 85), thus tying questions of justice to the concept of the common good. Thus, Tawney shares with Green the view that questions about rights and justice are unintelligible except by reference to the common good which is their source and foundation.

Both Green and Tawney are unclear as to the precise meaning and application of the concept of the common good. It would be useful, therefore, to reconstruct certain features of the arguments involved. Since the theory of the common good has usually been developed in connection with criticisms of various forms of individualism I will suggest a reconstruction of collectivist arguments insofar as they emerge from a theoretical critique of individualism. I shall suggest that the concept of the common good supplies critical leverage on both Rawls and Nozick.

The major theoretical claim of individualism – for both Rawls and Nozick – is that the social order exists in order to promote individual ends. The individual is primary, and society and state provide the framework within which individual ends can be pursued. Individualists are committed to the priority of individual aims, and stress the inadmissability of collective aims which cannot be explained in terms of the freedoms and choices of individuals. Both Rawls and Nozick subscribe to such a *general* view insofar as the underlying assumptions of both are individualistic. But what is striking is that both thinkers hold very different *particular* theories regarding the nature of rights and the role of the state. Rawls sees the interventionist state as the key to freedom and justice, whereas Nozick regards intervention as an attack on the fundamental freedoms and rights of individuals. There are at work two very different conceptions of society and state. However, what is interesting for us is that these *different* conceptions stem from the *same* general underlying theoretical assumptions – those of *individualism*. Rawls is less uncompromising in his hostility to collectivism than is Nozick (see Rawls, 1972, section 79), but his underlying theoretical framework is broadly the same.

What critical conclusions can be drawn from the above? We can argue that individualist assumptions *underdetermine* any particular theory of justice and the state since these assumptions are not sufficient to establish the case for a particular theory; individualist assumptions are not sufficiently determinate. Thus, on individualist grounds there do not appear to be ways of straightforwardly adjudicating between Rawls's and Nozick's conclusions.

Rawls, in fact, makes strenuous efforts to demonstrate why *his* theory of justice ought to be accepted. He constructs what he calls an 'original position'. This idea is a modern and sophisticated version of the state-of-nature theory, and reflects the influence upon Rawls of some contemporary economic and rational choice theory. Rawls hoped to show that the distributive principles he advocates are ones which rational persons concerned with furthering their own interests would choose if they were in an original position and had no knowledge of their particular talents and advantages. In this way Rawls aimed to show that from behind this 'veil of ignorance' there are certain principles which *all* rational persons would choose and which must therefore be agreed to.

However, Rawls's ingenious scheme has been criticized on the grounds that it is not self-evidently the case that his principles are the ones that all rational persons *would* choose; and that what he is doing is invoking a particular conception of rationality which is contestable (Barry, 1973). Thus, the objection remains that individualism cannot generate firm and uncontestable conclusions concerning the just organization of society.

It is conflict within individualism that collectivists complain about (MacIntyre, 1981, ch 17). Moreover, this theoretical critique is given more concrete expression in criticism of those societies in which an individualistic outlook is dominant. Individualism is taken to be indicative of the fragmentation and atomism of contemporary society, its splintering into diverse and competing ideologies and social groups, each selfishly promoting its own interests, and rationalizing that promotion by reference to some 'convenient' theoretical stance. What is required is a more reliable criterion on which to base public policy, something which is not subject to the whims and interests of particular groups, and which rests on theoretical foundations which are sufficiently determinate to yield compelling claims about justice and the state. What is needed is a conception of state and society founded on a recognition of the common good in relation to which public policy must be justified, and which legitimates the insertion of the state into the sphere of civil society.

But does such a conception mean that individual rights and interests are subordinated to the common good which is prior to them? Critics of common good theory have, from a liberal standpoint, suggested that once strictly individualist assumptions are relaxed freedom and rights are threatened. In section 1 of this chapter I suggested that a comprehensive conception of freedom required both negative and positive elements. I now wish to show that there is a further aspect of freedom which is connected to the concepts of community and common good, and consequently that collectivist concepts should not be construed as necessarily antithetical to freedom.

Theorists of the common good characterize society less as an aggregate of individuals and more in terms of its constituting a community. A society is seen as a system of shared values and commonly subscribed to practices and institutions. The emphasis is on how values, practices, and institutions form society as a whole and impinge on the lives of individuals. Moreover the common good can only be fully articulated in a society where its members are conscious of being part of a larger whole and understand the respects in which their rights and duties are implicated in that whole.

The above considerations bear on the issue of freedom in the following way. Theorists of community argue that a person's freedom is enlarged to the extent that he or she is able to identify with the values, institutions and practices of a society. If a society is perceived by its citizens to consist only of external constraints regulating individual or group action, then clearly the more state activity there is the less freedom there will be. Hence Nozick's view that social and political control must be kept to a minimum since such control is necessarily antithetical to freedom. If, on the other hand, institutions and practices can be identified with, and if the individual is able to recognize them as constitutive of a worthwhile way of life, they cease to have a purely coercive character. As one contemporary theorist of community has expressed this:

> In identifying with the purposes and standards embodied within these practices one experiences the activities within them as expressions of oneself, as projects, goals and norms that are one's own. If these identifications were to dissolve, some of the same practices and norms would be experienced as limits and obstacles to one's freedom.
> (Connolly, 1981, p. 164)

Thus, community enlarges rather than diminishes freedom. And this line of argument can forcefully be linked with the idea of democratic participation. The link between the individual and the community is secured through the widespread and active participation of the individual in the democratic process. Thus community and democracy are interconnected aspects of individual freedom. Moreover, while the state is crucial for securing the realization of the common good and has tasks beyond the minimal provision of peace and order, the determination of the common good is secured through the medium of participation within state institutions. However, it is worth noting that reformism has not developed an extensive participative conception of democracy, and has been content with traditional notions of representative democracy. But arguably representative democracy, through the medium of parliamentary institutions, has failed to check concentrated state power, and has allowed the increasing removal of policy-making from the active participation of citizens. Whether, however, the kind of freedom associated within the concept of community is realizable is one of several problematic issues concerning the adequacy of the concepts of community and common good. It is to these that we now turn.

The first objection is concerned with the *ontology* of the theory of the common good. We have already seen one version of the objection in Nozick who complains that there are no realities beyond individuals, society being construed as an aggregate of individuals. If true, this objection is very damaging, and renders foundationless an account of state intervention based on the idea of the common good. However, whether Nozick's objection is correct hinges on whether or not my earlier objection to his individualism carries substance. It will be recalled that I objected to Nozick's individualism on the grounds that it failed to account for the social basis of rights. The recognition of the social character of rights does not by itself provide sufficient grounds for a theory of the common good, but it does de-fuse one of the principle objections to the theory.

Secondly, theories of the common good can be criticized for being *unrealistic*. Even if there was some desirable ideal of a harmonious community, the realities of actual politics undermine its realization. On this view, politics is necessarily about struggle and self interest, power and domination. The best that can be done is, as democratic theorists such as Bentham argued, to set up democratic institutions which limit excessive power and make public policy as responsive to as wide a range of interests as possible.

Again, this is a persuasive objection, but its force depends upon the belief that conflict and domination are ineradicable. Theorists of the common good do not deny that empirically these things are part of social experience, but they would advocate an organization of society along lines which minimize such conflict. Marx was perhaps the most vigorous critic of the conflicts inherent in a capitalist society, and believed that a different social form – communism – could do away with conflict, at least in its repressive forms.

Thirdly, it can be argued, from the Marxist standpoint, that the idea of the common good performs certain important *ideological* functions. The origin of this argument lies in Marx's criticisms of Hegel. Hegel had argued that society was characterized by conflict and competition, but underlying these were unity and coherence which it was the role of the state to articulate.

Marx's objection, set out in the 1843 *Critique of Hegel's Philosophy of Right* (O'Malley, 1970), was that the idea of a common good in the context of, and in contrast to, the individualism and pluralism of civil society was illusory. Rather, the state should be seen as a reflection of the conflicts of civil society. Moreover, since those conflicts were deep social conflicts involving domination and subordination, inevitably the state, too, would have the character of domination, indeed of domination in the interests of some at the expense of others. In his later writings this idea was developed through an analysis of the class relations of capitalist society. But what is particularly important for us is the illusory character attaching to the representation of the state as a vehicle for the common good. Such a representation is held by Marx to be a part of bourgeois ideology; it is an ideological representation of the state as universal when in reality the state is tied to particular class interests.

However, the Marxist objection is not to the concept of the common good *per se*, since Marx supposed that communism provided the only social form capable of realizing the common good. The Marxist objection is that it is a mystification to suppose that there is a unity underlying conflicting interests, and in particular the class interests of a capitalist society. Indeed, whatever criticisms may justifiably be offered of aggregative individualist conceptions of society and of the view that a society is simply the sum of particular interests, one of the principal challenges to the theory of the common good concerns its inability to account for unity under conditions of diverse and conflicting interests.

The fourth area of difficulty concerns the significance of *bureaucracy* within the modern state. We have examined the idea of freedom in connection with the concept of community, and seen that there is a conception of freedom which stresses the extent to which individuals can identify with, and feel implicated in, the institutions and practices of their community. But supposing we could show that the institutions and practices of the community were dominated by the bureaucracy and subject to bureaucratic criteria of control. Max Weber identified bureaucratization as one of the dominant motifs of the modern age, but thought that bureaucracies could be checked by representative institutions. But suppose that we are more pessimistic than Weber about the effects of representative democracy and conclude that bureaucratic organization eludes democratic control and accountability, and that it is exclusively impelled by bureaucratic criteria of rationality and technical efficiency. If that was the case then what is defined as the common good turns out to reflect bureaucratic rationality rather than the genuinely shared values and ideals associated with the idea of community.

However, the above objection only holds to the extent that the domination of bureaucracies is accepted conservatively, as a fact of life. As I suggested earlier, however, the notion of the common good can be linked with a participative idea of democracy. From this standpoint increased participation and democratic accountability beyond the formalities of representative democracy are essential. In this way democracy supplies a persistent challenge to concentrated administrative power.

The above objections all raise formidable difficulties with the idea of the common good. In particular, there is the difficulty of explaining its adequacy as a concept under conditions of conflicting interests. However, I have attempted to indicate how the concept of the common good can be positively developed in relation to certain crucial flaws in individualist theorizing. Moreover, I have also argued that the idea of the common good is not necessarily antithetical to individual rights and freedoms; first, because it can be used as a way of explaining and legitimating rights, albeit on grounds different from individualistic natural rights theory; secondly, because it can be linked with a conception of democratic participation, moreover a conception which is more radical in its implications than representative democracy as we know it. When linked in this way to democratic participation, the concept of the common good can be invoked as a critical tool of analysis in relation to certain key features of contemporary societies, in particular their tendency towards bureaucratic rationality and centralization. The politics of reformism has not yet succeeded in developing a sufficiently extensive notion of democratic participation and accountability, and the implication of this is that the full realization of a politics of the common good which does *not* reflect a crushing collectivism depends upon the extension of democracy into sites from which it has so far been excluded.

References

Barry, B. (1973). *The Liberal Theory of Justice*. Oxford, Oxford University Press.
Connolly, W.E. (1981). *Appearance and Reality in Politics*. Cambridge, Cambridge University Press.
Daniels, R.V. (1975). (ed.) *Reading Rawls*. Oxford, Blackwell.
Gutmann, A. (1980). *Liberal Equality*. Cambridge, Cambridge University Press.
Held, D. *et al* (1983) *States and Societies*. Oxford, Martin Robertson.
Macintyre, A. (1981). *After Virtue*. London, Duckworth.
Macpherson, C.B. (1973). *Democratic Theory*. Oxford, Clarendon Press.
Nozick, R. (1974). *Anarchy, State and Utopia*. Oxford, Blackwell.
O'Malley, J. (ed.) (1970). Karl Marx, *Critique of Hegel's Philosophy of Right*. Cambridge, Cambridge University Press.
Rawls, J. (1972). *A Theory of Justice*. Oxford, Oxford University Press.
Sabine, G. (1963). *A History of Political Thought*. London, Harrap.
Sandel, M.J. (1982). *Liberalism and the Limits of Justice*. Cambridge, Cambridge University Press.

CHAPTER 5

The anatomy of communist states

Adam Westoby

This chapter attempts an overview of *general* conceptions of Communist states – ideas and theories which seek to elucidate their character, their overall relations to society, their essential principles of internal structure, and to place them within larger historical trajectories. Far from being comprehensive, the intention is rather to suggest, by comparison and contrast, some of the core problems which different thinkers commonly encounter.

An obvious feature of Communist states is the extent to which state and society interpenetrate. The party-state monopoly of tolerated political activity, and state control over almost all economic activity, provide the premises, but not the limits, of this intimacy. One result is that almost all theories of Communist states cannot avoid also being, in important measure, theories of Communist societies. And both political and social theories differ, notoriously, not only in the answers they provide but in the ways they pose their questions. Many arise within a relatively well defined tradition, which conditions their choice and framing of questions. Moreover theories of Communist states evolve not only in mutual contention but also in parallel with, and in reflection – if imperfect reflection – of the objects they conceptualize. The attempt to make analytical comparisons lucid, therefore, requires certain linkages of history and of intellectual history. It also, inevitably, involves a measure of critical assessment on the part of the author. Thus, like all *tours d'horizon*, this one has a point of view; however it is content to emerge, rather than claim precedence as an axiom.

This is a revised version of an essay which was earlier published in David Held *et al* (eds) *States and Societies*. (Martin Robertson, Oxford, 1983).

The scope[1] and approximate order may be summarized as follows.

(1) Marxism, seeing modern society as in travail between capitalism and socialism, generally conceives of Communist states through one or other of these categories: 'state capitalism', or a form (if 'degenerated') of 'workers' state'.

(2) The latter has affinities with criticisms from reform Communists, raising problems of distribution, economic, inequality and, perhaps, class; Western proponents of a *new* dominant class extend the implications to questions of exploitation and property.

(3) The concept of 'totalitarianism', set in a different framework, sees the concentration of political power, and not economics, as essential; 'bureaucratic collectivism' and related ideas attempt syntheses of economics and politics (or of property and the state).

(4) Ideas of 'convergence' raise questions of within what, if any, general historical sequences Communist states may be placed; ideas such as 'oriental despotism' exemplify concepts of a fundamentally different itinerary for East and West.

(5) Shifting from structure to genesis, various ideas argue the roots of the political volition that goes into the making of Communist states.

(6) Last, I review implications for Communist states' international action; and suggest some general conclusions.

In Communist states it is the state which owns and controls most major components of the economy. State planning, rather than private investment, is the motor of industrialization and economic development. This substitution is central to most Marxist theories of Communist states (as, indeed, it is to many socialist political programmes). The most important ideas are those of 'state capitalism', and of various types of 'workers' states'. Two linked preoccupations recur in them: the sense that state types are apposite or functional to particular forms and/or levels of economic development; and that the state acts as guardian of the property of the dominant class.

'State capitalism'

The notion of Communist states as state capitalist goes back many years. From the first months of the Soviet regime, the Bolsheviks' opponents protested that the revolution had resulted in a new state capitalism, with the new regime bringing back into authority the managers, and even the proprietors, of capitalist enterprises.[2] The term 'state capitalism' was also taken up in this period, by Lenin, but not derogatively; it expressed his view that the New Economic Policy (1921 on) could advantageously emulate the German state's amplified economic role during the war, assuming control over private enterprises in the interests of the nation as a whole.[3] (Hilferding, followed by Bukharin, analysed the fusion of state and private structures and interests in this sense before and during the First World War.[4]) Lenin varied the usage: he regarded the German state as representative of the German bourgeoisie, while the Soviet government exercised a 'dictatorship of the proletariat and peasants'.

Later development of ideas of 'state capitalism', though, have almost always had a critical edge. The Menshevik current within Russian social democracy had always argued that it would be impossible, or at least disastrously mistaken, to short-cut the necessary next phase of Russian economic development: capitalist industrialization within a bourgeois–democratic political system. The smallness of the Russian working class, and the generally low level of economic development and culture, would make a mirage of any direct push for socialism. Mensheviks interpreted the state the Bolsheviks built in this light, though the man who spelt out this view most fully in the early 1920s was their mentor Karl Kautsky. Bolshevik terror during the civil war (1918–20) impressed him not only morally, but sociologically. It reflected the state's attempt to substitute for social classes, and it facilitated a fusion of the new state and party officialdom with former capitalist managers and proprietors.[5]

The idea of 'state capitalism' recurred repeatedly during the interwar years.[6] For example in the 1930s the then social democrat Lucien Laurat amended Marx's schema of distribution in *Capital* to account for the privileged salaries of the Soviet élite.[7] But its most systematic development, applied not only to the Soviet Union but to the satellite states formed in Eastern Europe after the war, and to Communist China, came from dissident Communists (mainly Trotskyists) after the Second World War. The best known is that which Tony Cliff put forward from 1948, in which he tied the notion more directly to the impetus for industrialization.[8] According to Cliff capitalism was *restored* in the Soviet Union about 1928, only not in the form of private capital but as its agglomeration into state property. This was the significance of Stalin's turn to forced collectivization and industrialization during the first five-year plans. The growth of the state's bureaucracy was, together with Stalin's personal ascendancy, the necessary mechanism in substituting state coercion for market forces and extracting the surplus for industrialization from the peasantry. Cliff also depicted the Russian state (in particular) as an *imperialist* 'state capitalist' state, colonizing Eastern Europe and imposing on it similar structures and similar programmes for industrialization.[9]

As a *Marxist* theory, 'state capitalism' faces the problem of how to account for economic accumulation in the absence of the main mechanisms Marx examined in *Capital* – profits, market competition among independent capitals; more generally the operation of the 'law of value'. Thus Cliff and his co-thinkers, such as Michael Kidron, developed the idea of the 'permanent arms economy': *economic* competition between private capitals is being superseded (to differing extents) by miliary–political competition between capitalist states.[10] In Communist societies internal competition is entirely suppressed and the arms race is the main spur pushing, for example, Soviet planners to raise the productivity of their 'one big factory'.[11]

Variants of the Marxist theory of imperialism have also been applied to Soviet industrialization. Alvin Gouldner's concept of 'internal colonialism' posited a relationship of industrializing Soviet cities and their dominant political bureaucracy to the exploited countryside, analogous to that between metropolitan countries and their exploited colonies. The surplus for industrial accumulation was realized by political control which allowed the imposition of low agricultural sale prices, and high prices for factory-produced consumer goods, upon the peasants. Gouldner's account is close, in its essentials, to the idea of the 'scissors' invoked by Soviet planners in the 1920s: a free grain market inflates agricultural prices and causes industry to founder, as happened during the civil war and war communism (1918–21).[12] Soviet planners, however, employed the notion with a distinct political thrust: to one degree or another they favoured extraction of a surplus from the countryside.[13]

Ideas of 'state capitalism' have also been applied to Chinese industrialization after the Second World War. But the main point of departure remained the Soviet Union.

'Degenerated workers' states'

If Communist states are not capitalist, perhaps they must be socialist? The other main group of Marxist views forms a spectrum, shading from these states' own official fictions to more realistically critical conceptions of them as quasi- or proto-socialist.

Perhaps the most influential example among the latter is the notion of the 'degenerated workers' state' developed by Trotsky after his exclusion from power in the 1920s.[14] Trotsky, an eloquent defender of the regime up to the early 1920s, identified the essential 'degeneration' of the Soviet state in the growth of a privileged bureaucracy which found its political representative in Stalin. Economic backwardness, shortage, and the isolation of the Russian revolution had produced, not a new type of capitalist ruling *class*, but a bureaucratic *caste*. This rested both on the existence of socialist economic foundations (state control of the economy, which Trotsky saw as dependent on the Party's monopoly of political power) but also on the insecurity of these foundations, and the hostile pressure of a surrounding capitalist world.[15] The essential antagonism (or 'deformation') is between socialist production and unequal distribution. With very long queues, it is necessary to appoint a 'policeman' to keep order: the state bureaucracy becomes 'a bourgeois organ in a workers' state' and draws off the cream for its own use'.[16]

Ideas of a 'degenerated workers' state' resemble those of 'state capitalism' in that both link the privileges and the dictatorial methods of the state bureaucracy to economic backwardness: the state, directly or as a surrogate for the market, must coerce the surpluses for industrialization. But the further question thus arises of why the political regime endures once industrialization is achieved and extreme shortage recedes. There is also the related problem of how the working class can be (as one of Trotsky's modern followers puts it) 'institutionally excluded from the administration of its own state'[17] by a stable regime in the very long term. Analogies have been proffered (for example by Ernest Mandel) with the great variety of state forms (liberal republic, monarchy, military dictatorship, Fascism) which have proved consistent with the social domination of the capitalist class.[18] If the German bourgeoisie suffered under 'their' Hitler, might not Russian or Chinese workers suffer under 'their' Stalin or Mao? The effect of such arguments, though, is to attenuate almost to invisibility the Marxian dependence of political superstructure upon economic base.

In Trotsky's earlier version, however, the stress was on *im*permanence. Inequality and the political regime alienated the working class from the state even though it remained, in an historical sense, a 'workers' state'. This increased the dangers to both the political regime and the economic base by defeat in external war, a military coup, recrudescence of private property rights, or some combination of these. (Similar dangers have often been invoked by the rulers of Communist states.)

Reform Communists' ideas

Trotsky offered a vivid portrait rather than a clear-cut theory. Where he depicted Stalin's regime as specific to the earlier stages of industrialization he anticipated a number of post-war reform Communists who have argued the need for political and intellectual liberalization as a precondition of economic reform, especially with the expansion of creative mental work central to 'post-industrialism'. The concept of a state formed by its need to control the economy as the essential lever of industrialization leads, naturally, into ideas which distinguish different phases of industrialization and see some of the crucial strains within Communist states as arising from transition from earlier into later ones. The difficulties of centralized 'command' economies multiply as the number and variety of products increase, and the relationships between them do so much faster. Thus, in the 1960s, stagnating rates of industrial growth brought home to economic planners in the Soviet Union and Eastern Europe problems both of decentralized control, and of effective accounting, which led them to reinstate ideas in which freer markets were seen as complementing state direction.[19]

Something of a renaissance, albeit brief, resulted in several related fields: economic and planning theory; public administration; aspects of law. These provided the intellectual underpinnings of the moves towards market decentralization widely prepared in the Soviet bloc during the 1960s, but thoroughly enacted only in some countries, such as Hungary. In Czechoslovakia, where the economic reform was aborted when it began to unwind into political liberalization unacceptable to the Soviet leadership, ideas were pushed even further. Paralleling notions of 'post industrialism' put forward by sociologists in the West, a group of reform-minded Czech social scientists argued that in industrially advanced societies (such as theirs) industrial production would be progressively overshadowed in importance by science and technology as independent factors in the productive process, and more generally by creative mental employment. Increasing numbers of highly skilled intellectual workers would require, ever more insistently, a more liberal regime and freer interchange of ideas if their input to production were to be realised effectively.[20] This was an argument somewhat distinct from the (slightly earlier) economists' arguments for decentralization, which did not necessarily involve political relaxation, but rather devolution of practical measures of control. Such arguments, from those with official and/or academic status within Communist states, did not, of course, directly challenge official characterizations of the state. Nonetheless, on slightly different and more concrete planes, they questioned both the capacity of the socialist state to substitute itself for markets, and the 'leading role' of the industrial working class throughout the transition from capitalism to full Communism.

Inequality, exploitation, class, property

Czech (and other) economic reformers were viewed with reserve by industrial workers. One reason was their advocacy of pay differentials. Like owners and their managers in capitalist societies, the efforts of the administrators and 'intellectual workers' of socialism were to be spurred by economic rewards. The linked questions of differences in pay and other benefits and of the mechanism (if any) of exploitation in socialist society have been central to many theories of Communist states, including several quasi-Marxist ones. Marx originally provided a theoretical justification (most fully in the *Critique of the Gotha Programme*, 1875) in which he linked economic inequality to the persistence of the state for some time after the capture of political power by the working class. The impossibility of eliminating scarcity immediately meant that labour would have to be rewarded not 'according to need' but in accordance with 'bourgeois right' (by which he meant paying more skilled or energetic workers more, rather than profits on capital).[21] It would be necessary for a state to regulate rights of distribution and their inequalities. The idea is continued by Lenin, even in his most 'anarchist' essay on the state, *State and Revolution* (1917).

There is in these ideas, however, no suggestion that economic inequality will assume the form of *exploitation*, or that social differentiation linked with it will give rise to an antagonistic social structure, or new *classes*. However, from rather early in the life of the Soviet regime it began to seem to some that its institutionalized and linked inequalities of income and power denoted precisely this. Yet the economic mechanism involved, linked as it evidently was to the state's overwhelming role in employment, did not easily lend itself to a general theoretical account.

Modification of the Marxist theory of capitalist exploitation seemed to offer one solution. But there is a crucial difference between, for example, early theories of 'state capitalism', which see a fusion between the bureaucracies of state trusts and persistent and growing private capital, and later ones (such as Cliff's) which recognize the elimination of large-scale private property as permanent.[22] But in the latter case the essential mechanisms Marx postulated, of commodities exchanging at or near their labour values, and the competition of capitals in quest of profit, is lacking. State direction overrides many prices; during Soviet industrialization in the 1930s, for example, labour and other resources were channelled into heavy industry despite exceedingly low 'prices' for its outputs.

The notion of the 'degenerated workers' state', on the other hand, denies that exploitation is — as it would be under capitalism — rooted in the system of production. It results only from 'deformation' of the system of *distribution*, in antagonism with the (potentially socialist) organization of production. The state bureaucracy enjoy their privileges as, so to speak, a form of organized pilferage. And this is what makes them a *caste* rather than a class. In Marxism's view of previous social formations, the systematic extraction of a surplus by a minority has involved not only a specific mechanism of exploitation, but also an exploitative class reproducing itself from generation to generation, usually through property inheritance. Thus discussion of whether it is possible to identify a 'ruling class' in Soviet-type societies has often turned on its self-reproduction, its property forms, and their relations with the state. Trotsky's account of the 'degenerated workers' state', for example, saw systematic inheritance as dependent on the re-emergence of private property and, thus, on the eventual restoration of capitalism over the socialist economy.

Clearly, however, significant inheritance of privilege has developed without private property. One family of conceptions (broadly speaking that of 'bureaucratic collectivism', see below) accounts for this through notions of 'class' property, collectively controlled (and therefore 'owned') by a ruling stratum through the state. The question of *individual* family inheritance does not arise. Most versions of 'state capitalism' argue similarly. And a somewhat distinct line of thinking — with roots which pre-date the Russian revolution — stresses the joint capacity of educational differences and the social division of labour to form the basis of a generalized differentiation of the social structure, reproducing itself across generations.[23] Among recent writers, for example, Alvin Gouldner argues the global rise of a 'new class' distinguished by its 'culture of critical discourse', embodied in a form of 'human capital'.[24] This is the basis both of its higher productivity and its higher salaries. Gouldner's 'new class' in Communist societies resembles the growing scientific élite described by Czech theorists of 'post industrialism', but seen under a more critical aspect.

Where Gouldner identifies discrete divisions, the East German dissident Rudolf Bahro analyses the social division of labour as a continuum through a hierarchical pyramid.[25] There is a ranking of social locations, but no divisions into a small number of classes. Education acts as a multiplex factor of inheritance: not only have more upper-class children the cultural 'head start' enjoyed by the middle classes in the West, but education's associations with state or party office bring opportunities for direct manipulation of one's offspring's education and life chances.

Marx, seconded by Lenin, licensed higher economic rewards in so far as these reflected greater productivity. But, especially in the absence of the market, privileged positions of office can arise in the state or party bureaucracy which have no sensible connection with the productivity of the individual and since, in many cases higher education leads to bureaucratic office, the two effects – even if they were conceptually distinct[26] – are almost impossible to disentangle empirically. The elaborate state-party hierarchies of appointment and promotion are thus seen by 'new class' theorists both as an essential *part* of economic differentiation, and as *representative* of those who benefit from it.

'Totalitarianism'

The concept of 'totalitarianism', by contrast, emphasizes the capacity of state bureaucracy to dominate society directly, independently of roots in property forms or ruling classes. The general sociology of bureaucracy, in particular of its internal mechanisms, has a large, but unfortunately largely oblique, bearing on theories of Communist states. Much of it is (for obvious reasons of accessibility) derived from studies of corporate and state bureaucracies in the West. Moreover much of 'organization theory' is pragmatic, aimed at improving administration and work organization, and therefore focuses more on the alterable than the quintessential features of bureaucracy. Weber commented on the effects of the simultaneous growth of state and private bureaucracies and the 'unchecked' development of state bureaucracy that was to be expected if private property was eliminated.[27] The scope he saw for liberal politics to control bureaucratic structures lay largely in their mutual counter-balancing. His view may be taken as preamble to theories of 'totalitarianism' as the characteristic form of Communist states. The concept comes with many variants and nuances, but all shift their primary emphasis from the economy and property relations to political and administrative structures and the disposition of power. Power, when too far concentrated, ceases to be limitable by other powers, and destroys institutional and social pluralism throughout society.

The word 'totalitarianism', although it came to be one applied mainly to Communist states by their liberal critics, was actually launched as a term of approbation. Mussolini, from the mid-1920s, made '*lo stato totalitario*' (the totalitarian state) part of the language of Italian fascism, denoting by it his intention of principle to eliminate political rivals and form a one-party state. German Nazis similarly referred to their regime as '*totalitar*' in the 1930s (though Hitler preferred the word '*authoritar*').[28] 'Totalitarianism' was then adopted by social scientific literature before the Second World War as descriptive of Stalin's one-party state as well (though Soviet writers did not, of course, accept this).

The post-war development of the term in application to Communist states consists of a mixture of description and theory, embracing a family of linked characteristics, though not necessarily taken as defining conditions of 'totalitarianism' in the state.[29] Because the nature of *political* regimes has varied more than property relations both over time and as between different Communist states (and because politics is a less exact discipline than economics) the attempt to define a single category primarily via the polity rather than the economy necessarily produces even less clear-cut and general results.

Concentration of political power is essential to the idea of totalitarianism. In the sense of many of its exponents, it implies a concentration not only in one party but in the hands of the individual leader who, subordinating the party to his own purposes, rules through a network of more personal connections. Fascist states are particularly clear examples of this, but the 'Führerprinzip' is present also in the cults of Stalin's, or Mao's, personality. This recrudescence within a contemporary state of earlier forms involves – what is rather general in Communist parties – the recurrence of conflict between individual leaders or aspirants and the administrative apparatuses. It has affinities with the ascendancy of a single political leader in, for example, nineteenth-century France – Bonapartism – though the domination of totalitarian leaders in and through the party is distinct from Bonapartism's rule 'above party'. Linked with the concentration of power in the state is the attempt to destroy it at other and alternative levels. Totalitarianism, in this sense, aims also at the elimination, containment, neutering or assimilation of intermediate social institutions which could act as rival sources of power. The elimination of private capital and employment is, thus, one specific – if centrally important – case of something more general, which includes the assimilation of religious institutions, or trade unions, for example. At a more microscopic level, totalitarianism seeks also to weaken direct connections and solidarity between individuals, atomizing society so that the state's monopoly of control over the major, and formal, institutions renders the individual more directly dependent upon it, without personal connections in civil society to fall back on.

There are two other important shifts in the relations between state and society. First, the subordination of law, understood as an impersonal and independent system of adjudication: even though legal forms are preserved, the legal system is, in effect, under the control of the party leadership. And, secondly, the enforcement of an official 'ideology', provided by the state with a monopoly of authority in many areas of intellectual life, and claiming validity as a universal system of doctrine: Marxism–Leninism. The doctrine must be the more energetically defended by the state in that its democratic formulae are in tension with the actual political regime; it sets limits to private, as well as public, intellectual life.

If these features characterize totalitarianism as an ideal type, it is clear that many Communist states, in many periods, do not conform to it. The concentration of political power in one single leader is often circumscribed by a ruling oligarchy's wish to avoid the dangers of a 'cult of personality'. In respect of the state's pressure on the individual, there is clearly an enormous gulf between, say, high Stalinism and the relatively low-profile rule of Janos Kadar in Hungary. Similarly, the elimination of other powers is not a necessary condition of Communist rule: Polish Communism has co-existed ever since the war (as Mussolini earlier did) with a deeply entrenched Catholic church with which it has had to discover and continually renegotiate a *modus vivendi*. Whether, however, Communist rule could for long tolerate, for example, independent trade unions, which tend more directly to rival its economic and social powers, is more doubtful – as the case of Poland again testifies. The independence of the judiciary appears to be only a temporary and unstable phenomenon – as, again, in brief periods in Poland, or in Czechoslovakia before the Soviet invasion of 1968. But there are several instances when the political authorities have relaxed too stringent a control of intellectual life, and have allowed assent to Marxism–Leninism to decline to the point where it is merely polite, or less. Nonetheless, rival intellectual currents do, it is clear, always act as irritants of Communist states; as with independent social institutions the authorities have, if not an absolute intolerance of them, at least an 'allergy' towards them.

Suppressing rivalry creates its own problems for state authorities, partly analogous to those of eliminating free markets:[30] they lack the sort of 'sounding boards' which give democratic states warning of social pressures and shifting interests, and allow them to respond. Defence of the political monopoly imposes, as one of its costs, a species of 'numbness' in the perception of social processes; the tension between these is a perennial problem of Communist states.

Most senses of 'totalitarianism' see social atomization as a means for direct control of the central state power over individuals. Recently Alexander Zinoviev (an exiled Soviet logician and student of his former society) has urged a corrective emphasis on the individual's more immediate social environment: what social atomization produces is, in fact, an *active* (though rather cynical) participation.[31] The individual lives his life not in the state alone but within much smaller 'communes', the 'cells' of social life; within these his life chances depend on competition with others for leverage within a structure of power. Unlike economic competition in the West, where the performance of one individual does not necessarily worsen the situation of others, competition for power is a 'zero sum game'; consequently, in Communism's war of each against all, mendacity and mistrust are endemic. These are fought out within, and reinforce, the larger official frameworks of control. There is a curious and pessimistic asymmetry: where, in much political theory, the state is morally enlarged by its affinity with the people, in Zinoviev's account the totalitarian state, in imposing an affinity with its own ethos on the people, morally diminishes them.

'Bureaucratic collectivism'

Zinoviev's view (like Bahro's) reminds us that the social structures and interdependencies within Communist states (and the difference among them) elude neat categorization into a small number of classes. The problems of pinpointing a (politically) ruling class and an (economically) exploiting one have often been linked, and sometimes identified. The striking but very rough correlation of privilege and power, and the absence of any simple criterion (such as private property) have led to much involved discussion. The problems involved have produced a strand (with roots in Marxism, but growing well beyond it) which depicts – sometimes metaphorically and sometimes almost literally – the state power itself as a form of property capable of appropriation, if not by individuals then by a class collectively. The alignment of political with economic primacy is thus, so to speak, semantically assured. Christian Rakovsky developed a comment of Marx on the Prussian bureaucracy ('owns the state as private property') along these lines in characterizing the Soviet system in 1930.[32] The Italian Brumo Rizzi, in 1939, described the 'class property' of a new 'bureaucratic collectivist' ruling class as the hallmark of a distinct social form, to which modern societies, led by the Fascist and Communist states, were tending.[33] A similar, but more famous view was echoed a little later by James Burnham in *The Managerial Revolution* (1941).[34] In his construction two (perhaps over-determining) elements are combined: the managers owe their ascent to their necessity in production, but secure their position by the monolithic possession of the state power. The internal metabolism of the ruling group, and their relations to the rest of society, are little discussed.

Historical sequences and 'convergence'

Rizzi and Burnham offer early examples of the idea of a general 'convergence' of different state types towards a common condition[35] – which they both took Stalin's Russia in the 1930s to have approximated most closely. Evidently questions of Communist states, placing within sequences of historical development relate, but in a complex way, to those of their location within the world system of states. We take the former first.

For Marxist theories, historical sequences pose problems. Most variants take as fundamental a definite succession for modern societies, each defined by its characteristic mode of production: feudalism yields to capitalism, which in turn is transformed into socialism. More or less complex interrelations and combinations between these forms are recognized; for example, in Russia after the 1905 revolution, Parvus' and Trotsky's theory of 'permanent revolution' recognized the late and feeble development of economic capitalism within a political order inherited from the past, and envisaged that the bourgeois-democratic 'stage' might, in this national instance, be largely by-passed; many Russian Marxists before 1917 also anticipated (or feared) that economic backwardness would require dictatorial methods for any attempt to leap a stage direct to socialism. But as far as contemporary Communist states are concerned, Marxism's fundamental scenario tends to impose on its adherents a view of them as either a form (the last?) of capitalism – 'state capitalism' – or else as a variant (even if early, atypical, or deformed) of socialism. To view them as a social form distinct from either capitalism or socialism, or even an intervening stage between the two, disrupts the logic of Marx's analyses of capitalism, which see the premises of socialism being created organically within it. Certain Marxists – Rizzi, for example – do bluntly interpose 'bureaucratic collectivism' as an extra stage, but most opt either in the direction of 'state capitalism', or for a sort of proto-socialism..

Most ideas involving a notion of 'totalitarianism' have, however, a less closely defined historical sequence as background. The period of apparently greater liberalism under Khruschev in the Soviet Union, especially, gave rise to a distinct post-war sense of 'convergence' of which Talcott Parsons' functionalist sociology may be taken as an instance.[36] For Parsons, world history has evolved through three stages: primitive, intermediate and modern, and both Communist and Western states are now obliged to adapt to the exigencies of the modern period, with increasingly sophisticated industrial production and patterns of life. The increasing weight of the state and the bureaucratization of social functions in the West is reflected in a mirror-opposite evolution of Communist societies, towards greater differentiation, liberalization of the political regime, the emergence of competing interest groups, and so on.

Convergence in this sense, however, need neither lead to close similarities, nor affect all portions of society: in particular, industrial society may rely very heavily, or far less, on state direction of economic activity. This sense of 'convergence' – to a degree away from 'totalitarianism' – is distinct from that advanced, for example, by Marcuse: here high levels of technological development both require and secure integration of the mass of the population, not only into work but mentally, into functionally useful patterns of feeling and thought.[37] Deviance need less and less be repressed since it is increasingly isolated: one-dimensional thought rules. Like Parsons, Marcuse projected a reduction in state coercion in Communist societies, but in an account with a far more pessimistic coloration. Rather than the recurrent emergence of competing groups, he anticipated increasing passive homogeneity, East and West.

The idea of a sequence of modes of production with their corresponding states, each functional for traversing given levels of economic development, has difficulty with the parallelisms of, for example, industrialization. America and Russia, during the last hundred years, have both covered a great deal of common ground in basic industrialization, but the former with a capitalist mode of production and state, and the latter with 'socialist' ones.

One explanation of non-capitalist industrialization runs in terms of the order in which states industrialize. From the early 1880s the Russian socialist Vorontsov was putting forward the argument that 'the later the process of capitalization is commenced, the more difficult it is to carry it out along capitalist lines'.[38] For Russia, as a late developer, capitalist industrialization, even with sponsorship and subsidy by the state, could only be abortive or socially disastrous. The pressures of world markets and of the already industrialized nations, together with an unproductive and impoverished agriculture, meant that industrial capitalism could exist only as artificial islands of modern technology within a sea of depressed peasant demand, creating rural unemployment by the extinction of peasant crafts faster than it could ever absorb it in urban industry. However there was, Vorontsov argued, an alternative to this cul-de-sac: instead of forcing a hot-house capitalism, the state could develop both industry and the rural market by sponsoring collectivist economic forms; economic backwardness could prove to be an historical advantage. The influence among the Russian intelligentsia of Vorontsov and his fellow 'populists' (as Peter Struve was to dub them) later receded before that of the 'objectivist' Marxists, who could point to the boom of capitalist industry in the 1890s. But the basic idea that socialism could or should somehow by-pass the capitalist phase in such an under-developed country was common among Russian socialist intellectuals, some of its political implications later being codified in the Parvus–Trotsky theory of 'permanent revolution'.

Vorontsov's argument rested not only on backwardness in general, but also on specific features (Russia's cold climate, short growing season and surplus rural population, for example). It was also modern in its assertion that progressive economic development would not necessarily sit with political freedom: 'it will be Russia's destiny to bring about equality and fraternity, though she is not destined to fight for liberty'.[39]

A somewhat different explanation of political despotism grounded in specific conditions starts from Russia's longer-term history, and specifically from the non-feudal and 'asiatic' character of medieval Russia, with its state, rather than private, rights over land and peasants. Russia's thinkers frequently pondered her 'oriental' characteristics; this is a central theme of Plekhanov's *History of Russian Social Thought* (1909).[40] From his first Marxist writings, in the early 1880s, Plekhanov alluded to the possibility of a new form of oriental despotism, 'on communist foundations'; it was the fear of putting too much power in the hands of an 'asiatic' state which caused him, later, to oppose the policy of nationalizing the land.

The suggestion has been developed at length by the (aberrant) Marxist Karl Wittfogel, in *Oriental Despotism*,[41] which resurrects the 'asiatic mode of production' identified (but never examined in depth) by Marx. Russian social relations, both prior to and after Peter the Great's reforms, were only superficially feudal and 'Western'; fundamentally they were shaped by different relations of the state to society, in which strong intermediate proprietors were lacking, and the centralized state had a powerful role both in extracting an economic surplus (through taxes, etc.) and in the organization, or at least the regulation, of production.[42] And, following the Bolshevik seizure of power, these relations reasserted – or realized – themselves, only at a quite different, modern, technological level. The connected notions of oriental despotism and the asiatic mode of production emphasize the existence of forms of society in which both political dominance and economic exploitation occur through the state, without any substantial role for private property, and they stress that state forms can endure over the very long term, producing parallelisms across widely separated economic levels.

Wittfogel's outlook is that of an (anti-Bolshevik) Marxist; however, the conception of profound and long-lasting differences of state, culture and temperament dividing authoritarian East from liberal West is widespread.[43] Such views have a particular 'edge' for Eastern Europe: its states represent the imposition of an alien political order on societies and cultures which, having developed as part of Europe, are intrinsically unfitted for them; the broader extent of social and national rebellion in Eastern Europe compared with the Soviet Union since the war is taken as confirmation of this difference.

Wittfogel's view bridges two schools in that, while schematically loyal to Marx, he also makes fundamental use of the term 'totalitarian'. As a concept, 'totalitarianism' is more commonly associated with liberal political outlooks and hence, different views of the historical background from Marxism: different both in the historical phases perceived and in the senses in which they are regarded as necessary. 'Totalitarian' states are explicitly or implicitly contrasted with those enjoying parliamentary democracy and a 'pluralist' political order (an additional contrast is sometimes added between totalitarianism and 'authoritarian' states – such as many third world military regimes – which, while dictatorial, do not aim at ideological or psychological dominance).

The will to power

Much of the discussion so far has run in terms of Communist states as related to objective social structures. One can also tease out a strand of thinking which stresses the subjective characteristics, in particular the political volition, of a 'new class' – very variously defined – in both the genesis and internal development of Communist states. Usually the sources of the 'new class' are found in processes already under way in non- or pre-Communist societies: the growth of an educated but unpropertied middle class grounded in specialist professional and bureaucratic occupations, particularly in the state. Bakunin, in his polemical thrusts against Marx and Engels in the First International in the 1870s, accused them of aiming at the forcible despotism of experts and 'representative' politicians over the working class. The pioneer of this view as a systematic theory also deserves mention: the Russian–Polish radical Jan Makhaisky, exiled to Siberia in the 1890s, there discerned from reading *Capital*, not the benefits of socialism, but the dangers represented by the new class of 'white hands' with their 'intellectual capital', exploiting manual labour through their higher salaries, who aimed to ride the working class to power through socialism and, once there, establish both their dictatorship and their privileges through state offices.[44] The idea has often been renewed, often with greater sociological sophistication. Djilas' *The New Class*,[45] written from the privileged position of a former close lieutenant of Marshall Tito, emphasizes its conscious unity of will, so effective in gaining power. Gouldner's portrait of the 'new class' distinguishes the 'critical' educated strata, in scientific, cultural and social employment, from old-style managers. Its 'problem-solving' outlook and abilities explain its varied impulses and achievements from, for example, the Chinese Communist revolution to the American 'new left' of the 1960s. Ivan Szelenyi discovers represented in the Eastern European Communist states the interests of an historically much older stratum: an intelligentsia separated from both large-scale property and the mass of the population, but with a 'teleological' propensity for politics as 'rational re-distribution'.[46] Recent neo-conservative writers, particularly in the United States, have seen in the growth of state-financed middle-class occupations the roots of 'interventionism' and leftism aiming at their protection and expansion.[47] Similar interests are, it is argued, crucial to Communism as a political movement, and are embodied triumphant in its states. Students of intellectuals more narrowly defined have found in them both the wellspring of Communist state totalism and of the ideologies aiming at the rational-utopian reconstruction of society which enable them to mobilize much larger social forces.[48]

In the international arena

What implications do different theories of Communist states – most of which start from their internal structure – have for their international action? The range is considerable: from the picture of the 'degenerated workers' state' as essentially vulnerable and defensive, seeking an illusory isolation; through views that Soviet international conduct (for example) is a new form of imperialism; to Cornelius Castoriadis' characterization of the Soviet state as a 'stratocracy' – i.e. one in which the commanding military caste dominates society as a whole, dividing the economy into civilian and military sectors, siphoning off the best of the former to supply the latter, and in which geographical expansion and conquest (partly to appropriate the more efficient economies of capitalist rivals) is a fundamental objective of the system.[49]

Views of the international action of Communist states turn not only on their internal characteristics but also on wider questions of their relationships with other societies, in particular the developed market democracies of the West. Difference need not necessarily imply fundamental rivalry: it may equally entail a degree of complementary symbiosis, as in the 'Vodka-Cola' thesis popularized by Charles Levinson.[50] Equally similarity (as implied, for example, by many versions of 'state capitalism') need not entail mutually pacific relations. Ideas of the intrinsic defensiveness of *all* Communist states suffer problems in explaining hostilities between them: for example, the proxy Sino–Soviet war fought out between China and Vietnam, or the Vietnamese–Cambodian conflict. Equally, ideas which deduce foreign expansionism as fundamental, for economic or political reasons or a mixture of the two, cannot be applied in any common way to the very large Communist states, acting as world powers, and the smaller ones, generally dependent on one of the former. The analogy of a Soviet colonial system in Eastern Europe is limited in one crucial respect: there are no formal colonial relations, each Eastern European state remains, constitutionally, sovereign. (Several, however, include a clause prescribing 'friendship' with the Soviet Union in their constitutions.) Soviet control is a continuous system of guidance-suggestion-intervention through the upper reaches of the party apparatuses. It depends, thus, on the party and state's internal cohesion, and the authority of the state; it is when this is threatened that the Soviet leadership intervenes most directly. China has never acquired an analogous constellation of dependent powers, with the possible and temporary exception of Albania. It is doubtful whether one can provide a single framework of explanation of even Communist superstates' international action. Motives and pressures on many levels interact, and combine very differently for the first, and later, comers. A number of writers on the Soviet Union, such as Zbigniew Brzezinski,[51] pick up longstanding themes of specifically *Russian* historiography, and see Soviet imperialism and quasi-imperialism as the continuation in modern times of the Muscovite state's secular tendency to territorial expansion, arising from its militarized internal structure and its geographical conditions, lacking natural sea and mountain frontiers and with an endemic appetite for land.

One general point is, however, stressed by many writers (reversing economic accounts of capitalist imperialism): a basic impulse towards foreign expansionism lies in Communist states' economic inefficiency relative to market economies. While the state's monopoly of power is – because of the inescapable inefficiencies of the planning system – a disadvantage on the economic plane, it is a pronounced advantage on the military and political ones. Nor do Communist governments have to fear the same sorts of internal opposition to external war as many Western ones.

Conclusions

What might be distilled from such very general 'models' as we have mentioned, of which there is now a considerable array? Authors repeatedly single out one or a few aspects – economic, political or social-psychological – as *the* decisive ones. Other theorists, criticizing or reacting against such one-sidedness, often over-emphasize other, equally partial features. From the interplay, however, certain consensuses-across-differences do emerge. The impossibility of conceiving of social positions and relations separately from political ones, the interpenetration of state with society, compels a 'seamless robe' approach: conceptions of the one very commonly extend into a general view of the other. The sense of a civil society and economy distinct from the state tends to dissolve, and with it a premise of many modern evaluative analyses of the state, according as how it serves needs and interests within society. The social and political merge, jointly embracing the psychological; even where, formally speaking, the author takes certain features, such as economic relations, to be fundamental, he generally finds himself drawn, for the sake of realism, into lengthy sociological, psychological or anecdotal asides.

If conceptual distinctions between state, society and economy tend to blur, so do those among classes or strata. Property ownership, for example, can no longer act even in principle as a main criterion of social differentiation (though there have been attempts to keep notional forms of it in service). Yet similar family structures endure and privileged social position continues to be strongly inherited, through mechanisms which generally combine access to education, political leverage and bureaucratic office. Even the direct inheritance of posts is widespread.[52] The mechanisms of both material privilege and political power are different in kind from those in market, electoral societies.

But the linkage is closer. Ascent to high privilege virtually requires political exertion; the state enters into the formation of social ordering with an intimacy that – in societies where economic difference turns largely on property – it need not necessarily do. What the two social forms share must perhaps be expressed at a very high level of generality: social production, with comparable technologies, but combined and in friction with individual appropriation; the centralization of actual economic and political power; and the atomization of the population *vis-a-vis* the foci of control.

If most general theories of Communist states interweave the social and the political, there also emerges from them, in parallel and in a way paradoxically, a sense of the state as a powerful social interest in its own right, of its having become – from a rational, functional or moral point of view, or some combination of these – superfluous to or parasitic upon the life of society. The extreme point this attains in Communist society is, perhaps, one of the things that the determination and comprehensiveness of the state's grip reflects.

Notes and References

1.   Even among general conceptions I have selected harshly and, in compression, been unfair to all – I hope equally so. More empirical and so-called 'middle-range' theories are entirely omitted. The expression 'Communist states' simply denotes the coverage.
2.   For examples of anarchist criticisms of this sort, see Paul Avrich (ed.) (1973) *The Anarchists in the Russian Revolution*, London, Thames and Hudson, and (1967) *The Russian Anarchists*, Princeton, Princeton University Press. Similar criticisms came later from certain left-wing Bolsheviks: see Robert V. Daniels (1960) *The Conscience of the Revolution*, Cambridge, Massachusetts, Harvard University Press. At this time the idea of 'state capitalism' was not clearly distinguished from that of a new, but non-capitalist, ruling class.
3.   See, for example (1921) 'The Tax in Kind' in *Collected Works* (1963–70) Moscow, Progress Publishers, Vol. XXXII.
4.   See Stephen F. Cohen (1975). *Bukharin and the Bolshevik Revolution*, New York, Vintage Books, Chapter 1. Bukharin developed ideas in Hilferding's *Finance Capital* (1910), concluding that in the modern 'imperialist pirate state' social organs tended to fuse with the state into 'a single all embracing organization'. He also mentioned the theoretical possibility of 'an entirely new economic form', neither capitalist nor socialist, but in which class rule was reinforced and which resembled 'a slaveowning economy where the slave market is absent'.
5.   See Karl Kautsky (1920). *Terrorism and Communism*, London, Allen & Unwin; his views on the Soviet state are discussed in Massimo Salvadori.

(1979). *Karl Kautsky and the Socialist Revolution, 1880–1938*, London, New Left Books.

6. Early views are described in Adam Buick and William Jerome (1967) 'Soviet State Capitalism? The history of an Idea', *Survey* No. 62, January.

7. His views are summarized in English in Lucien Laurat (pseudonym, i.e. Otto Machl) (1940) *Marxism and Democracy*, London, Left Book Club.

8. Republished (1974) as *State Capitalism in Russia*, London, Pluto Press. Cliff's views on China are in Ygael Gluckstein (i.e. Tony Cliff) (1957) *Mao's China*, London, Allen & Unwin, whose arguments are refreshed in Nigel Harris (1978) *The Mandate of Heaven*, London, Quartet Books. A more orthodox Marxist criticism is David Purdy (1976) *The Soviet Union – State Capitalist or Socialist?*, London, Communist Party of Great Britain.

9. Ygael Gluckstein (1952) *Stalin's Satellites in Europe*, London, Allen & Unwin; see also Chris Harman (1974) *Bureaucracy and Revolution in Eastern Europe*, London, Pluto Press.

10. Cliff (1957) 'Perspectives of the Permanent War Economy', *Socialist Review*, Vol. VI, No. 8, and Michael Kidron (1970) *Western Capitalism Since the War*, Harmondsworth, Penguin, Ch. III.

11. Cliff, *State Capitalism in Russia*, p. 209.

12. Alvin Gouldner (1977–8) 'Stalinism: a study of internal colonialism'. *Telos*. No. 34, Winter. The idea preceded the events: Bukharin warned in 1925 against the working class 'degenerating into a real exploiting class', treating the peasant economy 'as a "proletarian" colony' (quoted in Cohen, *Bukharin and the Bolshevik Revolution*, p. 172).

13. See Alexander Erlich (1960) *The Soviet Industrialisation Debate*, Cambridge, Massachusetts, Harvard University Press; also Moshe Lewin (1968) *Russian Peasants and Soviet Power, 1924–8*. London, Allen & Unwin.

14. It was developed mainly in opposition to the theory of 'socialism in one country', whose first chief advocate was Bukharin, and sponsor Stalin. Ideas akin to Trotsky's have recently been embraced by 'eurocommunist' theorists of Western Communist parties.

15. The main statement is (1972) *The Revolution Betrayed*, New York, Pathfinder Press, written in 1936. Trotsky's thinking is well surveyed in Baruch Knei-Paz (1978) *The Social and Political Thought of Leon Trotsky*, Oxford, Oxford University Press.

16. *The Revolution Betrayed*, pp. 112–13.

17. Paul Bellis (1979) *Marxism and the USSR*, London, Macmillan, p. 234 – a useful critical exploration. Post-war disagreements (more involved than fruitful) among Trotsky's followers on the nature of Communist states are overviewed by Bruno Bongiovanni (1982) 'The Dissolution of Trotskyism', *Telos*, No. 52, Summer.

18. See, for example, E. Mandel (1979) *On Bureaucracy: A Marxist Analysis*, London, The Other Press.

19. An interesting account, relating back to earlier arguments, is in Moshe Lewin (1974) *Political Undercurrents in Soviet Economic Debates*, Princeton, Princeton University Press. See also Michael Ellman (1969) *Economic Reform in the Soviet Union*, London, PEP.

20. Radovan Richta, *et al* (1969) *Civilisation at the Crossroads*, White Plains, New York, IASP.

21. Marx-Engels (1968) *Selected Works*, London, Lawrence and Wishart, Vol. I.

22. Recent variants, also recognizing the elimination of *private* capital as per-

manent, have seen Lenin as the architect of 'a particular type of capitalist revolution', the only type of which a backward country such as Russia was capable; see, for example, Charles Bettelheim (1982) *Luttes de Classes en URSS*, Paris, Maspero, Vol. 3 and (1982) *Le Monde Dimanche*, 3 Octobre.

23. Bakunin was an early example; for others see Adam Westoby (1981) 'Education, Inequality and the Question of a Communist "New Class"', in Roger Dale *et al.* (eds) *Education and the State*, Vol. I, Brighton, Falmer Press.

24. Alvin Gouldner (1979). *The Future of Intellectuals and the Rise of the New Class*, London, Macmillan.

25. Rudolf Bahro (1978) *The Alternative in Eastern Europe*, London, New Left Books.

26. A recent essay of theoretical economics, John Roemer's (1982) *A Theory of Exploitation and Class*. Cambridge, Massachusetts, Harvard University Press, distinguishes two forms of exploitation in socialism, due to greater skill and privileged office respectively.

27. 'Parliament and Government in a Reconstructed Germany', in Weber (1968) *Economy and Society*, New York, Bedminster, Vol. III.

28. Leonard Schapiro (1969) 'The Concept of Totalitarianism', *Survey*, No. 73, Autumn.

29. More a term than a theory, 'totalitarianism' has long had a momentum of its own in ordinary parlance, outside the voluminous academic literature. Classic post-war statements are Hannah Arendt (1951) *The Origins of Totalitarianism*, New York, Harcourt Brace, and Carl Freidrich and Zbigniew Brzezinski (1957) *Totalitarianism Dictatorship and Autocracy*, Cambridge, Massachusetts, Harvard University Press.

30. An early and influential criticism of state economic monopoly is Ludwig von Mises (1920) 'Economic Calculation in a Socialist Commonwealth' (originally published in German) in F.A. Hayek (ed.) (1935) *Collectivist Economic Planning*, London, George Routledge.

31. Zinoviev's views are set out in (1981) *Communisme comme realité*, Paris, Julliard, and in his satirical novel (1979) *Yawning Heights*, Harmondsworth, Penguin. An interpretative summary is Philip Hanson (1982) 'Alexander Zinoviev: totalitariansim from below'. *Survey*, Vol. 26 No. 1, Winter.

32. Statement translated (1930) in *Luttes de Classes*. Paris. September–December.

33. (1939) *La Bureaucratisation du Monde*, Paris, Hachette.

34. Brumo Rizzi. Max Shachtman, co-dissident with Burnham among Trotskyist intellectuals in the 1930s, further developed the Marxist 'bureaucratic collectivist' criticism of the Soviet Union; see his essays in (1962) *The Bureaucratic Revolution*, New York, Donald Press. Among later variants Antonio Carlo (1974) in 'The Socio-economic Nature of the USSR', *Telos*, No. 21, Fall, sees it as a phase in the regression of the Soviet Union to capitalism, while Moshe Machover and John Fantham (1979) *The Century of the Unexpected*, Liverpool, Big Flame, view 'state collectivism' as specific to underdeveloped societies.

35. Writings on 'convergence' are reviewed in Alfred G. Meyer (1970) 'Theories of Convergence', in Chalmers Johnson (ed.) *Change in Communist Systems*, Stanford, Stanford University Press.

36. See, for example, Talcott Parsons (1960) *Structure and Process in Modern Societies*, Glencoe, Illinois, Free Press.

37. Marcuse, H. (1968) *One Dimensional Man*, London, Sphere Books.

38. Walicki, W. (1980) *A History of Russian Thought from the Enlightenment to Marxism*, Oxford, Oxford University Press, pp. 299–305.
39. Ibid, p. 431.
40. Samuel H. Baron (1963). *Plekhanov* Stanford, Stanford University Press, pp. 299–305.
41. Karl Wittfogel (1957) *Oriental Despotism*. New Haven, Yale University Press; revised edition (1981) New York, Vintage Books; his was an important influence on Bahro's view, mentioned above.
42. The adventures of Marx's 'asiatic mode of production' within Marxism are recounted in Marian Sawer (1977) *Marxism and the Question of the Asiatic Mode of Production*, The Hague, Martinus Nijhoff.
43. A recent example is Robert Conquest's (1980) *We and They*, London, Temple Smith. The conception of the Soviet regime as a specific outcome of the Russian state's 'patrimonial' relation to society is set out in Richard Pipes (1977) *Russia under the Old Regime*, Harmondsworth, Penguin.
44. See Marshall S. Shatz (1968) 'J.W. Machajski and "Makhaevshchina", 1866–1926'. PhD) thesis. Columbia University: extracts from Machajski's main work, *The Intellectual Worker* (1898–1905) are in Alexander Skirda (ed.) *Le socialisme des intellectuels*, Paris, Le Seuil.
45. Milovan Djilas (1968) *The New Class* (2nd edn) London, Allen & Unwin.
46. Ivan Szeleny, and George Konrad (1979) *The Intellectuals on the Road to Class Power*, Brighton, Harvester.
47. A selection is in B. Bruce-Biggs (ed.) (1979) *The New Class?* New Brunswick, New Jersey, Transaction Books.
48. See, for example, Raymond Aron (1957) *The Opium of the Intellectuals*, London, Secker and Warburg, and Lewis Feuer (1975) *Ideology and the Ideologists*. Oxford, Basil Blackwell.
49. Cornelius Castoriadis (1981) *Devant la Guerre*, Paris, Fayard. Castoriadis' earlier views are in (1973) *La Société bureaucratique*, Paris, Union Générale d'Editions.
50. Charles Levinson (1980) *Vodka-Cola*, Horsham, Biblios. The central idea is that Western capital, through loans and co-ownership of plants, shares in the exploitation of Communist states' more disciplined labour force, realizing profits through exports to the West.
51. See, for example, Zbigniew Brzezinski, 'Tragic Dilemmas of Soviet World Power: the limits of a new-type empire', *Encounter*, December 1983.
52. A recent press account reported that in the south west Chinese province of Guizhon more than 4000 young people had been dismissed from jobs they inherited from their parents (*The Times*, 9th February 1984).

CHAPTER 6

Imperialism

Diane Elson

Introduction

'Imperialism' suggests the aggressive actions of a state in the international arena, and has been associated with a number of diverse concepts and feelings. Most commonly, perhaps, imperialism conjures up images of colonialism – the British Raj, Dr Livingstone and so on. Consequently, it appears to be a somewhat outdated idea for considering the contemporary framework of relations between states. Yet imperialism can exist without colonialism, since some states can dominate and exploit others without military intervention and the creation of colonial regimes (Fieldhouse 1981, pp. 1–10). But we may go further and suggest that imperialism cannot fully be understood at the level of a *single* state or society. This has led the more systematic theorists of imperialism to define imperialism as an international *system* characterized by relations of domination and subservience, and to seek to analyse this system by reference to some underlying causal processes.

In this chapter, I want to consider one such theory of imperialism: the theory which argues that the underlying process is the *internationalization of capital*. By the internationalization of capital is meant the tendency for capitalist firms to engage in transactions which go beyond the boundaries of the state in which they are first formed. The process may involve any or all of the following forms:

i. *international trade*: foreign countries provide markets and raw materials for domestic firms;
ii. *export of capital*: domestic firms invest abroad; this can take the form of lending to foreign firms or governments; or buying shares

in firms established abroad; or setting up firms abroad, for example, to develop mines or plantations;

iii. *multi-national corporations*: large capitalist firms plan their operations on an international scale and carry out production in several countries, blurring the distinction, to some extent, between 'domestic' and 'foreign' firms.

In the first section of the chapter, I examine the 'classical' theory of imperialism, initiated by the English liberal J.A. Hobson, and developed further by the Russian Marxist, V.I. Lenin. Then I discuss criticisms of that theory. The third section probes the implications of the theory for the functioning of the state; and fourthly I consider whether it is applicable to the world today.

1. The classical theory of imperialism: Hobson and Lenin

Hobson's book on imperialism was published in London in 1902. It was prompted by concern at two developments of the last quarter of the nineteenth century: the spurt of colonial expansion, especially in Africa, and the growing rivalry between the leading industrialized capitalist countries.

Hobson concentrated on a critique of British imperialism. He claimed that the new colonies were not valuable from the point of view of trade, nor did they provide many new jobs to which unemployed British workers might migrate. His argument was that from a national point of view any gains resulting from the colonial expansion were small and precarious and far outweighed by the enormous expenditures entailed in procuring and protecting them. For Hobson, the central question was:

> How is the British nation induced to embark upon such an unsound business? The only possible answer is that the business interests of the nation as a whole are subordinated to those of certain sectional interests that usurp control of the national resources and use them for their private gain.   (Hobson, 1971 edition, p. 46)

What might those 'sectional interests' be? Hobson's answer was: the industrialists and financiers who need outlets for new investments, and the upper classes whose income is derived from the profit on these investments. He wrote:

It is not too much to say, that the modern foreign policy of Great Britain has been primarily a struggle for profitable markets of investment. To a larger extent every year Great Britain has been becoming a nation living upon tribute from abroad, and the classes who enjoy this tribute have had an ever-increasing incentive to employ the public policy, the public purse, and the public force to extend the field of their private investments, and to safeguard and improve their existing investments.   (Hobson, 1971 edition, pp. 53–4)

But why were there insufficient profitable outlets for investment in the domestic economy? Why was there any need to look abroad? Hobson's answer was that there was insufficient demand at home, in comparison with the ever-increasing productive capacity of the economy. The reason for the insufficiency of demand, according to Hobson, was the unequal distribution of income, in which some people had 'a consuming power vastly in excess of needs or possible uses, while others are destitute of consuming power enough to satisfy even the full demands of physical efficiency' (Hobson, 1971 edition, p. 83). But if the distribution of income were reformed, then the real cause of the 'new imperialism' would be removed because sufficient outlets for investment would be available at home. The answer was to tax away the unearned income of the upper classes, derived from loans made abroad; and to redistribute it to wage-earners or spend it on public welfare. Thus, within Britain, there was, according to Hobson, a definite antagonism between the interests of the imperialists and the interests of the people. What was required to end imperialism was 'popular government' rather than 'class government'.

The assumption that the internationalization of capital is linked to imperialism by the class character of the state is one that Hobson shares with Marxist theorists of imperialism, such as Lenin. Where Hobson's approach differs from the Marxist approach is in assuming that the class character of the state could be changed without changing the underlying economic system. For Hobson, imperialism was an unfortunate *policy* with very powerful backing; but a policy which might be changed with sufficient political mobilization and far-reaching reforms. It was not a *systematic phase* of capitalism with deep roots in the very existence of the division between capital and worker. For the Marxist writers, imperialism is not a policy but an in-built development of the capitalist economic system, a definite phase or stage of capitalist development.

Lenin wrote *Imperialism, the Highest Stage of Capitalism* in the spring of 1916, while in exile in Zurich. He himself described it as a 'pamphlet' and it was subtitled 'A popular outline'. It was written as an intervention in European socialist politics in the middle of the First

World War. Lenin was horrified at the support given to their national governments by socialists and working class militants, who abandoned internationalism and fought on opposing sides in the war.

His aim was to explain the nature of the war, in the hope that the working class would appreciate the necessity of overthrowing the system that Lenin considered responsible for the war. 'There are different kinds of wars,' wrote Lenin, 'including revolutionary wars.' To the widespread idea that the war was about defending 'national interests', the national interests of Germany, for instance, or the national interests of Britain, Lenin counterposed the idea that it was an imperialistic war; imperialistic in the sense of a war between the imperial powers over the division of the spoils of imperialism. In a particularly polemical passage, Lenin described it as 'war to decide whether the British or German group of financial marauders is to receive the most booty' (Lenin, 1916, p. 12).

Lenin was perfectly aware that imperialism existed before the end of the nineteenth century, and well before capitalism itself. He was not trying to explain imperialism *per se* in terms of the development of the capitalist system. Rather, he argued that the specific forms taken by imperialism at any time were related to the particular socio-economic conditions of that time. The argument is not 'capitalism created imperialism' but that 'the form of imperialism depends upon the socio-economic conditions'. So that 'Even the capitalist colonial policy of *previous* stages of capitalism is essentially different from the colonizing of finance capital' (Lenin, 1916, p. 139).

'Finance capital' was one of the terms that Lenin used to describe late nineteenth-century/early twentieth-century capitalism. He wanted to distinguish the form that capitalism took at this time from earlier forms, and to argue that a distinctly different stage of capitalist development had emerged. He argued that instead of banking being a separate activity from manufacturing, banks had merged with industrial firms, creating large holding companies with many subsidiaries, raising money by issuing shares on the stock market. The holding companies were dominated, argued Lenin, by financiers rather than by production managers. Rentiers, who lived entirely on income obtained from money capital, such as interest and dividends, predominated over entrepreneurs who were directly concerned with the production process, and who lived from the profits of their own manufacturing businesses. The development of finance capital, argued Lenin, had been made possible by the transformation of conditions in manufacturing industry itself: free competition between many small firms had given way to the concentration of production and monopoly.

How did Lenin connect his claims about the development of monopolies and the dominance of finance capital to imperialism? Think back to our earlier discussion of Hobson. How did *he* make the connection between economic developments and political developments? He pointed to the export of capital. Lenin was very much influenced by Hobson's study, and came up with the same answer:

> Typical of the old capitalism, when free competition had undivided sway, was the export of *goods*. Typical of the latest stage of capitalism, when monopolies rule, is the export of *capital*. . . An enormous 'surplus of capital' has arisen in the advanced countries. . . The necessity for exporting capital arises from the fact that in a few countries capitalism has become 'overripe' and (owing to the backward state of agriculture and the poverty of the masses) capital cannot find a field for 'profitable' investment.
>
> (Lenin, 1916, pp. 102–4)

So Lenin was claiming that the dominant *form* of the internationalization of capital had changed. Whereas previously international trade was the dominant factor, in the last quarter of the nineteenth century, according to Lenin, export of capital was the dominant factor. Following Hobson, Lenin argued that the reason for this shift was lack of profitable investment opportunities at home.

Lenin differed, however, from Hobson in his interpretation of the significance of export of capital. For Hobson, as we have seen, it was a regrettable *policy*, adopted by certain dominant interests. For Lenin, it was an inevitable tendency, given the socio-economic relations of the capitalist system, which he argued prevented redistribution of income mopping up the surplus capital.

Hobson's argument has been criticized on the grounds that the export of capital from Britain did *not* go mainly to the territories newly added to the British empire. Lenin rather glossed over this point, claiming that capital exports from Great Britain did go primarily to the colonies, without distinguishing between the colonies proper, and the self-governing dominions such as Canada. However, he did recognize that the other two major capital exporting countries did not export capital primarily to the colonies. France, he pointed out, exported capital mainly to other European countries, while German capital exports were divided between Europe and America.

The conclusion that Lenin drew was that export of capital not only led to a renewed spurt of colonial acquisition, but that it also led to a division of the world into the 'spheres of influence' of large capitalist firms, and of leading capitalist states.

Just as the home market was no longer an arena of 'free competition', so the world market was no longer an arena of free competition. It was divided into the *fiefdoms* of monopoly firms. As an example, Lenin pointed to the relationship between GEC of the USA and AEG of Germany. Both were giant electrical companies – electrical 'Great Powers', Lenin called them. In 1907 the two companies concluded an agreement to divide up the world between them. The GEC was allocated the United States and Canada; the AEG was allocated Germany, Austria, Russia, Holland, Denmark, Switzerland, Turkey and the Balkans. There was to be no competition between them in these two separate areas and, to help make this stick, they were to exchange technical know-how.

Agreements to divide up the world market had also been made in the oil industry, shipping, railway manufacturing, the steel industry, and the zinc industry. These agreements had sometimes collapsed; but Lenin's point was not that particular agreements, once reached, were final but that attempts to regulate competition between giant firms through the subdivision of the world economy were a permanent feature of the new stage of capitalism.

In describing this 'division of the world' Lenin both points to the ways in which the large firms are taking on some attributes similar to attributes of states – negotiating with each other at international conferences, behaving like 'Great Powers'; and also points to the involvement of states themselves in this process. For instance, the backing given by the German government to the Deutsche Bank in its struggle with Rockefeller's American Standard Oil Company over the division of the world oil economy.

It was through this concept of the 'division of the world' that Lenin saw a connection between international economic developments and international political developments. By the beginning of the twentieth century, there were no areas of the globe that were not claimed by, and under some degree of control by, a modern state. Thus territorial expansion by one modern state was not possible without disputing the rights of another similar state.

Lenin argued that the growth of productivity was unlikely to remain in conformity with any particular political division of the world economy. He had particularly in mind the disparity between Great Britain and Germany. Great Britain had much vaster colonies than Germany, but by the beginning of the twentieth century Germany had completely outstripped Britain in industrial development. The world economy, argued Lenin, was no longer 'open' to new expansionary capitals. To accommodate changes in the underlying development of productivity there would have to be changes in the partition of world markets and of investment opportunities; and this, Lenin believed, could only be accomplished by force.

The disparity between the development of productivity and the division of the world amongst the large capitalist firms, and the 'great powers', was for Lenin the key characteristic of the form imperialism took at the beginning of the twentieth century. It was an imperialism in which the most important aspect was the tension and rivalry between the leading capitalist states, given that there were no longer any 'open spaces' for capitalists to expand into; and that the 'last frontier' had been defined. This rivalry, Lenin believed, was the product of a distinctly new form of internationalization of capital. Here is how he summarized the main features of this form:

1) the concentration of production and capital has developed to such a high stage that it has created monopolies which play a decisive role in economic life;
2) the merging of bank capital with industrial capital, and the creation, on the basis of this 'finance capital', of a financial oligarchy;
3) The export of capital as distinguished from the export of commodities acquires exceptional importance;
4) the formation of international monopolist capitalist combines which share the world among themselves, and
5) the territorial division of the whole world among the biggest capitalist powers is completed.

Imperialism is capitalism in that stage of development in which the dominance of monopolies and finance capital has established itself; in which the export of capital has acquired pronounced importance; in which the division of the world among the international trusts has begun, in which the division of all territories of the globe among the biggest capitalist powers has been completed. . . .

(Lenin, 1916, pp. 151–2)

This kind of imperialism, according to Lenin, represented a special stage in the development of capitalism: not only a new stage, but also the 'highest' stage, the 'final' stage. Yet at the same time – paradoxically – it was capitalism in transition, moribund capitalism.

Lenin suggested two main arguments in support of his contention. First, he argued that monopoly led to 'immense progress in the socialization of production'. That is, the allocation of resources and organization of production was guided less and less by the 'invisible hand' of the market, and more and more by the conscious planning systems of large firms. The material means for planning were being developed – though the gains from planning remained in the hands of the few who owned and controlled large firms.

Secondly, he argued that monopoly resulted in a strong tendency to stagnation in technical progress, so that the rapid increases in productivity produced by nineteenth-century capitalism would not continue into the twentieth century. He suggested that if firms could sustain their profits by securing monopoly access to investment opportunities they would no longer have an incentive to develop new technology. They would even have an incentive to deliberately retard technical progress.

Dominated by rivalry between the Great Powers, capitalism as a social system had lost, Lenin contended, any claim to be capable of improving people's lives. Division of the spoils, not development of productive capacity, was the essence of twentieth-century imperialism.

2. Criticisms of the classical theory of imperialism

Much criticism of Lenin's (and Hobson's) theory has centred on the emphasis placed on the export of capital. Empirical evidence has been marshalled to show that the export of capital was not especially characteristic of a specific, late nineteenth-century and early twentieth-century phase of capitalism; and that it was not decisively connected with the scramble to acquire new colonies. Based on a wide-ranging survey of the evidence of economic historians, Warren (1980) makes the following points:

(i) The export of capital was a significant feature of British industrial capitalism from the 1820s onwards – and Britain was by far the largest foreign investor throughout the nineteenth century. In 1915, British investments at least equalled the combined total of those of the rest of Europe – they were twice those of France and nearly three times those of Germany, the two other major foreign investors.

(ii) There is no particular point at which foreign investment showed a significant upward acceleration. In fact, the rate of growth of foreign investment between 1820 and 1870 was probably even higher than between 1870 and World War I. This is precisely the opposite to the assumptions made by Lenin.

(iii) Several of the leading imperialist powers were net importers, not net exporters, of capital. From the 1880s to the outbreak of World War I, the USA, Japan, Russia and Italy were net capital importers. But all were engaged in the acquisition of new territories – the USA in the Pacific and Caribbean; Japan and Russia in the Far East; Italy in East and North Africa. It was these powers, together with Germany, which led the new outburst of colonialism, rather than Britain, the major capital exporter.

Criticisms have also been made of the explanation that Lenin gave for the export of capital. According to Lenin, the growth of monopoly was the causal link. The growth of monopoly was argued to lead to a surplus of capital and a lack of profitable domestic investment opportunities. Hence, capital had to be exported. But, as Warren points out, empirical studies show that the leading capital exporters, Britain and France, had the *least* concentrated and monopolized industrial structures. It was the countries with shortages of capital, such as USA, Germany, Russia and Japan, whose industries were earliest to be dominated by large corporations. Germany, it is true, was a net exporter of capital, but it was not really a case of surplus capital seeking outlets abroad that were unavailable at home. So great was the internal demand for capital in Germany that foreign investment always faced strong competition from domestic needs. In fact, for a long time the German government actively discouraged foreign investment on the grounds that domestic needs must take priority. A great amount of German foreign investment was directly tied to financing German exports.

Warren argues that international trade remained the dominant form of internationalization of capital. Between 1874 and 1914, foreign trade became relatively more important than foreign investment for all three major capital exporters: Britain, France and Germany. Historical documents indicate that the statesmen of every major imperialist country were primarily concerned with trade and strategic considerations, and gave no special emphasis to foreign investment.

The weight of empirical evidence certainly refutes the theory that imperialism in the late nineteenth and early twentieth century was rooted primarily in an excess of capital in the imperialist countries seeking outlets abroad. Warren summarizes the position thus:

There is no evidence of any relationship between territorial acquisition and 'superabundance' of capital, nor indeed that a stage of superabundance had been reached by any of the imperialist powers. On the contrary, net capital inflows were a feature of some of these powers during the imperialist period, and gross outflows were generally characteristic of the early stages of capitalist industrialization. 'Monopolization', which Lenin took to be the link between 'over-ripeness' and capital export, was of no great importance in any imperialist state (with the possible exception of Germany), especially in the two most important, Britain and France, until well after the territorial scramble.

Furthermore, Lenin's assertion that the export of capital became more important than that of commodities in the imperialist epoch was incorrect, as the statistical evidence on trade and foreign investment shows.

(Warren, 1980, p. 70)

In so far as the classical theory emphasized an export of capital in the aggregate as the key process underlying imperialism, it was wrong. But side by side with Lenin's emphasis on export of capital in the aggregate went an emphasis on the internationalization of the activities of large corporations. Though the two concerns are not clearly distinguished in the pamphlet on imperialism, Lenin was not only interested in the *quantity* of foreign investment in the aggregate, but in the changing organizational form of foreign investment. He was interested in the birth of what we know today as the multinational corporations. Mixed in with his theory of imperialism are arguments about the volume of financial flows from one country to another, and arguments about the overseas expansion of large industrial firms. 'Export of capital' is an ambiguous phrase, because it can be used to cover overseas lending by financial institutions, such as bank, *and* overseas expansion by industrial firms setting up branches abroad or taking over foreign firms. Sometimes Lenin used it to refer to the former, and sometimes to the latter – and sometimes it is not clear what he had in mind. Moreover, when he described in detail the 'division of the world' into the fiefdoms of large capitalist firms he focused on the division of markets and sources of raw materials, just as much as on the division of investment opportunities.

Lenin was trying to analyse a new phenomenon, the birth of multinational corporations, using old concepts like 'export of commodities' and 'export of capital'. His theory is not a coherent whole and moves continuously and confusingly between the macro-economic level of net volumes of financial flows and the micro-economic level of the international strategies of large corporations.

The empirical evidence usually marshalled against the classical theory focuses on the macro-economic level of financial flows. But the fact that the USA, for instance, was a net importer of capital at the macro-economic level, is not incompatible with the fact that leading US corporations were expanding outwards and investing abroad around the turn of the century. It was the latter phenomenon that Lenin highlighted in his discussion of the division of the world.

The concept of surplus capital does not, however, provide a convincing explanation of *why* leading US corporations were expanding overseas. Overseas expansion was not forced by a shortage of domestic investment opportunities. Rather it was induced by the rivalry between large firms; it became a weapon in their constant search for an advantage that would put them ahead of the rest. For example, some firms were very dependent on raw materials produced abroad, and feared rivals might monopolize the sources of supply. By investing directly in foreign producing enterprises they could gain control over the supply of their raw materials, and increase their security. Other firms invested abroad so as to control marketing outlets. Some went abroad simply to forestall competitiors who might be thinking of doing the same. At the turn of the century, the characteristic way of going abroad was to buy shares in existing foreign firms, or even completely take them over, rather than to set up completely new branches abroad. So the overseas expansion of the large industrial corporations had some similarities to the overseas lending of banks. In both cases, the financial markets, like those in the City in London, played a crucial role. But the reasons why capital was invested abroad were varied and cannot be reduced to a single explanation such as a surplus of capital.

3. The theory of imperialism and the state

So far we have concentrated on the classical theory's account of the internationalization of capital. I now want to turn to Lenin's account of the relationship between the internationalization of capital and the behaviour of the state. He ends his chapter on 'The division of the world among capitalist countries' thus:

> The epoch of the latest stage of capitalism shows us that certain relations between capitalist countries grow up, *based on* the economic division of the world; while parallel and in connection with it, certain relations grow up between political combines, between states, on the basis of the territorial division of the world, of the struggle for colonies, of the 'struggle for economic territory'.
>
> (Lenin, 1916, p. 127)

The crucial words here are 'parallel and in connection with it': exactly what were the parallels and what was the connection? Lenin's first argument is that just as there is no 'empty' or 'ownerless' economic space, because the big capitalist firms have partitioned it between them, there is also no 'empty' or 'ownerless' political space.

He tried to establish the *connection* by means of two types of argument; the first is an argument about the timing of events; the second an argument about the interests of monopoly capital. An example of the first type of argument is the following:

> We saw above that the development of pre-monopoly capitalism, of capitalism in which free competition was predominant, reached its limit in the 1860s and 1870s. We now see that it is *precisely after that period* that the tremendous 'boom' in colonial conquests begins, and that the struggle for the territorial division of the world becomes extraordinarily sharp. It is beyond doubt, therefore, that capitalism's transition to the stage of monopoly capitalism, to finance capitalism, *is connected* with the intensification of the struggle for the partition of the world.
>
> (Lenin, 1916, p. 131)

Yet there is a slide in the logic here, from an argument that A and B occur together, to an argument that there is a connection between the two. Lenin seems to be confusing correlation with causation. Correlation may make us suspect causation, but it needs to be supplemented with some reasons why there should be a causal connection; and some explanation of how that connection is actually made.

Lenin's second type of argument supplies some reasons suggesting why there might be a connection. For example:

> . . . monopolies are most firmly established when *all* the sources of raw materials are captured by one group, and we have seen with what zeal the international capitalist associations exert every effort to deprive their rivals of all opportunity of competing, to buy up, for example, iron ore fields, oilfields, etc. Colonial possession alone gives the monopolies complete guarantee against all contingencies in the struggle with competitors.
>
> (Lenin, 1916, p. 139)

We are offered as reasons for supposing a connection between the economic and the political partition of the world, the fact that the political partition of the world might assist the economic partition of the world; in particular the partition of present and potential raw material supplies and of markets. We should note that though this argument might establish a *prima facie* case for the connection that Lenin wants to make, it does *not* establish that the economic partition of the world *necessitates* the political partition of the world. In fact Lenin supplies no analysis of *how* the connection between the economic and political division of the world is actually made.

Though Lenin supplies no *explicit* theory of the state, several assumptions about the state are implicit in his theory of imperialism.

The most obvious is the assumption that the actions of the leading 'great powers' necessarily reflect the interests of finance capital. The state is implicitly seen as a direct instrument of finance capital, which in turn is conceived as a *unified monopoly* within each imperialist country. Monopoly capital and the state are assumed to have coalesced so that no analysis of precisely how they are connected is necessary. If finance capital requires monopoly over as much economic territory as possible, then, the assumption is, the state will act to secure that monopoly through political means. This type of Marxist argument had been discussed in earlier chapters as a form of reductionism, and it suffers from analytical weaknesses that other Marxist writers have tried to avoid by stressing the relative autonomy of the state from the immediate interests of particular firms.

Yet in spite of its reductionism, Lenin's theory of imperialism does not downgrade the importance of the state, nor does he dissolve the specificity of the *nation* state. Finance capital is assumed to exist in national blocs; and to require its own national state to further its interests abroad. National state action is seen as vitally necessary to the maintenance of profit. The constraints on state action are the actions of other states, each impelled by its own bloc of finance capital. The possibility of supernational agencies regulating the international economy and constraining the actions of states is not entertained. For Lenin assumed that the coalescence of interests stopped at the boundaries of the nation state. He was very scornful of the theory of ultra-imperialism put forward by the Austrian Marxist, Karl Kautsky. Kautsky proposed the possibility of a union of the imperialist powers, a phase when wars had ceased, a phase of the 'joint exploitation of the world by internationally united finance capital'. On the theme of international rivalry and conflict versus international co-operation and alliance between leading capitalist states, Lenin came down firmly on the side of rivalry and conflict. He argued that even if a particular division of the world appeared to be settled, this would only be temporary. It would be undermined by changes in national economic strength. Disparities between political spheres of influence and economic strength could only be resolved, according to Lenin, by force. The negotiated settlement, the supranational regulating body, had no place in his account.

To a large extent, this was because Lenin focused on the control of territory, not on the control of systems of economic and political relationships. Lenin's vision of the new phase in the internationalization of capital was one in which large corporations struggled to secure monopoly control of economic territory, of raw materials and markets. The best way of securing such control, he argued, was for national blocs of finance capital each to have 'its' state take political control of economic territory, and the most secure way of doing this was to establish colonies.

He certainly recognized that the world was not simply divided into 'great powers' and 'colonies', for he specifically mentions politically independent states which were not 'great powers', such as Argentina and Portugal. But he claims that Argentina was a 'semi-colony' and Portugal a British 'protectorate', and as the following passage shows, suggested that these are 'transitional forms':

> As to the 'semi-colonial' states, they provide an example of the transitional forms which are to be found in all spheres of nature and society. Finance capital is such a great, it may be said, such a decisive force in all economic and in all international relations, that it is capable of subjecting, and actually does subject, to itself even states enjoying the fullest political independence . . . Of course, finance capital finds most 'convenient', and derives the greatest profit from, *such* a subjection as involves the loss of the political independence of the subjected countries and peoples.
> (Lenin, 1916, p. 138)

But far from the situations of Argentina and Portugal being 'transitional forms', they have come to be the norm for the countries of Latin America, Asia and Africa. It is colonies which have proved to be 'transitional forms'. The last thirty years have shown that modern capitalism seems to be able to get along quite well without colonies. Direct territorial control has proved not to be a permanent necessity.

It was certainly important at the time when Lenin was writing, precisely because of the absence of the capitalist system of economic and political relationships in many parts of the world. Direct control of land was essential where a capitalist system of land ownership and economic contracts did not exist. An important function of the colonial state was indeed to impose capitalist property relations.

What Lenin did not see was that once a capitalist form of state had been established in the colonies, by its own actions it would tend to render the direct metropolitan control of territory less important. Once investors were confident that the (capitalist) rule of law would be enforced and contracts honoured, there was far less need for either direct ownership of raw materials or direct political control by a colonial state.

This is particularly the case given the continued ability, in the twentieth century, of the capitalist system to develop its forces of production. Lenin over-emphasized territorial control because he under-emphasized the dynamic character of what he called finance capital. In discussing the strategies of large corporations, he emphasized cartel agreements, and the manipulations of financial markets, and argued that these had superseded technical innovation as a way to secure profit. In this he was completely wrong. Technical innovation has become more and more, not less and less, important in the strategies of large corporations. Control of know-how has become much more important than control of raw materials and markets. What matters is that economic and political systems be maintained that permit multinational corporations to exploit their know-how on a world-wide scale. Control of territory was an important form for *developing* such social relations, but it is the social relations themselves which are the crucial factor.

4. The theory of imperialism in the world today

The world today is, in many ways, a very different place from the world of 1915; but it remains divided, though the nature of the divisions has changed. There are hardly any colonies of significance left; and the major competition for 'spheres of influence' is between the West and the Soviet Union. The internationalization of capital has become even more significant. Its dominant form today is the multinational corporation, which doesn't just acquire financial assets and exercise financial control, on a world-wide basis; but fragments its production process between factories in half a dozen different countries, so that it is impossible to give a national label to its final product. The Ford Motor Corporation is building a 'world car', with its gearbox made in one country, its doors in another, its chassis in another, and which is finally assembled yet somewhere else.

How does the theory of imperialism cope with these events? How far has it been developed? The analysis offered by Ernest Mandel illustrates one contemporary Marxist view. In *Late Capitalism* (1975, Ch. 10) Mandel distinguishes three forms of relation between capitalist states and three corresponding forms of the internationalization of capital. The first is *super-imperialism*. This refers to the dominance of a single, advanced capitalist state, and corresponds to control over an increasing share of internationalized capital by a single national class of capitalists. The second – *ultra-imperialism* – is the emergence of a supra-national imperialist 'world state' and corresponds to the international fusion of capital. It is the same idea as that put forward by Kautsky, and rejected by Lenin. Thirdly, according to Mandel, there is *inter-imperialist competition* between three blocs of imperialist states: the US bloc (including Australia and Canada),

Japan, and the Western European bloc. It corresponds to the fusion of capital on a continental basis, but not a fully international basis.

A concept employed by Mandel is that of the 'fusion of capital'. When he first introduces the term he writes of 'the international fusion of capital without the predominance of any particular group of national capitalists' and describes such capital as 'really multi-national'. What he seems to have in mind here is a multinational company that could not be described as a *British* multinational or a *Dutch* multinational or a *French* multinational, because the ownership and control of the company is not predominantly in the hands of any one national group. Thus:

> the international fusion of capital has advanced so far that all critical differences of economic interest between capital owners of different nationalities disappear. All major capitalists have spread their capital ownership, production of surplus value, realization of surplus value and capital accumulation (new investments) so evenly over different parts of the world that they have become completely indifferent to the particular conjuncture, the particular course of class struggle and the 'national' peculiarities of political development in any particular country. (Mandel, 1975 p. 332).

Mandel also introduces the concept of the 'indifference' of inter-national capital to particular states. This is the idea that a multi-national firm does not care which capitalist state is acting to try to safeguard its conditions of capital accumulation, the political and economic relations of the capitalist system, so long as *some* capitalist state is doing this. Mandel concedes that this would be characteristic of a complete fusion of capital.

Some writers have claimed that the big multinational corporations are already 'indifferent' to the 'nationality' of the state. Mandel also notes this:

> The example of big British, Canadian and some Dutch companies, in particular, is often cited in this connection. It is customary to emphasize that these companies have internationalized their activities to such an extent, and produce and realise surplus value in so many countries, that they have become largely indifferent to the development of the economic and social conjuncture of their mother country. (Mandel, 1975 p. 328–9)

The emphasis here is on the internationalization of the *production activities* of large corporations, rather than upon the ownership and control of large corporations. The argument is that some multi-nationals have such a high proportion of their production located outside the country of which their owners and controllers are citizens that they are 'denationalized' or 'state-indifferent'.

For Mandel, however, it is the internationalization of ownership and control which is the critical factor. He turns the argument round – if a multinational corporation is 'indifferent' to the state, in the sense of having no particular attachment or interest in any one specific state, then, argues Mandel, it is likely to find that the state is indifferent to it; that is, it is likely to find that no particular state has any particular commitment to safeguarding the interests of that corporation. Consequently,

> the position of 'state-indifferent' companies is liable to become increasingly threatened by those corporations that enjoy the real support of the local State apparatus (Mandel, 1975, p. 329).

Mandel thus predicts that multinational companies will not be state-indifferent, arguing that the internationalization of capitalist production does not transcend the national state, but in fact makes the role of national states even more important. He argues that a national state will only have a commitment to safeguard the interests of corporations whose owners and controllers have in turn some commitment to that state. To the extent that there is 'capitalist fusion' (i.e. ownership and control shared jointly by the citizens of several countries), to that extent there is a basis for supranational forms of capitalist state power, which will act on behalf of the capitalists of several nations.

Mandel concludes that supra-national forms of capitalist state power are likely to be established in Western Europe, but that inter-imperialist competition is likely to continue between the USA, Western Europe and Japan. This conclusion rests upon the assumption that capital fusion proceeds between Western European firms, creating integrated, genuinely 'European' multinationals. It also implies a belief that the activities of the leading capitalist states will reflect the interests of multinational firms.

Mandel's important argument can be questioned, in two main ways. Its assumption of a European fusion of capital implies a new breed of firms whose top boards of management are staffed by individuals from a variety of different European countries; whose shareholders are distributed fairly evenly between different European countries; and which cannot be identified as having a particular 'home country'. But in my view, there is no evidence to suggest that such fusion is taking place between British, French, German, Dutch, Belgian, Italian, etc., multinationals. There have been some celebrated attempts to create such fusions, celebrated not least because of their rarity. But they have been neither numerous nor very successful. The British and Italian multinationals, Dunlop and Pirelli, attempted a link-up which came close to Mandel's idea of fusion. But after a few years it was abandoned as a costly mistake after it proved impossible to achieve a genuine fusion.

Far more widespread than fusion is the formation of alliances, for specific purposes, between multinationals which still retain their national identity in terms of the nationality of their boards of mangement and location of their head offices. An example of such an alliance is the one formed in 1983 between the Dutch multinational, Philips, and the American multinational, American Telephones and Telegraph (AT & T). The two firms have set up a joint venture company to sell AT & T's digital public telephone exchange in markets outside the USA. The attraction of this alliance is founded in the huge research and development expenses involved in producing such high technology products. AT & T spent about $1 billion developing its digital exchange. Philips also spent a very large sum trying to develop its own digital exchange before it abandoned the attempt and joined with AT & T. Few companies can afford to bear alone the huge overhead costs of developing and marketing such products; and therefore seek to establish joint ventures to spread the costs. AT & T hope that the link with Philips will give it much better access to non-American markets where the European company has superior marketing expertise. For Philips, it represents a better alternative than leaving the market for this product altogether.

Such cross-national alliances are increasingly common, though certainly in the electronics and electrical goods industries European companies show a marked preference for alliance with US and Japanese firms, rather than with each other. The important point to note is that they are limited alliances; they express the duality of the relation between multinational corporations, a relation of both co-operation and competition.

Mandel also assumes that the activities of leading capitalist states will reflect the needs of multinational firms. He identifies the interests of the multinationals as being 'a successful struggle against crises and recessions', to be achieved through an international form of anti-cyclical economic policy (Mandel, 1975, p. 328). This is a crucial step in his implicit reduction of state policy to an economic foundation. It is crucial because it represents the interests of multinatinal firms as simple and straightforward, and capable of satisfaction by appropriate state action. Multinational firms are assumed to be interested in the successful deployment of economic policy to smooth out crises and recessions in the economy of their home territory. If multinationals fuse together they will be interested in smoothing operations not just in one country, but in all the countries from which the fused elements originate. From this Mandel deduces the need for a common supra-national imperialist state in Western Europe – and without much more ado assumes the need is likely to be met. Again, this seems a weak, reductionist claim. But Mandel's assumptions about the interests and needs of multinational firms are also open to criticism.

The interests of multinational firms are complex and contradictory, rather than simple and straightforward. For instance, a recession means fewer sales, but it also puts downward pressure on wages and disciplines the labour force: it bankrupts the weakest firms and tends to encourage centralization of capital. It can strengthen as well as weaken multinational firms.

Multinational firms, whether fused or not, have a long-term interest in international economic co-operation between states insofar as this co-operation safeguards the fundamental 'rules of the game' of the capitalist system. But they have an immediate interest in their 'own' state acting to protect their particular competitive position, even to the extent of breaking the rules of the game. They have an interest in sufficient internationalism to prevent the breakdown of the international financial system – but also an interest in sufficient nationalism to secure protection against competitors from other countries: two interests which conflict, in that increasing protectionism tends to worsen the problems of the international financial system.

I would argue that there is an interest of multinational firms in international economic policy harmonization, irrespective of any tendency towards international fusion, but that this is never absolute. There is also an interest in breaking the harmony through national economic policies to safeguard particular, immediate market positions. Moreover, the particular, immediate market positions of multinationals are different, even among multinationals with the same home base. There *is* no one, single interest of multinational corporations for the state to reflect, even should the state wish to do so.

My evaluation of Mandel can be summarized thus: Mandel's argument that the internationalization of capitalist production does not dissolve the specific importance of the state is valuable, but he fails to provide a satisfactory account of the relationships between post-war development of the multinationals and the changing forms of imperialism. To a large extent this is because he does not recognize the continual interplay of both competition and co-operation in the strategies of both multinational firms and of leading capitalist states.

Co-operation between the dominant capitalist states is not confined to EEC members, but neither does it exist outside rivalry, even within the EEC.

Decolonization and imperialism

We have already noted that the control of colonial territory has proved, on the whole, to be inessential to the maintenance of the profits of large western-owned firms. Since the end of the Second World War, most colonies have become politically independent. A vast number of new states have been created. Yet there is a wealth of evidence to show that western multinationals find the independence of former colonies no barrier to their continuing ability to make profits. Mining and agricultural multinationals have been quite prepared to yield ownership of their mines and estates to independent governments – in exchange for 'satisfactory compensation', of course. The multinationals often continue to operate the mines or estates, for a substantial management fee. Or they provide technical and marketing services – again, for a substantial fee. The power of the multinationals resides in their control of know-how. This makes them indispensable. Even governments of socialist countries like Cuba and China have concluded that they cannot do without some form of investment by multinational corporations. An independent government of Namibia, for example, would not be able to exploit its minerals without some participation by multinational corporations. It would not be able to sell its diamonds on the world market except through the Central Selling Organization, run by De Beers. Even the USSR, which supplies about twenty per cent of the world market, has used the Central Selling Organization to market its diamonds in the West. So western multinationals do not run the risk of immediate expulsion upon Namibian independence. It is more important to them that the railways run on time, and that the government bureaucracy functions with reasonable continuity and efficiency, than that South Africa continues to control Namibia. Hence the emphasis on stability.

But there are other overtones to the concept of 'stability' that need exploring. When Conservative minister at the foreign office Richard Luce claims that what really matters to the British government is that there should be stability in Namibia, for example, the notion of stability goes beyond 'absence of chaos', 'efficiency', and 'continuity'. Stability means 'reliability', not just in the sense of being able to rely on the presence of a state with some degree of organization, but also 'political reliability'. More important than whether the state bureaucracy carries out its functions to a reliable timetable is whether it can be relied upon to maintain the capitalist system. Stability means remaining within the sphere of influence of the dominant capitalist states, particularly, today, the sphere of influence of the USA. If Namibia is not yet independent, this does not mean it is an exception to the rule that control of territory is inessential to contemporary imperialism. Rather, it reflects a lack of confidence of the western imperialist powers that an independent Namibia will remain securely within the western sphere of influence.

For the most part, the newly independent former colonies have remained within the sphere of influence of the former colonial powers. Those that have sought decisively to remove themselves from this sphere of influence, and to begin to dismantle the capitalist social system internally, have found that the interest of the dominant capitalist states switches from 'stability' to 'destabilization'. In Chile, for instance, in 1973, destabilization took the form of the US government, in collusion with US business interests, acting to create internal dissension and to mobilize armed opposition to overthrow the democratically elected government. In other cases, where the fire power was not so decisively in the hands of those sympathetic to American interests, American combat troops have themselves been deployed, most massively in Vietnam in the 1960s, and more recently in Grenada (in 1983). The character of US imperialism has been acutely diagnosed by the American economist Arthur MacEwan (1972), and his twofold analysis is worth quoting at length.

> The internationalization of capital is a process which does not take place in a political vacuum. Capital requires direct protection and the institutions through which it operates must be protected. Thus the expansion of the area of operation of capital is always associated with an expansion of the political influence of the state with which that capital is associated.
>
> Coincidentally with the rising international power of U.S. business, the U.S. government engaged in numerous military interventions around the beginning of the century. The Spanish-American War led to the establishment of formal U.S. colonies in Puerto Rico and in the Philippines (an important stepping stone for establishing influence in China) and virtual colonial control over Cuba (only nominally independent). In each of these areas, the extension of U.S. political control was followed by a rapid increase of U.S. economic interests.
>
> In 1912 the U.S. intervened militarily in Nicaragua in order to assure that the interests of U.S. banks financing a railway were not interfered with. In 1915 the U.S. occupied Haiti in order to insure that the Haitian government 'honor' its obligations to U.S. bankers. In 1916, the U.S. Marines were sent to Santo Domingo and seized control of the customs and treasury of that nation in order to insure that obligations

to American companies would be fulfilled. And again in 1916, when U.S. oil interests were threatened in Mexico, the Marines were sent to the scene. While the majority of U.S. military interventions in this period were in the Caribbean, they were by no means limited exclusively to that area. In 1911 and 1912, and later in 1924 and 1926, U.S. armed forces made their presence felt in China in order to protect U.S. private property during civil disturbances there; these military actions provided the backdrop for the growth of U.S. trade and financial intersts in China.

Military interventions, however, should not necessarily be taken as typical of the operation of U.S. imperialism. More often than not, control has been exercised through economic power or through non-military political pressure.

On the level of particular interests, for example: the U.S. diplomatic mission in India sees to it that U.S. pharmaceutical companies are allowed to produce and sell under 'reasonable' conditions; in Bolivia and Peru, when U.S. owned oil companies are nationalized, it is the business of the U.S. government; when Brazilian coffee producers begin to sell instant coffee below the price at which U.S. companies can produce, the U.S. government 'encourages' the Brazilian government to impose an export duty. On a broader level, the government provides mechanisms for the general expansion of U.S. interests abroad: the U.S. government encourages foreign governments to lower tariffs for U.S. goods and to enter reciprocity arrangements with the U.S.; the U.S. government provides insurances against nationalization or other political 'disasters' in unstable areas; the international sections of various government departments – e.g., commerce, labor – devote themselves to providing U.S. business with investment and trade information on countries throughout the world. Finally, on the broadest level, the role of the government in protecting the international business interests of its citizens is the protection of the system that allows those interests to operate, i.e., the protection of international capitalism. (MacEwan, 1972, pp. 410 – 13).

In the traumatic case of American intervention in Vietnam, Mac-Ewan argues that US business had relatively few direct economic interests. The military involvement was not so much in defence of particular capitalist profits. Rather, it was in defence of the capitalist system itself. Similarly, he suggests, US interventions in Iran in 1953, in Guatemala in 1954, in Cuba in 1961, and in the Dominican Republic in 1965, were attempts to prevent those countries opting out of the international capitalism system.

But, American intervention apart, *is it* possible to opt out of the international capitalist system? The 'world systems' theorists, discussed in the next chapter, would answer that it is not. In their view *all* countries are part of the same world system, dominated by production for the market. Even if it is possible to opt out of the international capitalist system, is it possible to opt out of imperialism? Or is it only possible to switch from one sphere of influence, that dominated by the USA, to another sphere of influence, that dominated by the USSR? This issue again raises the problem of whether political influence and might qualifies as 'imperialist' in the same sense as economic – and specifically capitalist – domination and exploitation.

The USSR and imperialism

The USSR has to a considerable extent made itself the ally of Third World movements of resistance to western imperialism, providing military, economic and diplomatic support for those fighting against control by the major western states. But along side this support has gone the export of many features of the current social order in the USSR: the imposition of controls on emigration and internal movement, the establishment of Soviet party structures, the spread of Soviet theories of what constitutes Marxism and Leninism, and controls on the press. So the achievement of greater independence from western control has been counterbalanced by the creation of bureaucratic political structures mirroring those of the USSR.

There is no doubt that the USSR exercises outright dominance over the other countries of Eastern Europe. It regards them as part of its sphere of influence and has several times used its military power to ensure that they remain firmly within that sphere. This cannot all be ascribed to the idiosyncracies of Stalin. Since Stalin's death in 1953, Warsaw Pact troops have invaded Hungary and Czechoslovakia. The threat of Soviet invasion has served to repress the struggle of Polish workers for independent trade unions in the 1980s.

In the sense that the USSR regards the rest of Eastern Europe as its satellites, and is quite prepared to use force to maintain its sphere of influence, then it could be described as an imperial power. It regards itself as entitled to undisputed leadership of the communist world. It regards itself as entitled to extend its sphere of influence, and to intervene militarily in support of its allies in other countries, as it has done in Afghanistan.

The control the Soviet Union has exercised over Eastern Europe since the early post-war years (1946/9) is, however, of a particular type. In view of the crucial importance of the East European states for the defence of its western border – a border which twice this century has been crossed by invading German armies – the Soviet Union has been concerned and, since the end of World War II, has been militarily able to control those states in line with its own preferences. It has viewed those states rather as an aspect of its domestic security rather than as elements in any strategy of global imperialism. Much the same views came to prevail over Afghanistan in the late seventies. A pro-Soviet regime was already in place in Afghanistan: the Soviet role was to prevent it from being overthrown.

Along with this military dominance has gone some degree of economic dominance. Three forms of Soviet 'economic imperialism' are distinguished by Barratt-Brown (1974). They are the mixed Russian–East European enterprises of the early post-war years; price discrimination by the USSR against other members of the Soviet bloc; and the use of Comecon, the Council of Mutual Economic Assistance, by the USSR and the richer members of the bloc to exploit the poorer members, such as Cuba and Vietnam.

The mixed Russian–East European enterprises were criticized by the East Europeans as being based on unfair valuations of the investment of the two parties, and as being designed to restrict development that did not fit in with Soviet plans. In addition, they were used by Russia to monopolize the local markets at the expense of independent local operators.

But the main form of Soviet economic imperialism, it has been suggested, was not through such enterprises, but through trade. Eastern European countries frequently complained of price discrimination. They argued that the USSR has tended to charge them more for its exports than it charges to the West; and to pay them less for its imports than it pays to the West.

However, there is evidence that the nature of the economic relations between the USSR and Eastern Europe changed since the early years of Soviet dominance over that area. Until 1956 there was clearly an aspect of exploitation in Soviet economic control. It is estimated that the Soviet Union made a net gain of $20 billion (or milliard) from economic relations with Eastern Europe during the period 1945–56 (Brzezinski, 1967, p. 286). But of this total $15 billion was drawn from East Germany and could to a large extent be considered war reparations from a defeated aggressor to the devasted victor. After 1960, though, the Soviet Union appears to have lost in economic terms in dealings with Eastern Europe and to have taken advantage of the post-1973 energy crisis not to secure economic gains but to enhance political and strategic advantages (Lavigne, 1983, pp. 136 and 149).

On some occasions, reports Barratt-Brown, less developed members of the Soviet bloc have complained that trade between them and the more developed Comecon countries is unequal because it takes place at the prices set on the capitalist world market, rather than at prices derived from a socialist planning process. If trade at these prices is exploitative when it takes place with capitalist countries, then, it is argued, it is equally exploitative when it takes place with socialist countries. On the other hand the support of the USSR has been of vital importance in the face of American-lead assaults on revolutionary Third World states. It is unlikely that the governments of Cuba, South Yemen and Ethiopia would have survived without Soviet aid. (Halliday, 1983, p. 98).

It is easy to describe examples of Soviet domination; but how to explain it? We have explored explanations of the imperialism of the western powers that point to the expansionary drive for profit, the internationalization of capital, as the important underlying process. This clearly will not do as direct explanation for Soviet imperialism, because the Soviet economy is not motivated by the drive for profit. There have been some attempts to explain Soviet imperialism in terms of the *physical* requirements of the Soviet economy. For instance, the Czech economist, Ota Sik, has argued that it stems from the direct economic interest of large firms in the Soviet system in securing control over their inputs and outputs, so as to fulfil their plan requirements. It has been suggested that the Russian invasion of Czechoslovakia in 1968 was based on the need to ensure that Czechoslovak industry remained geared to the needs of the USSR; and that the intervention in Afghanistan was motivated by a supposed Soviet need for Persian Gulf oil. Halliday (1983) argues that this explanation is baseless, and finds little evidence to suggest that economic requirements as such determine Russian foreign policy.

So what does? In the previous section we concluded that American intervention in the affairs of other states was best seen as a policy directed to the preservation and strengthening of the capitalist system, rather than a narrow furthering of the interests of particular American multinationals. A parallel explanation is possible of Soviet interventions in the affairs of other states: it is directed to the preservation and strengthening of the Soviet bloc as a whole, rather than the narrow furthering of the interests of large state enterprises.

The important distinction to be made between American and Russian domination lies in the difference between the two systems which their respective exercise of 'imperial' power is designed to strengthen. American imperialism is in furtherance of the capitalist system, the power and privilege of capital. Russian imperialism is in furtherance of the Soviet system; of the power and privilege of a self-appointed and secretive bureaucracy. Each type of power contains significant contradictions. The defence of the capitalist system involves the defence of the liberal democracies of Western Europe – but also of the dictatorships which rule in many capitalist countries of Latin America, Africa and Asia. The only freedom guaranteed and enjoyed in both is the freedom of capital itself. The defence of the Soviet system involves the defence of bureaucracies which tend to stifle popular democracy – but also genuine attempts to liberate peoples from the tyranny of capitalist dictatorships and from poverty; attempts to go beyond capitalism in an effort to make provision for needs rather than profits the central organizing principle of the system.

Capitalist imperialism is often characterized as 'economic' imperialism, and Soviet imperialism as 'political' imperialism, on the grounds that economic power is the primary factor in the capitalist system and political power the primary factor in the Soviet system. In one sense, this is correct. But we should be careful not to jump too quickly to the conclusion that this means that Soviet imperialism has to be analysed with a wholly different set of conceptual tools. The point of departure in my discussion of Lenin's theory was that the specific forms taken by imperialism were related to prevailing socio-economic conditions. The implication of this is that we should also seek to explain *differences* – why capitalist imperialism is 'economic' and Soviet imperialism 'political' – by referring to the different socio-economic conditions of the two. The hypotheis would be that political power is primary in the Soviet system, and Soviet imperialism is 'political', precisely because of the particular socio-economic conditions that prevail in the USSR: the state ownership or control of all significant economic enterprises.

Perhaps the most controversial question raised by the experience of Soviet imperialism is whether it constitutes evidence that imperialism is as endemic to socialism as it is to capitalism. Arthur MacEwan's argument can certainly be cited to suggest that imperialism is endemic to the capitalist system:

> Within a capitalist economic system there are basic forces which push that system toward expansion. This expansion carries with it an extension of control; hence, a capitalist system necessarily develops into an imperialist system.

The 'basic forces' arise from the competitive struggle for profit, which continually drives firms to seek new markets, new sources of raw materials, and new sources of labour supply, expanding their activities internationally. In a socialist economy, by contrast, it might be argued there is no competitive struggle for profit, and hence no impulse to expand overseas. Thus in a socialist society, it might be concluded, there is no economic pressure internal to the system for the state to control what happens overseas.

However, the countries which have been trying to create socialist economies in the twentieth century find themselves caught up in quite another kind of competitive struggle: the competitive struggle between capitalist and socialist systems. As things stand at the moment this is a profoundly unequal struggle, as Halliday points out:

(i) The two systems are unequal militarily. For instance, both the USA and the USSR have enormous destructive potential in their nuclear arsenals – but overall the USA is considerably stronger than the USSR.

(ii) The two systems are unequal economically. For instance, the overall gross national product of the USSR is 40%–50% that of the USA; and its per capita GNP is equivalent to that of Ireland, Spain or Greece. The combined GNP of all the Warsaw Pact countries as a whole is only one third of that of the major capitalist states. Of course, they started the contest from a much lower level of economic development.

(iii) The two systems are unequal in the fund of democratic experience on which they could draw. The capitalist system has the democratic experience of North America and Western Europe to draw upon. Of all the countries in which attempts have been made to establish socialism, only East Germany and Czechoslovakia had any significant experience of democracy prior to the attempt.

The socialist states have so far failed to realize either the political or the economic potential yielded by their rejection of the drive for profits. As Halliday puts it:

> Far from going beyond capitalist political freedom, something for which socialism has the capacity, they have established systems that in most visible dimensions still fail to match their competitors. They have removed many forms of economic, social, racial and sexual oppression characteristic of capitalist societies, but in the realm of political democracy, in voting, publishing, organising, criticizing as established activities these countries have, as yet, failed to produce liberties that compare with those achieved under capitalism. In the language of Western political theory, the communist states offer 'substantive' freedoms – to work, housing etc – but not 'procedural' freedoms to criticize and so on. On the economic front, the record of the communist countries has been rather a good one, and certainly far better than most western argument used to suggest. But there has still been a great gap between the potential of planned economic growth and the results, and there

has been a special gap in the realm of those consumer goods which are the most tangible and universally valued inlet of individual, family and class enrichment. (Halliday, 1983, p. 39)

It could be argued that the impulse of the Russian state to exercise dominion over other states stems from the present stage of the competitive struggle between the capitalist and socialist systems; and from the failure of the Russian state to make greater progress in the construction of socialism. While not *directly* stemming from the internationalization of capital, it could be seen as *indirectly* stimulated by the power of the international search for profit, and the determination of the most powerful western states to keep as much of the world as possible open to that search.

5. Some hypotheses about the international context

In this chapter I have discussed and criticized the classical theory of imperialism, and examined some modern developments of it. By way of conclusion, I want to summarize some hypotheses about the international context which are yielded by the theory of imperialism.

(i) Relations between capitalist states are linked to the internationalization of capital. There is a continual tension between the boundedness of the capitalist state, its sovereignty over a definite area of land, and the expansionary tendency of capital to pursue profit wherever it can be made. This creates a pressure for the state to reach out beyond its territory to provide the conditions for capital accumulation in areas beyond its jurisdiction.

(ii) Different forms and phases of international expansion of capital tend to provide characteristically different forms of state 'outreach'.

(iii) The internationalization of the operations of large firms tends to take the form of conscious regulation and 'division' of the world economy, both through agreements between firms, and through agreements between states.

(iv) No one set of regulations and agreements for the 'division' of the world economy can be expected to last for ever. Uneven development of productivity both between firms and national economies tends to undermine any given set, producing instability, and possibly crisis. There is no 'invisible hand' which can be relied upon to revise smoothly the regulations and agreements in line with developments in real economic strength.

(v) The division of the world through colonial control of territory has been superseded by the division of the world into the spheres of influence of the western imperial powers, especially the USA, and the spheres of influence of the USSR.

(vi) Direct state intervention by western imperial powers in the affairs of another state has become more related to the overall strategic goal of safeguarding the international capitalist system, than to the narrowly economic goal of protecting national businesses.

The theory of imperialism certainly gives grounds for thinking that the national state, especially the United States of America, remains essential to the operation of the international capitalist economy. It rejects the idea that there are trans-national institutions, though it accepts, and indeed emphasizes, a tension between national and international economic and political forms.

References

Barrat-Brown, M. (1974). *The Economics of Imperialism*. Harmondsworth, Penguin.

Brzezinski, Z. (1967). *The Soviet Bloc*. Harvard University Press.

Fieldhouse, D.K. (1981). *Colonialism 1870–1945*. London, Weidenfeld & Nicolson.

Halliday, F. (1983). *The Making of the Second Cold War*. London, Verso.

Hobson, J.A. (1971). *Imperialism: a study*. University of Michigan Press, Ann Arbor; first published in 1902, London, James Nisbet.

Lavigne, M. (1983). 'The Soviet Union inside Comecon', *Soviet Studies* XXXV, No. 2.

Lenin, V.I. (1916) *Imperialism, the Highest Form of Capitalism*. Moscow, Foreign Languages Publishing House.

MacEwan, A. (1972). 'Capital Expansion, Ideology and Intervention' in R.C. Edwards, M. Reich, and T.E. Weisskof (eds), *The Capitalist System*. New Jersey, Prentice Hall.

Mandel, E. (1975). *Late Capitalism*. London, NLB/Verso.

Warren, B. (1980). *Imperialism: Pioneer of Capitalism*. London, New Left Books.

CHAPTER 7

Nation state and international system: The world-system perspective

Roger Dale

Like the theories of imperialism (which are discussed by Diane Elson in chapter 6), the world-system perspective seeks to get behind and beyond the surface appearance of international relations. The two approaches share some features, but differ on others. Where the world-system perspective differs most basically from imperialism is that it takes a 'monist' rather than a 'dualist' view of the world system. Proponents of the world-system perspective hold that there is a single world system into which all nations are integrated. Understanding this is the key to understanding not only what happens between nations, but also within nations. What gives this perspective special piquancy in the context of this book is its implicit, and frequently explicit, claim that the effect of the world system upon individual nation states is so great that there is little point in analysing them in isolation. If we want to understand what goes on in any particular nation state, according to world-system theorists, we will find that its central characteristics derive from its place in the overall world system.

In this perspective analysing the nation state as if it were the locus and level at which problems are both generated and solved is to accept an *ideological* account of it, to analyse the appearance, not the reality. Certainly for Immanuel Wallerstein, the leading proponent of the world-system perspective, selecting the nation state as the appropriate place to focus our attention involves assuming what we should be seeking to uncover. His own assumptions about where we should focus attention, which are discussed below, are very different.

The plan of this chapter is as follows. In Part I I shall briefly outline the world-system perspective. In Part II I shall look at 'the nation state in the world-system' and in Part III at the 'world-system in the nation state'.

Part I The World-System Perspective

The origins of world-system theory are to be found in the theoretical discussion of the causes of 'underdevelopment' in the 1950s. Very briefly, the 'modernization' theory dominant at that time held that the causes of 'Third World' underdevelopment lay within the Third World itself. The way out of underdevelopment lay in following the path laid down by the already developed nations. Underdeveloped countries could and should be as like developed countries as possible, in every way, economically, politically and culturally. They should aim to be free enterprise, (preferably two-party) democracies peopled by responsible citizens with high 'achievement motivation'. And they could be speeded along this path by western aid, both economic and cultural. Furthermore, as Eric Hobsbawm points out in his review of recent work by W.W. Rostow, a very influential figure in the modernization theory of the 1960s, this view 'sees the world economy as essentially a collection of dynamic interacting national economies which are essentially similar in their objectives . . . (and which) can be either regarded or essentially analysed as a complex of national economies. It is a world in which the basic problems, which are those of growth, are essentially soluble everywhere by the same methods of economic engineering because they are all equally 'economies'' (1979, p. 307).

Just as modernization theory saw the world economy as an aggregation of fragmented but similar units, albeit to some extent interdependent, so too the contemporary international relations theory saw the world as essentially divided into a set of units controlling particular territories. These units, or nation states, each made the pursuit of their own self-interest the principal guide to policy. That they did so with relatively greater or less power to back up that pursuit was acknowledged, but any tendencies towards inordinate concentration of power were countered by an international state system which encouraged a tendency towards a balance of power between those states capable of exercising overall dominance. This view of international relations as essentially concerned with balances of power between individual nations or blocs of nations is as much, or more, a part of our commonsense thinking about 'foreign affairs' (the very words reinforce its separateness from the central activities of the state), as is the hierarchical developmentalism of modernization theory.

One key characteristic of both these approaches was that they treated countries as wholly separate from each other, and as having a good deal of autonomy. Relations between countries were confined to a specified international sphere, where transactions between two or more essentially similar entities were carried out on the basis of implicitly agreed rules.

This central notion of separateness was challenged by the so-called 'dependency' school. Particularly influential was the critique of Andre Gunder Frank and the concept which he popularized of 'the development of underdevelopment' (Frank, 1971). This suggested that underdevelopment did not result from factors internal to underdeveloped societies, but was in fact the direct result of their relationship with the developed countries. Links with the developed nations caused and intensified underdevelopment. The exploitation of the underdeveloped world was the basis and condition of the prosperity of the developed world; the 'developed' world only became 'developed' by creating an underdeveloped world.

Crucially for our present purposes, this approach suggested that it was futile to study the development of either developed or underdeveloped societies in isolation from each other. They were more than interdependent. In dependency theories there was a single world economic system; nations in centre and periphery were in a kind of parasitic relationship, with the growth of the one dependent on what it could suck from the other.

However, while dependency theories moved beyond the ideas of the separateness of nation states, accepting a notion of a permanently imbalanced, mutually influential, relationship they saw these still as essentially external relationships for both set of countries. Indeed, the idea that the peripheral, or Third World, nation-state, could (and probably would and certainly should) develop along totally different lines from those imposed on it by the centre, was absolutely central to dependency theories.

The way that the world-system perspective differs from dependency theories — as well as from imperialism — is caught in its very title. It refers to a *system* because the relationships between its parts (the nation states) are not taken to be random, arbitrary or haphazard. Rather, there is an interdependence of a regular and systematic kind between the parts. This interdependence is such that changes in one part of the system necessarily have implications for other parts of the system; the relationships between the parts keep the whole system functioning. It is a *world* perspective, rather than an international one, because it views the world as a single whole, rather than as an aggregate of overlapping, but separate, sets of relations between states. And it is a *capitalist* world-system because it is capitalism which provides the logic of the system, the basis for its essential interdependence. This capitalist world-system is more than the sum of its parts, and constitutes the level at which any effective analysis of any individual component states must begin. In this perspective, 'national states are *not* societies that have separate, parallel histories, but parts of a whole' (Wallerstein, 1979, p. 53); the structure of the world system as a whole broadly determines relations both between and within nation states.

Wallerstein distinguishes the world-system perspective as follows:

> A developmentalist perspective assumes that the unit within which social action principally occurs is a politico-cultural unit – the state, or nation, or people – and seeks to explain differences between these units, including why their economies are different. A world-system perspective assumes, by contrast, that social action takes place in an entity within which there is an ongoing division of labour [you will discover the significance of this in the next section, R.D.] and seeks to discover *empirically* whether such an entity is or is not unified politically or culturally, asking *theoretically* what are the consequences of the existence or non-existence of such unity (Wallerstein, 1979, p. 155. Emphasis in original).

The world-system perspective has been developed in a number of different ways, some of which we will briefly consider below. It is, though, possible to list some basic propositions common to all its major adherents. The following extract is by four leading adherents of the perspective, Samir Amin, Giovanni Arrighi, Andre Gunder Frank, and Immanuel Wallerstein; it comes from the introduction to a book in which they each present their own separate analyses of the current world 'crisis'.

> While each of us does not present exactly the same picture, we share a number of important premises. These mark off our mode of analysis, our approach to the subject, from many (quite probably most) other analysts in the world today, and so it is important to present them at the outset.
>
> 1. We believe that there is a social whole that may be called a capitalist world-economy. We believe this capitalist world-economy came into existence a long time ago, probably in the sixteenth century, and that it had expanded historically from its European origins to cover the globe by the late nineteenth century. We believe it can be

described as capitalist in that endless accumulation is its motor force. We believe that the appropriation by the world bourgeoisie of the surplus value created by the world's direct producers has involved not merely direct appropriation at the marketplace, but also unequal exchange, transferring surplus from peripheral to core zones.

2. We believe that we cannot make an intelligent analysis of the various states taken separately without placing their so-called internal life in the context of the world division of labor, located in the world-economy. Nor can we make a coherent analysis that segregates 'economic', 'political', and 'social' variables.

3. We believe that, throughout the history of this capitalist world-economy, there has been increasing organization of oppressed groups within the world-system and increasing opposition to its continuance. The capitalist world system has never been under greater challenge. Despite, however, the unprecedented political strength of the world's working classes and peripheral countries, both the praxis and the theory of the world socialist movement are in trouble.

4. After World War II, the United States was the hegemonic power, having commanding power in the economic, political, and military arenas, and able to impose relative order on the world system − a fact which correlated with the world's unprecedented economic expansion. We believe that this hegemony is now in a decline, an irreversible (though perhaps slow) decline − not, we hasten to add, because of any weakness of will among U.S. leaders, but because of objective realities. This decline is manifested in many ways: the increased competitiveness of Western European and Japanese products, the frittering away of the old Cold War alliance systems and the emergence of a Washington-Tokyo-Peking axis, and wars among states in the periphery, including states governed by Communist parties.

5. We do not believe that the struggle between capitalist and socialist forces can be reduced to, or even symbolized by, a struggle between the United States and the USSR, however much the propaganda machines of both assert this. Nor do we think the analysis of the crisis can be made by looking at the core countries alone, as though the crisis were located only there. What is going on in the USSR, Eastern Europe, China, etc. is not external, or in contraposition, to what is going on in the rest of the world. The 'crisis' is worldwide and integral, and must be analyzed as such.

(Amin *et al*. 1982, pp. 9–10)

The best known version of the world-system perspective is that of Immanuel Wallerstein. A brief account of his work forms the core of this chapter. It is valuable, though, to consider, also, at least the contribution of one other leading world-system theorist, Samir Amin.

It is possible to see Amin's as a relatively 'soft' version of the world-system perspective, insofar as his acceptance of its 'monism' (where everything belongs, or is explained, within one single system) is not always complete. This results largely from his unremittingly 'Third World' viewpoint.

His purpose is to understand the system that oppresses the poor peoples and nations of the world in order to replace it. He takes a determinedly 'anti-Eurocratic' line. This leads him to seek explanations of, and solutions to, the problem of underdevelopment, an agenda not at all dissimilar from that of dependency theories. What distinguishes him from them is his unwillingness to isolate or differentiate the fate of particular underdeveloped countries from the fate they all share equally as a result of their position in the world economy. That position he categorizes as peripheral. The periphery is contrasted with the centre (or core). His system is therefore constructed principally by the relations between 'centre' and 'periphery' states. Centre and periphery are differentiated in terms of the market relationships that integrate them into the world capitalist system, whose expansion brought about their differentiation. The centre develops on the basis of the expansion of its home market and in it the capitalist mode of production becomes the only mode of production. The capitalist mode of production is imposed on the periphery from outside, but in such a way that its penetration is incomplete.

It does not become the exclusive mode of production, but combines with existing pre-capitalist modes of production. The nature of these pre-capitalist formations, together with the state of capitalism at which they were integrated with the world system, gives peripheral societies their particular character.

In peripheral states, the capitalist mode of production's domination is secured by and for the absentee bourgeoisie of the centre. Crucially, then, there is no base for independent development; development of the periphery is shaped by, for, and under conditions (eg. world prices) created by and for the centre. Furthermore, the centre has internal market relationships within itself as well as with the periphery, while the periphery has no internal relationships within itself, relating only in dependent ways to the centre. This one sided and dependent relationship to the centre denies to peripheral states the possibility of indigenous capital accumulation. It both defines their peripheral status, and prevents them from being able to break out of it.

There are clear affinities between Amin's division of the world into centre and periphery and the kind of 'dualist' perspective which characterizes both dependency and imperialism theories. One further important difference from the more thoroughgoing world-system theorists lies in Amin's treatment of the socialist countries. They are placed outside both centre and periphery, for while they may be part of the world capitalist market, their internal market relations are not dependent upon it.

The point of including this very brief reference to Amin's work, however, is that, unlike theorists of dependency or imperialism, he does not single out particular countries, or groups of countries, within either centre or periphery, for analysis, but contends that the significance of their central or peripheral status (and his attention is confined almost entirely to the periphery) far outweighs any individual differences there may be between countries within each category. That is to say, in his treatment of individual nation-states, he resembles world-system theorists more than dependency or imperialism theorists.

In understanding underdeveloped societies, then, those of their characteristics that derive from their common status in the world system are more important than any superficial differences between them, though we should not underestimate the range of different positions within that common status. For instance, though they are all 'peripheral', Brazil is very different from Chad, and Hong Kong from Tanzania. However, Amin takes this not as a denial but as a confirmation of his thesis, for none even of the 'newly industrialized countries' (eg. Brazil, South Korea, Mexico) has achieved independent development. They have, instead, suffered new kinds of internal problems (eg. increasing inequality of incomes) and became bound to the centre in new ways (eg. through external debts) with the consequence, for Amin, that 'none of the features that define the structure of the periphery is weakened as economic growth proceeds. On the contrary these features are accentuated' (Amin 1976, p. 292). (This argument is further exemplified in the extended quotation below.) One reason why Amin gives overwhelming priority to 'position in the system' may lie in his commitment to change the situation of underdevelopment. If the source of that underdevelopment lies not within any particular country, or in its relationship with another country or group of countries, but at the level of the world capitalist system, then it is irrelevant and even misleading to concentrate on either the situation within any particular country or to point to major apparent differences between peripheral countries. Given Amin's premises, focusing on the world level does provide a more effective account of any particular peripheral country and especially of the conditions for changing it, than examining its peculiarities in isolation.

One major problem with this approach is that it denies the importance of the kind of national data typically available; it is apparently not applicable at any but the most general level of analysis. This makes it difficult both to test and to exemplify. The following extract from a recent article does, though, shed some light on the distinction between centre and periphery, and between periphery and dependence, in Amin's thinking. It emphasizes the importance of the one-sided relationship of periphery to centre for the social structures of central and peripheral countries, and for their capacity to achieve non- dependent development.

> The hypothesis that development within the world system is inevitable is based on a confusion between 'peripheral' and 'dependent'. A comparison of examples from the periphery (Brazil and South Korea, for example) and examples of 'backward core powers' (Spain, Portugal, Greece), or of 'nonperipheral dependence' (Canada) is necessary to clarify this.
>
> The 'peripheral/dependent' confusion has gradually led to the obscuring of the main point of the analysis, the internal class relationships that underlie peripheral development. The comparison between Spain and the Third World is enlightening. During the 1950s and 1960s. Spain developed rapidly, largely as a 'dependent' zone development implied an opening to the outside world that increased the country's integration into the international – and especially the European – division of labor, mainly financed by foreign capital. This was accompanied by an almost parallel increase in the real wages of workers and employees, and in the real incomes of small-scale peasants (with large regional and sectoral differences, however). Parallel increases of this sort do not exist in any example of rapid growth in the Third World – neither in Brazil, where growth has been accompanied by a fall in wages and rural pauperization, nor in South Korea, where incomes have at best stagnated (Iran is a similar case), nor in such radical bourgeois experiments as Egypt. This contrast therefore forces us to distinguish between the social dynamic of the backward core powers and that of the peripheral countries.
>
> This same distinction applies to Canada, which although totally dependent economically, in the sense that it is simply a province of the United States and its growth is almost exclusively due to accumulation within the U.S. monopoly system, is not 'peripheral'. Workers' incomes increase in the same way they do in the United States.
>
> (Amin, 1982, pp. 193–4)

This example does appear to provide a basis for distinguishing between centre (or 'core') (Western Europe, North America, Japan and Australasia) and periphery (Africa, Asia and Latin America), though how well that would hold up in some cases, say South Africa, is not certain. But the crucial question is, even granted a finer distinction between centre and periphery, does the basis of that distinction as contained within the passage quoted justify the concentration on the world rather than the national level? Or, to put it another way, is what that passage tells us about Spain, Brazil, South Korea and Canada what we most need to know about those countries? Putting the question like that forces us to ask just how, ie. with what kinds of evidence, the priority given to the world system could be justified.

Wallerstein's world-system perspective

Wallerstein takes the defining characteristics of a social system to be 'the existence within it of a division of labour, such that the various sections or areas within are dependent upon economic exchange with others for the smooth and continuous provisioning of the needs of the area. Such economic exchange can clearly exist without a common political structure and even more obviously without sharing the same culture' (1979, p. 5). However, for him, the only kind of social system is a world system, a unit with a single division of labour and multiple cultural systems. There are two kinds of world systems, world empires and world economies; the former have a common political system, the latter do not. Since the sixteenth century, there has been only one world-system in existence, the capitalist world economy.

What is crucial for Wallerstein is that 'capitalism and a world economy (that is, a single division of labour but multiple polities and culture) are obverse sides of the same coin. One does not cause the other. We are merely identifying the same indivisible phenomenon by different characteristics' (ibid, p. 6).

This raises the issue, which is a point of contention between 'Wallersteinians' and many of their critics, of exactly what constitutes capitalism. For one of the most prominent critics of the definition assumed by Wallerstein, Ernesto Laclau, 'the fundamental economic relationship of capitalism is constituted by the free labourer's sale of his labour-power, whose necessary precondition is the loss by the direct producer of ownership of the means of production' (1977, p. 23). That is to say, it is in its production relations that we find the defining characteristic of capitalism (or any mode of production). Hence, while wage labour was found in Europe from the sixteenth century on, other forms of labour – slave and other types of forced labour, peasant production, and so on – were dominant in other areas of the world, making it impossible, for Laclau, to call them capitalist.

Wallerstein's response is to argue that the essential feature of a capitalist world economy lies not in the production relations but in

market relations. Production for sale in a market in which the object is
to realize the maximum profit is what defines capitalism. It is not
essential that production be *industrial* production, nor is wage labour
a defining characteristic of capitalism. His second response is to ask
whether, in any case, each separate nation-state has its own 'mode of
production'. He argues that it does not. The world economy as a
whole is characterized by a single mode of production. If that is so,
what is (and has been) the mode of production of this world economy?
Wallerstein does not deny that different forms of labour compensation
are found in different regions of the world economy. However, he
does not appear to regard wage labour as crucial even in the origins of
the capitalist world economy. Rather, its prominence is merely one of
the results of the 'series of accidents – historical, ecological, geographical – (by which) Northwest Europe was better situated in the 16th
century to diversify its agricultural specification and add to it certain
industries than were other parts of Europe' (op. cit. p. 18).

Central to Wallerstein's approach is the idea of three positions in
the capitalist world economy, core, semi-periphery and periphery,
which he argues had become stabilized by about 1640. They form the
basic and necessary structure of the world capitalist system, with all
individual nation-states located in one or another of them. Mobility
between the three positions is possible – the United States was not
always a core power, for instance – but only on a 'one up, one down'
basis. The *structure* of core, semi-periphery and periphery is crucial to
the survival of the capitalist world system, of which it is a normal and
necessary part.

The semi-periphery is needed to make a capitalist world economy
run smoothly; it is one of the factors (along with the military strength
of the core and ideological commitment to the system as a whole)
maintaining political stability in an intrinsically exploitative system.
The existence of this middle stratum means that the upper stratum is
not faced with the unified opposition of all those outside it, because
the middle stratum is both exploited and exploiter. This three layered
structure is a normal and necessary condition of a world system.

Furthermore, the strength of state machineries is a function of their
structural position in the world economy rather than of internal
conditions. As Wallerstein puts it,

> States in which core activities are located have achieved the most
> efficacious state structure relative to other states. That is both the
> consequence of the nature of their economic activity [which required
> extensive protection in the world market,|R.D.] and of the socio-
> economic groups located within its limits, and the cause of their ability
> to specialize in core-like activities. States in which peripheral activities

are concentrated are conversely weak [because dominant groups' interests lay in maintaining an open economy, R.D.], and are weakened by the very process of economic peripheralization. The semi-peripheral *state* is precisely the arena, where, because of a mix of economic activities, conscious state activity may do most to affect the future patterning of economic activity. In the 20th century, this takes the form of bringing socialist parties to power (ibid, p. 274).

And this is what underlies what is perhaps Wallerstein's most pointed comment on 'the State'

One cannot reasonably explain the strength of various state machineries at specific moments of the history of the modern world-system primarily in terms of a genetic-cultural line of argumentation, but rather in terms of the structural role a country plays in the world-economy at that moment in time. (ibid, p. 21)

Wallerstein divides the history of the capitlist world economy into four stages. The initial stage lasted until almost the middle of the seventeenth century. In the second stage, which lasted until the late eighteenth century, England became a hegemonic core country through a process of mercantilist struggle with first the Netherlands and then France.

From the beginning of the third stage onwards, industrial production became increasingly pervasive and had a number of significant implications. It led to the further geographic expansion of the European world economy to include the whole globe (in search of both raw materials and markets). It meant the elimination and absorption of remaining minisystems and of other world-systems (of which Russia was the most important). It meant the end of slavery. The manufacturing sector in the U.S. and Germany gained ascendancy and enabled the transition to core status. Core countries became much more industrialized and intra-core competition for even peripheral markets created a new world division of labour, with the core now the provider of machine tools and infrastructure (railways, etc.) rather than manufactures. And finally, industrialism created for the first time a large scale urban proletariat and with it 'anti-capitalist' forces. The threat that this posed, and the simultaneous recession of the latter end of the nineteenth century, was solved by expanding the purchasing power of the core countries' proletariat and the beginnings of a welfare state ideology.

This stage ended with the First World War and the fourth stage, that of consolidation, began in 1917 with the Russian Revolution. Wallerstein regards the Russian Revolution as essentially that of a semi-peripheral country whose internal balance of forces had been such that from the late nineteenth century it began to decline towards peripheral status, because of the penetration of foreign capital, the resistance to the mechanization of agriculture, and the decline of military power. While Britain's decline (which started in 1873) continued, the U.S. took on its hegemonic role and Germany fell further behind following military defeats. Following the Second World War, the U.S. achieved clear primacy and her spectacular growth required new markets. With what has become the 'Soviet bloc' closed to U.S. exports, three alternative areas were developed. (1) West Europe was reconstructed under the Marshall plan. (2) Latin America became an almost wholly American market. (3) The remaining colonies had to be made independent, both to reduce the surplus going to the Western European colonizing powers, and to fully mobilize their productive potential. Since 1965, U.S. hegemony has declined as the cost of political imperium (Russian military challenge, European economic resurgence and cumulated Third World pressures) has become too high economically.

The emergence in this stage of many countries where there is no private ownership of the basic means of production has brought about not only international reallocation of consumption. It has also created a clear threat to the ideological justification of capitalism, by exposing the political vulnerability of capitalist entrepreneurs, and by demonstrating that private ownership is irrelevant to the rapid expansion of industrial productivity. *But*, Wallerstein argues, 'to the extent that (what is commonly known as the socialist bloc) has raised the ability of the new semiperipheral areas to enjoy a larger share of the world surplus, it has once again depolarized the world, recreating the triad of strata that has been a fundamental element in the survival of the world-system' (ibid, p. 34). This new strength of the semi-periphery, together with the continuing economic expansion of the core, has led to the further economic and political weakening of the periphery.

Part II The Nation-State in the World-System

Reference to the function of the tripartite structural division of nation states in the world system neatly introduces our discussion of how the world system perspective handles the problem of the nation state. For Wallerstein, it is confusing to think of 'states' outside the world system. 'Stateness is not a generic category of political life but a historically specific category . . . distinctive to the relationally formed jurisdictions . . . of the initially European-centred interstate system.

It a category given by, because factually imposed by, the developmental process of the capitalist world-economy' (Hopkins and Wallerstein, 1981, p. 45). For Wallerstein, the nation-state post-dates capitalism, and is a consequence rather than a cause of capitalism. But what exactly is the role of nation-states in the capitalist world economy? Wallerstein argues that 'Capitalism as a system of production for sale in a market for profit and appropriation of this profit on the basis of individual or collective ownership, has only existed in, and *can be said to require*, a world-system in which the political units are not co-extensive with the boundaries of the market economy' (1979, p. 66. My emphasis).

Why, though, does capitalism require such a separation of political and economic units? What is it that these political units (nation-states) provide which is lacking from the logic of the capitalist world economy? And how do nation states perform this function? Wallerstein argues thus:

> The fundamental role of the state as an institution in the capitalist world-economy is to augment the advantage of some against others in the market – that is, to *reduce* the 'freedom' of the market . . .
>
> The modes of augmenting advantage are many. The state can transfer income by taking it from some and giving it to others. The state can restrict access to the market (of commodities or of labor) which favor those who thereby share in the oligopoly or oligopsony. The state can restrain persons from organizing to change the actions of the state. And, of course, the state can act not only within its jurisdiction but beyond it. This may be licit (the rules concerning transit over boundaries) or illicit (interference in the internal affairs of another state). Warfare is of course one of the mechanisms used . . .
>
> It is this realistic ability of states to interfere with the flow of factors of production that provides the political underpinnings of the structural division of labor in the capitalist world-economy as a whole. Normal market considerations may account for recurring initial thrusts to specialization (natural or socio-historical advantages in the production of one or another commodity), but it is the state system which encrusts, enforces, and exaggerates the patterns, and it has regularly required the use of state machinery to revise the pattern of the world-wide division of labor.
>
> (Wallerstein 1979, pp. 291–2)

That is to say, it is through state structures that particular groups are able to affect and distort the functioning of the market in their own favour. States act as agents, maximizing the division of the world surplus in favour of specific groups (located within, or outside, their borders). But it is not just in the distribution of surplus that the states affect the CWE (capitalist world economy). State structures intervene in the CWE at every stage, from procurement of the means of production, though transformation of material into commodities, and their sale and distribution, to the investment of the profit as accumulated capital. But the basic contradiction of the capitalist system, for Wallerstein, lies in the different ways that world supply and world demand are determined. Overall world production is the result of the individual decisions of individual producers, and there is a tendency toward expansion of production (supply) in order to maintain or increase profit levels. Overall world demand, on the other hand, is determined not by individual decisions, but by political decision about the distribution of income among various groups within a society – and specifically by the level of wages. As Wallerstein puts it,

> World demand is fundamentally determined by a set of pre-existing compromises within the various states that are part of the world economy, and which more or less fix for medium run periods (c.50 years) the modal distribution of income to various participants in the circuit of capital.
>
> (Wallerstein, 1980b, p. 168)

To summarize Wallerstein's view of nation-states in the world system, then:

1. They are an intrinsic, organic part of the whole world system, not separate from it.
2. The historical structural division of nation states into core, semi-periphery and periphery is an essential condition of the stability of the whole world system.
3. Competition between nation state machineries is the motive power which keeps the system moving. Without that it would be transformed either into a world empire, or a socialist world system.
4. They intervene in and distort the 'free' working of the capitalist world economy so as to increase the benefits (profits, wages, etc.) which some groups receive within it.
5. They are at least the sites of the political struggles and compromises which determine the overall level of world demand.

Critics of the world-system perspective have focused mainly on the first item on the list, the symbolic inseparability of the system of nation states and the capitalist world economy.

This is not, of course, a very common view of how politics and economics interrelate at the international or world level. Some approaches tend to subsume political factors under economic ones. Others assume that political and economic forces operate largely independent of each other. A further alternative view, which it is particularly appropriate to consider here because of its explicit, but not unsympathetic, contrast with Wallerstein's approach, is that put forward by Theda Skocpol. In contrast to Wallerstein's view that states, and indeed the idea of stateness, are brought into being by, and secure the purposes of, the capitalist world economy, Skocpol argues that 'the intersocietal network . . . incubated the first self-propelling industrialization of England' (Skocpol 1976, p. 179). And while she acknowledges that 'capitalism has from its inception developed within, around, and through a framework of "multiple political sovereignties" – that is, the system of states that originally emerged from European feudalism and then expanded to cover the entire globe as a system of nations,' she goes on to emphasize that

> this changing international system of states was not originally created by capitalism, and throughout modern world capitalist history represents an analytically autonomous level of trans-national reality, *interdependent* in its structure and dynamics with the world economy but not reducible to it. Indeed, just as capitalist development has spurred transformations of states and the international state system, so have these 'acted back' upon the course of capital accumulation within nations and upon a world scale.
>
> (Skocpol and Trimberger, 1977–8, p. 110)

An essentially similar critique of Wallerstein's view of the state in the world system informs Peter Worsley's important critique of Wallerstein (Worsley, 1980) which I now want to examine.

Worsley's basic strategy is to question whether Wallerstein's single capitalist world-system is in fact a totality, capitalist, global and systemic. In challenging the view that the only economic (and social) system in the contemporary world is the capitalist one, Worsley argues that the essence of the notion of system is that it refers not to a mere aggregation of various kinds of things into a whole, but to a whole whose various parts relate to each other in systematic ways. For Wallerstein, for instance, the core, semi-periphery and periphery in the capitalist world economy are essentially integrated with each other, rather than related in more or less random, or shifting ways. In Wallerstein's approach the 'systemness' of the capitalist world economy is a function of, is given by, flows from, its very capitalist nature.

The nature of the relationship between the parts is shaped by capitalism. Worsley tries to show that there is currently an alternative system to the capitalist. He argues that the most obvious feature of the contemporary world, indeed, is the conflict between two economic and social systems (capitalism and communism) of a fundamentally different kind. He argues that Wallerstein's approach entails avoiding the most critical socio-political questions, and ignoring, or depreciating the importance of, the most salient international differences in the contemporary world, which derive from this inter – rather than intra – system conflict.

The second thrust of Worsley's criticism of Wallerstein concerns his definition of capitalism. He broadly shares the major criticisms, noted above, of that definition of capitalism, which make it impossible to claim that the world has been 'capitalist' for the past 400 years. This is not the place to follow through this debate in any detail, but we should recognize that the different positions in it do contain different implications for the role, strength, and importance of the nation state in any kind of world system or world order.

For Wallerstein, following from his definition of capitalism, it is chiefly at the level of the market and the development of trade that the state 'distorts', 'intervenes in', or 'interferes with', the economic imperatives of capitalism. It is to the effect of the state in intervening in relatively unfettered world market forces that he pays an overwhelming amount of attention, compared to that he pays to the relationship between the state and production, or to the wider political arrangements which might faciliate or obstruct the development of capitalism. Worsley attacks this apparent subsumption of the polity under the economy, putting forward in its place the idea of political economy. Thus, Worsley argues, Wallerstein does not recognize that the development of the economy depended upon the *prior* conquest of political power, which then afforded opportunity for economic entrepreneurs to innovate and expand.

This has two major consequences for their analyses of the state. First, the role of the state (in the narrower sense of 'state apparatus') for Wallerstein is largely external. Nation-states' chief function is to facilitate the operation of the market, which Wallerstein sees as effectively creating all the conditions of its own successful operation, including production. For as, Skocpol has pointed out, there is a tendency on Wallerstein's part to treat the social relations of production merely as different 'modes of labour control', operating in a 'top down' fashion, with 'the dominant classes choos(ing) freely among alternative strategies of labour control by assessing rationally the best means for maximising profits, given the geographical, demographic, technological, and labour skill conditions in which they find themselves, and given the profitable possibilities they face for selling particular kinds of products on the world market.' (Skocpol, 1977, p. 1079) This effectively rules out discussion of much of what goes on within states.

The second consequence of the emphasis on market relations is that relations between nation-states tend to be seen only in that dimension. In contrast to Wallerstein, who spends little time analysing 'non-market' relations between nation-states, Worsley's central emphasis is on *political* economy and on the *pluri-dimensionality* of relations between nation-states.

The final aspect of Worsley's critique of Wallerstein I will mention concerns his view of the world system. Wallerstein sees an essentially simple world-system. It is based on the structure of core, semi-periphery and periphery, and though there may be fluctuations or even upheavals within that structure, they are not sufficient to transform its essential 'systemness' and simplicity. To this Worsley counterposes a view which emphasizes the complexity of the world. In place of Wallerstein's flexible and almost self-regulating single world-*system*, he sees an essentially precarious and shifting world *order*, where stability is not inherent but is constantly challenged by political and ideological forces as well as by economic ones.

Part III The World System in the State

One of the features that characterizes a world system perspective is its relegation of the importance of the kinds of features of social and political life within national societies that usually comprise the staple of discussions of 'the state'. This is not to say that inter-state differences are not recognized or that the presence of social and political conflict within each and any nation state is overlooked by world-systems theorists. Such things are acknowledged, but tend to be regarded as either relatively unimportant or as a function of the particular nation-state's location within the world system. As Wallerstein puts it:

> Since states are the primary arena of political conflict in a capitalist world-economy, and since the functioning of the world-economy is such that national class composition varies widely, it is easy to perceive why the politics of states differentially located in relation to the world-economy should be so dissimilar. It is also then easy to perceive that using the political machinery of a given state to change the social composition and world-economic function of national production

does not per se change the capitalist world-system as such. (1979, p. 293)

It is worth noting here a major difference between the approaches of imperialism and the world-system perspective. The former lays very much more emphasis on the role of particular nation states, imperialist powers, and their impact on particular sectors of the world which they exploited, than does the latter. In the world-system perspective a relatively anonymous system logic, independent of any nation-state, propels the system, and it is enough to know a country's structural location in the capitalist world economy, i.e. whether it has core, semi peripheral, or peripheral status.

The point of this final section is to ask what a world-system perspective contributes to attempts to understand what goes on within any particular nation-state, beyond leading us to investigate its place within the system. Would taking a world-system perspective limit us to explaining national social and political activity by reference to the structures of the world economic system alone? Or can we take the view while the world economic system may be indifferent to national boundaries, this does not mean that national frontiers signal *no* distinctions of any real importance? I think we can and should take that view. Only by doing so will we gain full value from the contribution that a world-system perspective can make to our understanding of individual nation-states.

However, before considering how we might do that, I would like to consider three assumptions which seem to underly the emphasis on the essential similarity of nation-states in similar world-system locations. It is important to recognize these assumptions and how they might be modified if we are to gain anything from world-system theory.

First there is the assumption of the irrelevance of pre-capitalist history. Nothing that happened anywhere before 'the long sixteenth century' and nothing that happened outside North Western Europe after that until a country's integration into the capitalist world economy, is of any contemporary importance. For Wallerstein, states (which, remember, he sees as being brought into being by capitalism) 'create in their wake peoples, nations, ethnic groups' (1982, p. 15). What this assumption means is that capitalism carries *all* before it. It sweeps away, neutralizes or ignores all existing institutions, ideologies groupings etc., and is not influenced in any significant way by any of them. Taking the assumption at face value would mean, for instance, that there were no relevant pre-capitalist differences between, say, Japan and Britain, and that such differences as we can see between them in, say, production relations, result only from the impact of capitalism.

It is clear that some institutions that predated capitalism in this country – for example, some legal forms and practices – have not been entirely swept away or reshaped by the rise and development of capitalism; on the contrary, they provided part of the framework within which capitalism developed. In the same way, it is not possible to consign all institutions and practices that predated – and often survive alongside – capitalism in peripheral countries to a box labelled 'traditions'. These institutions and practices are not homogeneous, nor do they all succumb in the same way to the arrival of capitalism. The point is neither to write them off or to assert their invulnerability, but to analyse the effect of the form of the spread of the capitalist world economy on each of them.

If the first assumption wipes the slate clean, the second, which we might call the assumption of identical impact, sees the capitalist world economy as having the same effect on all the territories it penetrates. All nation states have now been integrated into the same capitalist world economy. But his assumption appears to ignore very serious differences in the impact of capitalism. Some of these are located in differences between core countries and some between peripheral countries. To take one example of each: (a) would we expect a (lastingly) different impact on nation states whose first experience of the capitalist world economy came through the medium of British, as opposed to French, Portuguese or Dutch colonialism? This is clearly a complex and difficult question to which no easy answer either way is possible – and that, of course, is the point. We cannot assume that differences in the experience of colonialism were fundamentally irrelevant. We have rather to demonstrate that they were or were not. A similar argument can be made about differences in peripheral countries. Can we say that differences in their mineral wealth, for instance, have had no impact on their relations with core countries? Furthermore, we should not assume that the capitalist world economy affects all the sectors of any particular nation-state in the same way; that the same sectors in every nation-state are affected; or that the weight of its impact on the sectors it does effect is the same either within or across nation states. The nature and effect of the world economy has to be considered separately in each separate case.

The third assumption is one shared by many analysts of underdevelopment. A brief, if slightly pompous, label for it might be the assumption of the normative superiority of the indigenous. It is based on the idea of a 'natural' development path being open to any nation, and the necessary inferiority of any alternative imposed from outside.

The assumption seems to be that if it hadn't been for the capitalist world economy the world would have been filled with autarkic and independent nations. This seems another dangerous assumption that could only be justified on the basis of evidence which would be almost impossible to collect. And it is one that has particularly to be borne in mind when considering the effect of the world economy on peripheral countries.

I have spent some time on these assumptions because I feel that an awareness of them helps considerably to sensitize us to the issues involved in examining the message of the foregoing discussion, broadly that the impact of the world system on any particular state needs to be looked at in detail. But since the latter is very difficult to carry out in the space of a single introductory chapter, I will confine myself to considering briefly *how* the impact of the capitalist world economy is *mediated* to individual countries. This is another question to which world-system theorists have not paid a great deal of attention; they appear to assume that the impact is self evident and that its processes require no explanation. However, without trying to isolate at least some of the major ways through which these effects are mediated it is impossible to specify their form and impact in any particular case.

The two forms of 'mediation' I want to look at are international organizations and transnational or multi-national corporations. Both these have become prominent as the form of the capitalist world economy has changed from a point where it was dominated by national capitals and policed by individual nations.

International Organizations

There are thousands of international organizations. They differ in both their membership base (bilateral, multilateral, 'World') and their purposes. Here I want to consider, very briefly, the role of world organizations (though there is, of course, no organization, not even the United Nations Assembly, which includes every single nation state in its membership). These 'world' organizations (i.e. organizations with a potential comprehensive membership and intended world wide impact) are not all of a kind. Some of them are concerned broadly with setting down and helping to achieve minimum standards within their area of competence. In this group we would include, for instance, the World Health Organization and the International Labour Organization – and perhaps also UNESCO. Rather separately, the United Nations Assembly seeks to provide a world political forum, and its Security Council to achieve world peace. A third group consists of world economic organizations like the IMF and the World

Bank. It is this group which most obviously appear to have links with the capitalist world economy. The investigation of such links is, of course, an extremely difficult and complex matter – but a crucial question that at least points us in the direction such investigations would have to take is, 'who benefits'? What various kinds of national or international ends do these organizations serve? Are their activities instrumental in preserving – or changing – a particular world economic or political system? Or do they serve the interests of particular nations? Is there evidence of particular nations submerging their own immediate gain in the interest of the longer term stability of a particular economic or political system? Does the existence of these organizations in fact, 'prove' either Worsley's or Wallerstein's argument – or is it irrelevant to either or both of them?

One way of looking at this question is to regard international organizations as the sources of the 'hegemony' of a particular world system, that is to say of the process by which one particular way of ordering the world system comes to be regarded throughout that system as the only way of ordering it. It becomes a form of common sense which it is perverse or subversive to oppose. This view has been put forward by Robert W. Cox. He writes

> Hegemony at the international level is thus not merely an order among states. It is an order within a world economy with a dominant mode of production which penetrates into all the countries and links into other subordinate modes of production. It is also a complex of international social relationships which connect the social classes of the different countries. World hegemony is described as a social structure, an economic structure, and a political structure; and it cannot be simply one of these things but must be all three. World hegemony, furthermore, is expressed in universal norms and institutions which lay down general rules of behaviour for states and for those forces of civil society that act across national boundaries – rules which support the dominant mode of production. (Cox, 1983, pp. 171–2).

He goes on to argue that 'international organization is the process through which the institutions of hegemony and its ideology are developed'. This is expressed in a number of ways. First, 'International institutions embody rules which facilitate the expansion of the dominant economic and social forces but which at the same time permit adjustments to be made by subordinated interests with a minimum of pain'. Second, 'International institutions and rules are generally initiated by the state which founds the hegemony. At the very least they must have that state's support. The dominant state takes care to secure the acquiescence of other states according to a hierarchy of powers within the inter-state structure of hegemony'.

Third, 'International institutions perform an ideological role as well. They help define guidelines for states and to legitimate certain institutions and practices at the national level. They reflect orientations favourable to the dominant social and economic forces' (ibid, p. 172).

This represents a very sophisticated view of international organizations as both the sources and the 'carriers' of the hegemony of a particular world order. As such, it does seem to tie in with, and give considerable support to, Wallerstein's world-system perspective. But two questions at least must be asked of it. First, can we really talk of a hegemonic world order when Worsley, for instance sees the clash between two quite different conceptions of world order as the dominant feature of the contemporary world? And second, how are we to understand the threat of the dominant world power, the United States, to withdraw from one of the largest and most important international organizations, UNESCO, because of its 'counter-hegemonic' stance?

The Internationalization of Production

Theories of imperialism were developed during the period when national capitals were expanding to cover almost the entire world between them. The economically most powerful nations each had their own spheres of influence and directly controlled colonies. The role of the state in each of these countries was to protect and expand these markets – in the last resort by means of war. The central thesis, as Nigel Harris (1983) puts it, was of 'the fusion of State and the collectivity of companies, the two constituent elements of national capital' (p. 236). However, through a series of processes we have no space to go into here, by the 1970s the increasing internationalization of capital was threatening to bring to an end the era of domination of national capitals. As Harris puts it, 'The long promise of the market, of capitalism, was beginning to emerge – the competition of capitals for profit without the diversion of national 'identity'' (ibid, p. 131). Thus, at the very time when Wallerstein was beginning to elaborate his theory of the capitalist world economy, the plausibility of such a perspective was becoming greater than it had ever been.

In what ways, then, do the internationalization of capital and the internationalization of production affect what goes on in nation states? In Harris's fusion between state and capital the state is involved in (1) protecting markets for enterprises located within its boundaries; (2) the 'patriation' of profit to the company's 'home' territory and (3) providing a legal, economic, political, industrial and

military infrastructure within which production can flourish. However, the dissolving of that fusion, brought about by internationalization, had led to changes for the state in all three aspects of the
relationship. The importance of the protection of markets has probably waned somewhat, though the protection of sources of raw
materials less so. The growth of multinational corporations has quite
severed the links between market, production and profit as individual
states become incapable of legally controlling the activities and policies of companies with multiple national locations, but no unambiguous 'home base' to which profits will automatically be repat-
riated. One consequence of this is competition between nation-states
to provide the most favourable conditions − i.e. lowest tax levels −
for the patriation of profits.

It is, though, in the area of inter-state competition for the location
of production that the implications of the internationalization of
capital for particular nation states are most direct. Where a *national*
bond between a particular company and a particular state does not
exist, or ceases to exist, it is not enough for a state to provide an
infrastructure amenable to a particular company − it has to provide
one more amenable than competing states. Part of this infrastructure
has to do with conditions of (re)patriation of profits and other
financial attractions which are not, of course, without implications
for state policies and practices. But the impact of these is less direct
than the impact of policies and practices for the control of labour, for
instance. We should note that it is not only the 'repressive' regimes of
the Third World who are involved in this way. There have been
numerous examples in recent years − the most recent being the
wooing of Nissan − of British governments stressing the need for a
binding commitment to 'industrial peace' if a particular multinational corporation is to be persuaded to set up production in this
country.

Conclusion

What I have attempted here is a brief exposition of world-system
theory, emphasizing those parts of it that bear most directly on the
way we think about the state. In doing this I have tried to indicate the
kinds of questions with which the world-system theory confronts the
predominantly national focus of most 'orthodox' theories and studies
of the state, of whatever stripe. The world-system perspective does
not in itself imply that any such study is meaningless, but it does force
us to consider both the purpose and the limitations of nationally

focused studies. And even if we do not accept its most radical implications, the world-system perspective requires us to examine a broader and quite different range of 'external constraints on national freedom of manoeuvre' than theories which are based on relations between particular states or groups of states.

I have also sought to indicate some limitations on the value of the world-system perspective in the study of the state. The idea that its basic shape is given, by its function in the capitalist world economy provides a conception of the state which is both limited and distorted, as well as being excessively instrumentalist, while the associated insistence on the priority of the world system over any national historical or cultural differences does not always seem easy to justify. In a sense, what the world-system perspective does is to present almost a base-superstructure model on a world scale, and it shares the strengths and weaknesses of such models.

Bibliography

Amin, Samir (1976). *Unequal Development*. Brighton, Harvester.

Amin, Samir (1982). 'Crisis, Nationalism and Socialism' in Amin *et al*. 1982,

Amin, Samir; Arrighi, Giovanni; Frank, Andre Gunder; and Wallerstein, Immanuel (1982). *Dynamics of Global Crisis*. New York: Monthly Review Press.

Cox, Robert W (1983). 'Gramsci, Hegemony and International Relations: An Essay in Method', *Millenium* 12, 2, 162–75.

Frank, Andre Gunder (1971). *The Sociology of Development and the Underdevelopment of Sociology*. London, Pluto Press.

Harris, Nigel (1983). *Of Bread and Guns*. Harmondsworth, Penguin.

Hobsbawm, Eric (1979). 'The Development of the World Economy', *Cambridge Journal of Economics* 3, 305–18.

Hopkins, Terence K. and Wallerstein, Immanuel (1981). 'Structural Transformations of the World-Economy', in Richard Rubinson (ed.) *Dynamics of World Development*. Beverly Hills and London, Sage 233–61.

Laclau, Ernesto, (1977). *Politics and Ideology in Marxist Theory*. London, New Left Books.

Skocpol, Theda (1976). 'France, Russia, China: a Structural Analysis of Social Revolutions', *Comparative Studies in Society and History*. 18, 2, 175–210.

Skocpol, Theda (1977). 'Wallerstein's World Capitalist System; a Theoretical and Historical Critique'. *American Journal of Sociology* 82, 5, 1075–1090.

Skocpol, Theda and Trimberger, Ellen Kay (1977–8) 'Revolutions and the World-Historical Development of Capitalism', *Berkeley Journal of Sociology*, 22, 101–13.

Smith, Sheila (1980). 'The Ideas of Samir Amin: Theory or Tautology?' *Journal of Development Studies*, 17, 1, 5–21.

Wallerstein, Immanuel (1974). *The Modern World System Volume 1* New York, Academic Press.

Wallerstein, Immanuel (ed.) (1975). *World Inequality*. Montreal, Black Rose Books.

Wallerstein, Immanuel (1979). *The Capitalist World Economy*. Cambridge, Cambridge U.P.

Wallerstein, Immanuel (1980a). 'Imperialism and Development', in Albert Bergesen (ed.), *Studies of the Modern World System*. New York and London, Academic Press, 13–23.

Wallerstein, Immanuel (1980b). 'The future of the World Economy', in Terence K. Hopkins and Immanuel Wallerstein (eds) *Processes of the World System*. Beverly Hills and London, Sage, 167–80.

Wallerstein, Immanuel (1982). 'Crisis and Transition', in Amin *et al*, 11–54.

Worsley, Peter (1980). 'One World or Three: A Critique of Immanuel Wallerstein', in Miliband, Ralph and Saville, John (1980) *Socialist Register*. London, Merlin Press, 298–338.

CHAPTER 8

The future of the nation state

David Beetham

The nation state is the dominant political formation of our time. It is so central a feature of the political landscape that it is difficult to imagine its absence; to suggest the possibility of its demise may seem presumptuous, if not actually alarming. Historically considered, however, the nation state is a comparatively recent phenomenon. If we consider European history, then it is only the period from the sixteenth to the nineteenth centuries that saw the definitive emergence of the centralized *state*, successfully claiming a monopoly of law making and law enforcing power over a unified geographical territory, and independence from any external authority. Before that time political authority had been mainly local in its exercise, and subject to overlapping jurisdictions and multiple competences. States were generally much smaller than today, their boundaries were constantly shifting, and the control of the monarch or prince was relatively weak. Within his own territory he shared authority not only with a variety of local powers, but was also subject to the higher authority of the Emperor and the Church, which had its own system of courts and taxation in each locality alongside the secular ones. Jurisdiction was thus multiple and overlapping rather than unitary and monopolistic. It was over against these particularistic and many-layered sources of authority that the state gradually came to assert a jurisdiction that was uniform, centralized and exclusive, and independent of external control. Exclusive jurisdiction internally, and independence externally – these are summed up together in the idea of sovereignty.

If that process of *state* formation is comparatively recent in historical terms (from the sixteenth to the nineteenth centuries), it was only as late as the nineteenth century that the idea became widely accepted that the proper boundaries of the state should coincide, not with the particular territory that had been historically acquired by dynastic alliance or conquest, but with a given people, who constituted a *nation*. The people comprising a nation became the sole source from which the state could derive its legitimacy; and the nation became the sole legitimate object of their political allegiance. Nationalism in this sense was associated with the redrawing of the territorial map of European states in the course of the nineteenth century, whereby through a process sometimes of secession, sometimes of amalgamation, sometimes a combination of the two, the boundaries of state jurisdiction came to coincide more closely with that of peoples sharing the common characteristics of culture and historical identity that qualified them for nationhood. This was a process that continued into the twentieth century, with the dissolution of the Habsburg, Tsarist and Ottoman empires at the end of the First World War.

The nation state, then, is a historical product, not a fact of nature. It embodies two distinct ideas of sovereignty: sovereignty as the idea of the state's supreme and independent jurisdiction over a given territory; and sovereignty as the idea that the source of legitimacy for that jurisdiction derives from the people who constitute the nation. It also embodies two distinct but mutually reinforcing notions of exclusivity: the exclusivity of the *state* in its jurisdiction over its territory; and the exclusivity of the *nation*, both in the sense that the interests of its people are paramount (to use a recent phrase), and in the sense that the nation forms the exclusive object of their political allegiance.

It is only in the second half of the present century, since the break up of the colonial empires, that this formation has become universal across the globe. In the 1940s and 1950s European nationalism was transformed into anti-colonialism and served as a vehicle for securing independence against the European powers. Many of these new states were highly artificial constructions, states in search of nations still to be formed, in which the only national force remaining after the decay of the nationalist movements has been the army and the state bureaucracy. This fact reminds us that the relationship between nation and state is anything but a simple or uniform one. A nation can be as much the conscious creation of state policy as a pre-existing cultural entity demanding political autonomy within its own state boundaries.

Why is it that this particular political formation has come to prevail so universally? Why did the dominant political structure come to be located at this particular level of social space – greater than city states, less than empires? Why, within this social space, did the dominant political structure take the form of an exclusive sovereignty, rather than a loose federation or a pluralistic network of alliances? And why did it come to be associated with a division of the world's population into the differentiated groupings called nations? These are large questions, embracing a huge span of modern European history. A simple, no doubt over-simple, answer would be that the nation state came to prevail because it proved most successful in meeting the economic and military requirements of a changing world economy and international order. In the context of the growing world economy of the eighteenth and nineteenth centuries those states proved most economically successful, in which a free market was established over a relatively wide area, within a unified system of law, taxation and administration. In the context of military competition those states proved most effective which were able to rely on the resources of such an economy, and to count on the allegiance of a relatively unified population. Finally, the nation state was the only political structure that proved capable of containing the demands for national autonomy and unification which accompanied the incursion of the popular masses into the political arena, and of satisfying the demands of popular sovereignty. In this process the longer established nation states, especially England and France, proved most successful, and served as a model which others felt impelled to follow in order to catch up with the leaders. The prestige that the nation state form thus acquired in its European context ensured that it also served subsequently as a model in a very different context for societies seeking to establish their independence against the colonial powers, later in the twentieth century.

That is a very crude summary of a complex process. However it serves my present purpose, which is to argue that just as the nation state became universal, because a combination of economic, military and politico-cultural forces came to consolidate political structures at this particular level, and ensure their success, so a combination of the same forces, at a later stage, is now working to undermine the effectiveness of the political structures at that same level. In other words, the very period in which the nation state has become universal is the very period when we are beginning to see the process of its erosion.

Let me try and put the point more precisely. Implicit in the success of the nation state and its universality is a threefold claim: that this political formation is the one most effectively able to guarantee the economic well being, the physical security and the cultural identity of the people who constitute its citizens. My thesis is that, on each of these dimensions, economic, military and cultural forces are at work which increasingly call into question the sovereign nation state's capacity to make effective these claims. This thesis does not depend on there having been some golden age of the nation state, in which it was uniformly successful in satisfying these implicit claims; as we shall see its record has been ambiguous to say the least. All I wish to argue is that, whatever effectiveness it may have had in the past, is now increasingly being called into question.

Before I proceed to examine each of these three dimensions in turn, let me confront an objection, which if it could be sustained would seriously damage my line of argument. This is that there is simply no such thing as *the* nation state, only an immense variety of different kinds of nation states, some of which for reasons of size and internal organisation have always been better able than others to meet the requirements of their citizens. More precisely, it could be argued there have always been large or core states in the world system that have proved successful, and small or peripheral states that have proved unsuccessful and experienced a variety of forms of dependency upon the larger. One might also add for good measure a group of semi-peripheral states which have mediated the relationship between the two. Now I would concede a good deal of this argument. Of course there are massive differences among the species 'nation state'. But the issue is whether this political configuration will continue to work even for the most successful, let alone the rest; and whether there are not historical forces acting in common on all, and to which all are subject, just as there were common forces at work which led to the success of the nation state in the first place. That at any rate is the idea that I now want to substantiate.

1. Economic

Let me take first the economic dimension, and the claim of the nation state to be able to meet the economic needs of its citizens, or at least provide the framework within which these can be met.

The growth of the world economy in the eighteenth and nineteenth centuries came to favour the nation state as the most effective context for the development of the capitalist economy. Internally it provided a unified national market for the expansion of domestic industry; externally it provided protection against damaging competition and support for the conquest of overseas markets. Common to both liberals and interventionists was the idea of a 'national economy' located within a bounded political space. This national economy provided the necessary framework for economic expansion, and in the twentieth century for the development of the welfare state. Now it is doubtful whether the concept of a national economy is any longer so applicable in view of the development of the world economy in the late twentieth century. As many commentators point out, it is not a question of there now being a world market which did not previously exist; it is a question rather of a qualitative change in its character. It is no longer structured with national economies and national firms as its basic units, but in a manner that increasingly cuts across nation states and operates independently of them.

The most obvious and frequently commented on feature of this new development of the world economy is the multinational or transnational corporation, for which a single national market is now insufficient to provide the necessary economies of scale, and which is capable of organizing its production without reference to state boundaries. Its mobility and supranational scale of operations enable it to dictate terms for the location of its industries, and to evade state controls through its pricing policies and access to international finance. There is a huge disparity between the mobility and global reach of the world economy, and the immobility and national scale of the state. The latter is often reduced to participation in a beggars' auction, each state vying with the others to offer the most advantageous terms for the location of new industry at the expense of its own taxpayers.

Of course the transnational corporation still needs the nation state for the provision of human resources, material infrastructure and all manner of supporting services. And once located, its industries have to conform to the political conditions pertaining in the host country. To this extent it is dependent upon the state. But such dependence lasts only so long as the life of the particular investment. In the location of new capital the transnational corporation is unconstrained: it is able to optimize conditions for its operation on a world scale, without reference to the interests of particular national economies.

Now the scale of the transnational corporation is only one aspect, and probably not the most important, of the way in which control of economic activity within the nation state is escaping beyond it. Individual countries are relatively powerless in face of the operation of the international markets which determine the price of commodities, interest rates and the availability of finance. Changes outside their control can undermine their chosen economic policies, often in a short space of time. And those policies are themselves often influenced by such activities as currency speculation, or controlled in a more explicit manner by the requirements of international bankers. The conditions imposed upon debtor countries by orthodox finance are highly restrictive, and their interest payments alone can consume a large proportion of their export earnings. The threat of default may illustrate the power the weak have at their disposal. Yet it is a highly attenuated form of power which threatens only further hardship for a country's inhabitants by precipitating a collapse in the international banking system itself.

The distribution of power and powerlessness within the world economic system thus evades any overall control. The systematic consequences of a series of large scale economic actors, both transnational corporations and nation states, all independently seeking to maximize their economic interests, produces outcomes that are damaging to all, and beyond the scope of existing international agencies to deal with. Adam Smith's invisible hand simply does not work at the level of the world economy, not even when supplemented by the wagging of a more corporeal finger on the part of the IMF and the World Bank, or the flaccid gestures of a global Keynesianism. The consequences of this are manifest: in the short term world wide depression, financial crisis and mass unemployment; in the longer term resource depletion, pollution and ecological decay; in both short and long term the intensification of global inequalities which the nation state on its own can do little to correct.

Before I am accused of exaggeration, let me hasten to say that it is not my contention that nation states have no influence over their own economic affairs or that no policy changes are possible that would effect an improvement, for example, in existing levels of unemployment. That would be an untenable position. All I wish to assert is that such policies increasingly come up against the limits imposed by the structure of the world economy, at which level there are no political institutions capable of exerting effective control. The concept of the 'national economy' has not yet been superseded, but it is subject to considerable erosion, and to that extent also the capacity of the sovereign nation state to control its own economic destiny. Sovereignty, in other words, cannot be equated with power. My first contention, then, is that the nation state's ability to satisfy the economic requirement of its citizens is increasingly being called into question.

2. Military

The second dimension that I want to examine is that of physical security, the protection of which is generally regarded as the first responsibility of the state. Control of the means of violence is *par excellence* the business of the state. The modern state was the product of warfare, in the sense that its territorial sovereignty was achieved by a process of internal conquest and pacification, and its external boundaries defined through war or defeat in war. Similarly the physical security that the nation state promises its citizens has a dual aspect. Internally it claims to protect them from violence at the hands of each other (though they also need a guarantee of protection against the violence of the state). Externally it claims to defend them against the threat from other nation states. Of these two the state has more control over the internal than the external aspect, where it confronts other nation states simply as one actor among many pursuing equally exclusive national interests. The contrast between the internal and external security of the modern state was put in classic though exaggerated form by Thomas Hobbes, when he compared the external relations of that state to the state of nature from whose baneful effects its monopoly of violence protected individuals internally. Sovereign states confront each other much as individual egoists in the pre-governmental state of nature.

> In all times kings, and persons of sovereign authority, because of their independency, are in continual jealousies, and in the state and posture of gladiators; having their weapons pointing and their eyes fixed on one another; that is, their forts, garrisons and guns upon the frontiers of their kingdoms; and continual spies upon their neighbours; which is a posture of war. (Hobbes, 1961 edition, p. 83)

Hobbes's account is something of a caricature, in the sense that it ignores the normative consensus that is both necessary to internal order and a partial or intermittent feature of the international system. Nevertheless, that passage effectively captures the quality of 'external egoism' that is the characteristic posture of the modern state, powerfully reinforced by the nationalism that assigns exclusive priority to the claims of its own people over those of others. It is hardly surprising in view of such a posture that the history of the nation state has been one of repeated warfare, despite all the best efforts of diplomacy. The twentieth century, the century of the nation state, has also been the century of the most continuous warfare, though the location of those wars has shifted increasingly south and east. If you look at a map of war in the twentieth century you will find that during the first half century, following the establishment of the system of the major nation states in Europe, the wars were primarily European in origin. Since 1950 and the establishment of the system of independent nation states in Africa and Asia, the origin of wars has shifted progressively south and east, although some of those wars have been fought by the super powers or in proxy for them. Even when it is not actually fighting, the nation state has been arming itself in preparation for having to, and so further undermining its ability to provide for its citizens' welfare.

Now of course much of recorded human history has been a history of warfare. And all manner of potential conflicts would exist even within a different political structure from that of the nation state. I do not wish to argue any simple monocausal thesis. Yet, to to put it no stronger, the nation state within a system of nation states has hardly had an impressive record for minimizing war or guaranteeing security. Two features of the modern world make that security increasingly problematic. One is the shrinking of the globe in time and space, which causes wars at one point to have immediate repercussions at another. The second is the continuous developments in technology, that make war increasingly total and destructive. Of these developments, that of nuclear weapons and the increasingly sophisticated means for their delivery are clearly the most significant.

Of all twentieth-century developments, it is the discovery of the atom bomb that has most clearly rendered the exclusive sovereignty of the nation state anachronistic. Some argument could be advanced on behalf of the aeroplane; but it is the development of nuclear weapons that has finally put an end to the nation state's ability to guarantee the security of its citizens. The reason is well known. There is simply no defence against nuclear weapons, and the threat of mutual destruction which acts as a substitute for defence, depends entirely on the actions and mental processes of potential enemies, which are by definition outside the control of the individual nation state. Now it has often been said that it is the nuclear balance of terror that has kept the peace in Europe for the past 35 years. That is a proposition which it is impossible either to prove or disprove. But it would be a brave person who would argue that, because it has done so in the past, it must continue to do so in future, whatever the development of weapons systems or the attitudes of governments. That proposition is based upon the assumption that deterrence is a stable condition, an assumption which the last twenty years has proved to be erroneous, and not for accidental reasons, but for reasons that are intrinsic to nuclear deterrence itself. The same logic that is integral to the concept of deterrence also leads to an increasing proliferation of nuclear weapons, both laterally, to other nation states that do not have them, and vertically, in terms of an increasing complexity and sophistication of weapons systems on the part of those who do. If it is necessary for one nation state to possess nuclear weapons for its protection, then by the same argument it must be equally necessary for all to possess them who have the industrial capacity to construct them. If it is necessary to possess them, then it must be equally necessary to match a potential adversary's destructive capacity and sophistication of delivery systems, and not only those he has, but those he might conceivably develop. Nuclear deterrence is based on mutual fear, and it is a maxim of Hobbesian prudence in such a relationship to assume the worst about your adversary. In other words, the proliferation and escalation of nuclear weapons does not in my view require special explanation in terms of the power of the military industrial complex, or specially benighted statesmen – though no doubt these do not help. It is implicit in the dialectical relationship between sovereign nation states in a condition of continuously changing technology – a relationship of which statesmen themselves are as much the creatures as the controllers. The procession of retired ministers, Chiefs of Staff, etc., ready to deplore the policies they themselves pursued in office is eloquent testimony to this fact.

I do not want to convey the impression that I believe there is any simple solution to this problem. Indeed, if my analysis is correct, it is precisely because the process of nuclear escalation is so deeply embedded in the normal logic and posture of the nation state that its resolution proves so intractable. The dilemma can be put as follows: any resolution of the mutual insecurity can only be achieved through the structures of nation states; yet it requires nation states to behave in ways which run counter to their fundamental character: to surrender some at least of their exclusivity: the exclusive claim to sovereignty over their own territory; their excusive concern only for the welfare and security of their own citizens – an exclusive concern which under contemporary conditions only leads to their greater insecurity.

What we face here is the most acute example of a general dilemma within contemporary society – that is the huge discrepancy between the pace of technological change, and the capacity of social organization to adapt to or control that change. The fact that the discovery of atomic energy had made the exclusive sovereignty of the nation state anachronistic was clearly recognized by many of the scientists who worked on the construction of the first atom bombs – those that is who were able to transcend the intellectual excitement of solving technical problems at the frontiers of knowledge and reflect on the political significance of what they were doing. In the so-called Franck report submitted by a number of them to the Secretary of State for War in June 1945 urging against the use of the atom bomb against Japan, they argued that only the surrender of a certain measure of sovereignty to an international organization could prevent the development of an increasingly uncontrollable and expensive nuclear arms race, such as has indeed precisely occurred (Junck, 1960, Appendix B).

The nation state, then, claims as its most basic rationale to provide for the security of its citizens. Its record in the past on this score is ambiguous; it is doubtful whether it can effectively maintain this basic function in the future.

3. Cultural

Let me turn now briefly to the third claim implicit in the idea of the nation state – the claim to protect the cultural identity or distinctive way of life of its population.

The concept of the nation has always eluded entirely satisfactory definition. This is partly because there is an important subjective dimension to it: people constitute a nation when they consider themselves to be one. But that claim to be taken seriously must rest upon some historical identity, some geographical contiguity, some shared cultural characteristics, often linguistic, though not necessarily so. Now the idea of the nation state embodies a reciprocal conception: that nations require their own political institutions or states to protect their cultural identity, their distinctive way of life; and that states require a relatively unified population to ensure mass support. The theory is that nation and state should coincide. The reality of course is very different; there is no such simple coincidence almost anywhere. If you look at a world map of historical nationalities, they by no means coincide with the boundaries of nation states. And if you add other cultural communities – based on religion, language or ethnicity – then one could say that it is the exceptional nation state that does not have within its borders one or more minority nations or sub-nations if we may so call them. Some may be dispersed throughout the majority population, more usually they are geographically concentrated. These minorities have rarely settled easily into the nation state. They constitute a challenge to the nation state when they come to demand a measure of political autonomy for themselves, or outright separation, or incorporation in another already existing state. They become a special embarrassment when they appeal to that same principle of national self-determination on which the legitimacy of the wider nation state is itself based.

Now such problems of minorities asserting themselves against the nation state have always existed. The evidence suggests that they are becoming more rather than less frequent, and that they are posing an increasing threat to the integrity of nation states. In contrast to the previous challenges to the nation state that I have outlined – economic and military – this is a challenge as it were from below rather than above. For purposes of analysis let me briefly identify three different though interconnected factors at work, which lead cultural minorities to feel that their identity is threatened within existing nation states, and to assert themselves against it.

i) The first is oppression or discrimination at the hands of the majority population. A central feature of nationalism, as we have seen, is its exclusivity, its definition of itself over against others. This often expresses itself in a superiority and hostility towards the minorities within the nation state, who become treated as second class citizens. The baneful effects of that process over a lengthy period are all too familiar to us from the history of Catholics in N. Ireland and of blacks in mainland Britain, and do not require further elaboration.

ii) The second factor that brings minorities to rebel is the existence of strongly centralizing and assimilationist policies on the part of the nation state. The chief proponents of such assimilationist policies are the state personnel themselves, the military, the bureaucracy and so on, whose interests are those of the central state, and whose ideal is that of national unity and a homogeneous population. It is not surprising that the UN has never brought itself to give an unequivocal declaration on behalf of minorities – both Charter and Universal Declaration of Human Rights make reference only to the rights of individuals. The furthest it has got has been a declaration by one of its subcommissions to the effect that 'persons belonging to minorities shall not be denied the right [note the negative] to enjoy their own culture, practise their own religion, or use their own language' – though it also goes on to say that 'to qualify for any protection, a minority must owe undivided allegiance to the government of the state in which it lives' (Mackey, 1975, p. 16). Not surprisingly, such assimilationist and centralizing tendencies often have precisely the opposite effects from that which is intended, and bring the minorities concerned to the point of open rebellion.

iii) Thirdly are the forces of the world economy itself. It is often believed that as the economy becomes global in scale, so it will create an increasingly global identity, a kind of western consumerism writ large. That is at best a very partial truth. Economic development is not a gradual and uniform process, but a sudden and disruptive one, which brings all kinds of dislocations and disparities in its train. The rapid dislocation of traditional ways of life brings with it a reassertion of older forms of consciousness that have lain dormant for generations. The way in which the operation of the international economy reinforces regional disparities within countries, again leads to the re-emergence of regional nationalisms that have previously accommodated themselves to the larger nation state, and whose demands for greater political or cultural autonomy cannot be ignored or suppressed without increasingly bitter conflict. Now in the light of what I said earlier, the idea of a lot of smaller local self-contained economies, isolated from the operation of the world economy, is hardly realistic. But it does not follow that there is no room for forms of more local political autonomy that are consistent with an international division of labour. The alternative of increased centralization and assimilation merely offers the prospect of more intensive conflict and the threat of disintegration.

We see, then, that the nation state is now under challenge from a combination of historical forces, economic, military, and politico-cultural, both from above and below. These forces raise an increasingly serious question mark over the ability of the sovereign nation state to protect the economic welfare, the physical security and the cultural identity of its inhabitants. In the light of these developments, what possibilities present themeselves for the future?

One obvious possibility is that, in the face of these challenges and precisely because of them, we shall see a renewed assertion of the nation state: a reassertion of the exclusive sovereignty of the state over its own territory, of the exclusive claims of the nation both against those outside and against the minorities within its own borders. The more historical forces move beyond its control, the more the nation state may feel compelled to reinforce and solidify the power that it does have at its disposal. If my analysis is correct, such a development, however understandable, could only be a regressive one, because increasingly out of step with the necessities of the world in which we actually live. We could then experience the end of the nation state, not as a gradual erosion of its power, but as a final convulsion which would engulf its citizens.

Alternatively, we could postulate an ideal of a plurality of political structures, at a number of different levels, of which the national would certainly be one, but which would also comprise the sub-national, the regional and the global, each with different forms of popular participation and representation appropriate to the particular level. Of these, the development of effective supra-national institutions at the world level is the most urgent necessity. However, in the absence of any powerful social and political forces which could act as the bearers of this historical necessity, it has to be said that any proposal for a system of world government is at present merely Utopian. Certainly the institutions of the United Nations provide the framework and some of the potential elements for such a development; but it too obviously acts merely as an extension of the interests of individual nation states.

A third possibility is more modest. The most perhaps we can expect in the short term is a certain relaxation of the exclusive claims of the nation state – both upwards and downwards. A number of contemporary developments taking place in Western Europe, the heartland of the nation state, offer a pointer in this direction. In response to the widespread resurgence of national and sub-national movements, we have seen the willingness, albeit reluctant, on the part of some states to yield a portion of their sovereignty downwards, of which Spain is the most recent example. We have also seen the surrender of some sovereignty over economic affairs to a higher West European level in the EEC, however inadequate, limited and distorted those institutions may be. The regional level may just offer the most hopeful possibility of a learning process that will sustain a future experiment in supra-nationality at the global level.

Nevertheless, it must be said that these supranational developments are at the institutional level only, and have little implantation in the popular consciousness. This is hardly surprising in view of the potency of those cultural institutions which reinforce a purely national identity. Daily we are invited to regard the achievements of our own nation, whether in sport, industry or whatever, as especially noteworthy and meritorious, and to count the lives of our fellow nationals as of higher worth than the rest of humanity. It is the continuous reinforcement of such assumptions that provides the basis for the oft-asserted claim that the nation state 'has a lot of life in it yet'. But all of us have a number of different dimensions to our social identity – I will leave out mention of class, sex and so on for the purpose of this occasion and simply talk about levels – we each have a local, a national, a European identity (if we are European) and an identity as member of the human species. What the nation state does is to single out one of these identities, and assign it sole political validity, make it the exclusive basis of political allegiance. In so doing it denies the increasing interdependence of the world's peoples.

It is in this context that we see another kind of development taking place right across Western Europe, of popular movements for ecological protection, for peace and disarmament, for education in world development, and so on. Common to all of them is the affirmation of a species identity which transcends all the others, and the assertion of its supreme political validity. It is hardly surprising that the nation state views such movements with suspicion, and seeks to patronize or discredit them, because they challenge the exclusive national identity on which the nation state itself depends. Yet if my analysis is correct, that affirmation of a less exclusive political allegiance is one that is more appropriate, indeed more urgent, in the stage of world development in which we are now living. But these alternative popular forces are still relatively weak in relation to the power the nation state has at its disposal – for which the contrast between the web of wool and the barbed wire fence offers us a timely symbolic representation.

Let me sum up, with one final consideration. My argument has been an essentially simple one. It is that, just as the sovereign nation state developed because it was the political formation that corresponded most appropriately to the historical forces at work in the past centuries in Europe, so it is becoming increasingly inappropriate in face of the forces at work in the contemporary world. But as with all human history, we see a disjunction between the historical changes at work and the capacity of social institutions and forms of social consciousness to adjust to those changes. That disjunction, which is normal for human societies, has now been massively reinforced by the pace of technological change, and has assumed a character that can only be described as pathological. The nation state offers perhaps the most conspicuous example of this disjunction. Whether the necessary institutional and cultural transformations can be made in time is a crucial question for the future of the human species.

Bibliography

Breuilly, J. (1982). *Nationalism and the State*. Manchester, Manchester University Press.

Gellner, E. (1964). 'Nationalism' in *Thought and Change*. London, Weidenfeld and Nicolson.

Harris, N. (1983). *Of Bread and Guns*. Harmondsworth, Penguin.

Hellman, R. (1977). *Transnational Control of Multinational Corporations*. New York, Praeger.

Hobbes, T. (1961). *Leviathan*. Oxford, Basil Blackwell.

Hobsbawm, E.J. (1979). 'The Development of the World Economy', *Cambridge Journal of Economics*, pp. 305 – 18.

Junck, R. (1960). *Brighter than a Thousand Suns*. London, Penguin.

Kidron, M. and Segal, R. (1981). *The State of the World Atlas*. London, Pluto Press.

Mackey, W.F. (ed.) (1975). *The Multinational Society*. Massachusetts, Newbury House.

Nairn, T. (1977). *The Break-Up of Britain*. London, New Left Books.

Radice, H. (ed.) (1975). *International Firms and Modern Imperialism*. London, Penguin.

Schell, J. (1982). *The Fate of the Earth*. London, Cape.

Thompson E.P. and others (1982). *Exterminism and Cold War*. London, New Left Books.

Tilly, C.H. (1975). *The Formation of National States in Western Europe*. Princeton, PUP.

Tivey, L. (ed.) (1981). *The Nation State*. Oxford, Martin Robertson.

Wallerstein, I. (1979). *The Capitalist World Economy*. Cambridge, Cambridge University Press.

Young, N. (1983). 'The New Peace Movement in Europe' *Bulletin of Peace Proposals*, vol. 14, no. 2.

CHAPTER 9

Beyond liberalism and Marxism?

David Held

We live in a world punctuated by crises which affect the welfare and life-chances of countless millions of human beings. The upheavals of the twentieth century – the rise of fascism and nazism, the degeneration of the Russian revolution into Stalinism, the two World Wars, the struggles between West and East, North and South – have demonstrated the urgency, if it ever needed accentuation, of inquiring further into the nature of 'societies' and 'states'. Any such enquiry, however, must be incomplete if it does not pursue the question of 'how things might be otherwise'; that is, how the political world might and should be organized. This chapter, accordingly, offers an opportunity to reflect upon alternative directions for the state.

The chapter is divided into three sections. The first builds on earlier discussions in this volume of arguably the two greatest contributors to modern political thought, John Stuart Mill and Karl Marx. The juxtaposition of their rival diagnoses and prescriptions – and the conflicting strains within each of their work – brings into clear relief many of the issues that divide modern political thinkers. The next section attempts to assess the meaning of these competing positions for a country like Britain today. I offer a series of arguments which point to one possible resolution of some of the issues considered. Finally, I conclude with a brief account of the many questions which remain open and which are in urgent need of further thought.

Mill vs. Marx?

Mill offers one of the most significant and richest accounts of modern liberalism. His heritage may be summarized by the proposition:

representative democracy (skilled government accountable to an electorate) is the most suitable mode of government for the enactment of
laws consistent with the principle of liberty and moral self development, as the free exchange of goods on the market is generally the most
appropriate way of maximizing economic liberty and economic good.

Toward the close of *Representative Government*, Mill summarizes
the 'ends of government' in the following way:

> Security of person and property and equal justice between individuals
> are the first needs of society and the primary ends of government: if
> these things can be left to any responsibility below the highest, there is
> nothing, except war and treatises, which requires a general government
> at all. (1972, p. 355)

One need not be Karl Marx to ask whether Mill was trying to
'reconcile irreconcilables' (1970a, p. 16). For Mill's work entails the
attempt to link together into a coherent whole security of person,
property, equal justice and a state strong enough to prevent or
prosecute wars and sustain treaties. In fact, Mill's work lends itself to a
variety of interpretations concerning not only matters of emphasis but
the very political thrust of liberalism and liberal democracy. There
are, at least, three possible interpretations worth emphasizing.

First, Mill tried to weave arguments for democracy together with
arguments to 'protect' the modern political world from 'the democracy'. While he was extremely critical of inequalities of income, wealth
and power – he recognized, especially in his later writings, that they
prevented the full development of most members of the working
classes – he stopped far short of a commitment to political and social
equality. In fact, Mill's views could be referred to as a form of
'educational elitism', since they clearly seek to justify a privileged
position for those with knowledge, skill and wisdom. The leading
political role in society is allotted to a class of intellectuals, who, in
Mill's system of vote allocation, happen to have the most property and
privilege. He arrives at this view through his emphasis on the importance of education as a key force of liberty and emancipation. It is a
position fully committed to the moral development of all individuals
but which simultaneously justifies substantial inequalities of power
and reward in order for the educators to be in a position to educate the
ignorant. Thus, Mill presents some of the most important arguments
on behalf of the liberal democratic state alongside arguments which
would in practice cripple its realization.

Second, Mill's arguments concerning free-market political economy and minimal state interference anticipate later 'neo-liberal' arguments. According to this position the system of law should maximize

the liberty of citizens – above all, secure their property and the workings of the economy – in order that they may pursue their chosen ends unhindered. Vigorous protection of individual liberty allows the fittest (the most able) to flourish and ensures a level of political and economic freedom which benefits all in the long run.

Third, while Mill remained throughout most of his life firmly of the opinion that the liberal state should be neutral between competing individuals' goals and styles of life – individuals should be left as free as possible – some of his ideas can be deployed to justify a reformist view of politics (see chapter 4). For Mill's liberal state is assigned an active role in securing people's rights through the promotion of laws designed to protect groups such as ethnic minorities and to enhance the position of women. Additionally, if we take Mill's principle of liberty seriously, that is, explore those instances in which it would be justified to intervene politically in order to prevent 'harm to others', we have, at the very least, an argument for a fully fledged 'reformist' conception of politics. Occupational health and safety, maintenance of general health, protection from poverty – in fact, all those areas of concern to the post Second World War welfare state – might be included as part of the sphere for legitimate state action to prevent harm. In the *Principles of Political Economy*, Mill adopted such a line of reasoning and argued not only that all workers should experience the educational effects of ownership and control of the means of production but also that there should be many exceptions to *laissez-faire* economic doctrines. Taken together these views can be read as one of the earliest statements of the very idea of the welfare interventionist state (see Green, 1981).

Marx relentlessly attacked the idea of a 'neutral' liberal state and 'free' market economy. In the industrial capitalist world the state could never be neutral nor the economy free. Mill's liberal state may claim to be acting on behalf of all citizens, it may defend its claim to legitimacy with the promise to sustain 'security of person and property' while promoting simultaneously 'equal justice' between individuals. But this promise cannot, Marx argued, be realized in practice. 'Security of person' is contradicted by the reality of class society where most aspects of an individual's life – the nature of opportunities, work, health, life-span – are determined according to his or her location in the class structure. What faith can be placed in the promise to guarantee 'security of person' after a comparison is made between the position of the unemployed, or the worker in a factory doing routinely dull and unrewarding tasks in dangerous conditions and the position of the small and extremely wealthy group of owners and controllers of productive property living in conditions of more or less sumptuous luxury, often in houses and estates guarded by high walls and dogs? What meaning can be given to the liberal state's promise of 'equal justice' between individuals when there are massive social, economic and political inequalities?

In formally treating everyone in the same way, according to principles which protect the freedom of individuals and defend their right to property, the state may act 'neutrally' but it will generate, in Marx's view, effects which are partial; that is, it will inevitably sustain the privileges of those with property. By defending private ownership of the means of production the state has already taken a side. It enters into the very fabric of economic life and property relations by reinforcing and codifying – through legislation, administration and supervision – its structure and practices. As such, the state plays a central part in the integration and control of class divided societies; and in capitalist societies this means a central role in the reproduction of the exploitation of wage-labour by capital. The liberal notion of a 'minimal' state is, in fact, connected directly to a strong commitment to certain types of intervention to curtail the behaviour of those who challenge the massive inequalities produced by the so-called free-market: the liberal state is perforce a coercive or strong state. Security of person and equal justice cannot be reconciled with this state of affairs. The maintenance of private property in the means of production contradicts the ideals of a political and economic order comprising 'free and equal' citizens. The movement toward universal suffrage and political equality in general, was, Marx recognized, a momentous step forward but its emancipatory potential was severely undercut by inequalities of class and massive restrictions on real freedom.

Contemporary Marxism divides into at least three major camps: 'libertarians' (eg. Herbert Marcuse), the 'pluralists' (eg. Nicos Poulantzas) and the 'fundamentalists' (eg. Marxist–Leninists). Each of these groups (or schools of Marxism) claims, in part, the mantle of Marx.[1] I shall argue that they can all do this because Marx himself might have been trying to 'reconcile irreconcilables'. He conceived of the post-capitalist future in terms of an association of all workers, an association in which freedom and equality were combined through (1) the democratic regulation of society; (2) the planned use of resources; (3) efficient production; (4) greater leisure, etc. But is the democratic regulation of society compatible with planning? Is the model of the commune, of direct democracy, as advocated by him (1970b), compatible with a decision-making process that produces a sufficient number of decisions actually to coordinate a complex, large scale society? Is efficient production compatible with the progressive abolition of the division of labour and more leisure? Marx envisaged the full participation of all 'free and equal' workers in institutions of direct democracy and planning. But how exactly is such an association to function? How precisely is it to be secured? What happens if some people bitterly object to a decision of the central commune? Assuming the dissenters are a minority, do they have any rights (for instance, to safeguard their position)? What happens if people simply disagree on the best course of action? What happens if differences of interest persist between groups of different ages, regions, religions, etc? What happens if the new forms of association do not immediately work, or do not work at all adequately in the long run? (see Vajda, 1978) The rifts in contemporary Marxism are in part a consequence of Marx's insufficient reflection upon issues such as these. Marx left an ambiguous heritage.

Marx, it should be emphasized, was not an anarchist; hence he saw a lengthy period of transition to communism which deployed the resources of the state, albeit a transformed state. But libertarian Marxists argue that his position can be interpreted adequately only if we read it as a consistent critique of all forms of division of labour, state bureaucracy and authoritarian leadership (whether created by the 'Right' or 'Left'). They contend that Marx was trying to integrate the ideals of equality and liberty in his conception of the struggle for socialism and of the model of the commune and, hence, the aims of a non-coercive order must be embodied in the means used to establish that order. If the struggle isn't organized democratically, it will be vulnerable to decisions which can be exploited by new forms of despotic power. The end – a fully democratic life – necessitates a democratically organized movement in the struggle against capital and the state. Libertarian Marxists maintain, in short, that Marx was a champion of the democratic transformation of society and state and a consistent critic of hierarchy, centralized authority and all forms of planning in detail. The struggle for socialism must involve the creation of a mass movement, independent of the corrupting influence of the bourgeois state apparatus, to challenge all forms of established power. Libertarian Marxists make it clear that, in their view, there can be no associations or compromises with the state; for it is always everywhere the 'condensed power' and 'power instrument' of dominant economic interests.

By contrast, pluralist Marxists emphasize that Marx saw the transition to socialism and communism taking place differently in different countries. Following his conception of state institutions as to a significant degree independent (or 'relatively autonomous', as some would now put it) from the dominant class, pluralist Marxists stress the importance of the deployment of these institutions against the interests of capital. In countries where the liberal democratic tradition is well established, the 'transition to socialism' must utilize the resources of that tradition – the ballot box, the competitive party system – first, to win control of the state and, second, to use the state to restructure society. The principle of the 'ballot box' should not be overridden: one cannot create a new democratic order in a way which bypasses the achievements of past struggles to political emanicpation. Unlike libertarian Marxists whose position is consistently anti-state and anti-party, pluralist Marxists – from Eurocommunists to 'Left wing' social democrats – argue that the implications of Marx's critique of the capitalist state are that the party of the working class and its allies can and must attain a secure and legitimate position in the state in order to restructure the political and social world. They also argue (along with some libertarian Marxists) that Marx's concern to reduce non-coercive power to a minimum must not be interpreted – as Marx himself tended to do all too often – exclusively in terms of class related issues. The power of men over women, of one ethnic group over another, of so-called 'neutral' administrators or bureaucrats over subject populations, must be confronted and its implications pursued – including, crucially, the implication that not all differences of interest can be interpreted in terms of class. Additionally, they argue, the 'end of scarcity' is so far in the future – if it can be imagined at all – that there are bound to be major differences of position concerning the allocation of resources. Hence, the transition to socialism and the establishment of a socialist polity will for all intents and purposes be a long democratic road in which competing parties must – for all the reasons provided by liberal democrats – have a central role. In order to create the space for alternative ideas and programmes, and prevent power holders from 'transforming themselves into a congealed, immovable bureaucracy', there must always be the possibility of being removed from office.

Fundamentalist Marxists, finally, emphasize (in common with libertarian Marxists) that the modern representative state is a 'special repressive force' for the regulation of society in the interests of the dominant economic class. The liberal democratic state might create the illusion that society is democratically organized but it is no more than an illusion; for the exploitation of wage-labour by capital is secured within the framework of liberal democracy. Periodic elections do not alter this process at all. Thus, the state cannot simply be taken over and contained by a democratic movement; its coercive structure has to be conquered and smashed. Preoccupied by the problems of seizing power, fundamentalist Marxists argue that the transition to socialism and communism necessitates the 'professional' leadership of a disciplined cadre of revolutionaries. Only such a leadership has the capacity to organize the defence of the revolution against counter-revolutionary forces, to plan the expansion of the forces of production and to supervise the reconstruction of society. Since all fundamental differences of interest are class interests, since the working class interest (or standpoint) is the progressive interest in society and since during and after the revolution it has to be articulated clearly and decisively, a revolutionary party is essential. The Party is the instrument which can create the framework for socialism and communism.

One may say, then, that while Marx offers one of the most profound challenges to the modern liberal and liberal democratic idea of the state and one of the most potent visions of a free 'stateless' society, his views, like Mill's, contain ambiguities which lend themselves to a variety of interpretations. However, Marx's heritage, at the very least, is a powerful vision of the future as a world of unimpeded democracy – established with the destruction of social classes and ultimately the abolition of the state itself.

Beyond Liberalism and Marxism: A possible way forward?

How do we begin to adjudicate between Mills's and Marx's rival diagnoses and prescriptions? What sense can we make of these competing perspectives? Unfortunately, there is no simple way to analyse these issues. For each perspective forms a complex network of descriptive-explanatory and normative statements; each is concerned with how things are and how things should be. Within each 'network', moreover, only relative and pragmatic distinctions can be made between the 'theoretical' and 'observable' (Hesse, 1974). What is 'seen' and 'registered' as important is an effect of the general framework of interpretation. While each perspective can, of course, be subjected to theoretical and empirical appraisal – examining its clarity, coherence, comprehensiveness, empirical adequacy and general capacity to withstand argument and dispute – political perspectives, like scientific theories, are always, in the final analysis, underdetermined (that is, not fully accounted for) by this process of appraisal. This state of affairs, and along with it the virtual inevitability of endless political argument and disagreement, should not, however, be regarded as grounds for abandoning systematic political thought. For it testifies to the fundamental importance of political systems encouraging, promoting and tolerating argument, debate and openness in discussion of all public matters. The implications of this view will be drawn out later.

In what follows I would like to elaborate *one* strategy for moving beyond the current debate between perspectives. Before proceeding a few comments and qualifications are in order. First, it is important to stress that the position set out below does not present a tightly knit series of ideas; rather, it amounts to a number of suggestions for further examination – suggestions which try to steer discussion beyond the seemingly endless juxtaposition of liberalism or liberal democracy with Marxism. Second, my approach involves an attempt to reconceptualize a key notion common to these perspectives and to show that aspects of both could, indeed should, be integrated in an alternative society. I am not claiming, however, that this 'critical reintegration' suggests an immediate political agenda.

The Principle of Autonomy

The liberal democratic and Marxist traditions are both concerned with the development of people's capacities, desires and interests in freedom and democracy. Liberalism[2] is preoccupied with the creation of a world in which 'free and equal' individuals can flourish; this is a position maintained alike by, for example, Locke, Mill and Nozick. Marxism is preoccupied with the reduction of all forms of coercive power so that human beings can develop as free and equal. Put in this general and abstract way, there appears to be a convergence of principle. But, of course, there are very substantial differences of position. To name but one: liberalism ties the general goals of liberty and equality to individualist political, economic and ethical doctrines. The individual, in essence, is sacrosanct, and is free and equal only to the extent that he or she can pursue and attempt to realize, with minimum political impediment, self-chosen ends and personal interests. Only individuals can judge what they want, governments must protect their rights, etc., etc. By contrast, Marxism is committed to the achievement of social or collective goals which are distinguished from individuals merely pursuing private satisfaction in the capitalist market place. For Marx and Engels to take equality and liberty seriously is to challenge the view that these values can be realized by individuals in and through private enterprise + the liberal democratic state. These values, according to them, can be realized only through class struggle, the dictatorship of the proletariat and eventually through the complete democratization of society and the 'withering away of the state'.

What I want to argue – and I shall state my position bluntly to clarify its nature – is that liberalism and Marxism share in common a set of aspirations which can be stated in the form of a central principle. Additionally, I shall contend that both liberalism and Marxism are in general mistaken about the conditions under which these aspirations can be enacted, and the institutions most suitable to their enhancement. I cannot put my case at length here, but I shall at least indicate the broad reasons for my view, bringing in arguments elsewhere in the volume which support the case I want to make.

The aspiration of the liberal and Marxist traditions to a world characterized by free and equal relations among mature adults reflects, above all, a concern to ensure the:

1. creation of the best circumstances for all humans to develop their nature and express their diverse qualities (involving an assumption of respect for individuals' diverse capacities, their ability to learn and enhance their potentialities);
2. protection from the arbitrary use of political authority and coercive power (involving an assumption of respect for privacy in all matters which are not the basis of potential and demonstrable economic or political 'harm' to others[3]);
3. direct and equal involvement of citizens in the regulation of public life (involving an assumption of respect for the dignity and equal worth of human lives[4]);
4. provision for the consent of individuals in the legitimation or justification of regulative institutions (involving an assumption of respect for the authentic and reasoned nature of individuals' judgements);
5. expansion of economic opportunity to maximize the availability of resources (involving an assumption that when individuals are free from the burdens of unmet physical need they are best able to develop themselves).

There is, in other words, in both liberalism and Marxism a commitment to what I shall call the 'principle of autonomy'.[5] The principle can be stated as follows:

> *individuals should be free and equal in the determination of the rules by which they live; that is, they should enjoy equal rights (and, accordingly, equal obligations) in the specification of the framework which generates and limits the opportunities available to them throughout their lives.*

Both liberalism and Marxism prioritize the development of 'autonomy' or 'independence'. But to state this – and to try and articulate its meaning in a fundamental but highly abstract principle – is not yet to say very much. For the full meaning of a principle cannot be specified independently of the conditions of its enactment. Liberalism and Marxism may prioritize 'autonomy', but they differ radically over how to secure it and, hence, over how to interpret it.

The specification of a principle's conditions of enactment is a vital matter; for if a perspective on the future of the modern state is to be at all plausible, it must be concerned with both theoretical *and* practical issues, with philosophical as well as organizational and institutional questions. The consideration and espousal of political principles, independently of considering the conditions of their realization, encourages an arbitrary choice between them and seemingly endless abstract debates about them. I have already claimed that both liberalism and Marxism are mistaken about the conditions in which the principle of autonomy can be enacted. It is, therefore, important to identify and explain these conditions.

Enacting the Principle

One cannot begin to consider the conditions or practical requirements of the principle of autonomy independently of historical and political circumstances. I should, therefore, like to stress from the outset that the discussion has as its backdrop Western capitalist countries and, in particular, Britain. My argument is that the conditions of enactment of the principle of autonomy can be specified adequately only if one (a) draws upon aspects of both liberalism and Marxism and (b) appreciates the limitations of both perspectives.

By way of a starting point consider Table I. The point of Table I is to indicate that the principle of autonomy can only be realized adequately if we take seriously some of the central prescriptions, and thus some of the central arguments, of both liberalism and Marxism. Equality and liberty – the interconnections of which the principle tries to specify – can only be guaranteed if one appreciates the complementarity of liberalism's scepticism about political power and Marxism's scepticism about economic power. To focus exclusively on the former or the latter is to negate the possibility of realizing the principle of autonomy. Liberalism's thrust to create a sovereign democratic state, a diversity of power centres and a world marked by openness, controversy and participation is radically compromised by the reality of the so-called 'free market' – the imperatives of the system of corporate power and multinational corporations, the logic of commercial and banking houses and the economic and political rivalry of the power blocs.[6] Marxism's embodiment in East European societies today is marked by the growth of the centralized bureaucratic state; its claim to represent the forces of progressive politics is

TABLE I. *Justified Prescriptions of Liberalism and Marxism*

Liberalism	Marxism
1. Hostility to and scepticism about state power, and emphasis on the importance of a diversity of power centres;	1. Hostility to and scepticism about concentration of economic power in private ownership of the means of production;
2. separation of state from civil society as an essential prerequisite of a democratic and social order;	2. restructuring of civil society, i.e. abolition of private ownership of (large-scale) means of production, as an essential prerequisite of a flourishing democracy;
3. the desirable form of the state is an impersonal (legally circumscribed) structure of power;	3. the 'impersonality' or 'neutrality' of the state can only be achieved when its autonomy is no longer compromised by capitalism;
4. centrality of constitutionalism to guarantee formal equality (before the law) and formal freedom (from arbitrary treatment) in the form of civil and political liberties or rights essential to representative democracy: above all, those of free speech, expression, association, belief, one person-one vote and party pluralism;	4. the transformation of the rigid social and technical division of labour is essential if people are to develop their capacities and involve themselves fully in the democratic regulation of political as well as economic and social life;
5. protected space – enshrined in law – for individual autonomy and initiative;	5. the equally legitimate claims of all citizens to autonomy is the foundation of any freedom that is worth the name;
6. importance of markets as mechanisms for coordinating diverse activities of producers and consumers.	6. unless there is careful public planning of investment, production will remain geared to profit, not need.

tarnished by socialism's equation in practice with bureaucracy, surveillance, red tape, hierarchy and state control. If liberalism's central failure is to see markets as 'powerless' mechanisms of coordination and, thus, to neglect – as critical pluralists, among others, point out – the distorting nature of economic power in relation to democracy, Marxism's central failure is the reduction of political power to economic power and, thus, the neglect – as pluralist Marxists, among others, point out – of the dangers of centralized political power and the problems of political accountability (cf. Chapter 3). Accordingly, liberalism's account of the nature of markets and economic power must be doubted while Marxism's account of the nature of democracy must be questioned.

It should be clear by now that, in my view, the conditions of enactment of the principle of autonomy are the institutions and organizations of a fully democratic order – a democratic state *and* society. In order to specify this order further it is important to take note of some of the critical limitations of both liberalism and Marxism. Generally, these two political perspectives have failed to explore the impediments to full participation in democratic life other than those imposed – however important these may be – by state and economic power. The roots of the difficulty lie in narrow conceptions of 'the political'. In the liberal tradition the political is equated with the world of government or governments alone. Where this equation is made and where politics is regarded as a sphere apart from economy or culture – that is, as governmental activity and institutions – a vast domain of politics is excluded from view: above all, the spheres of productive and reproductive relations. A similar thing can be said about the Marxian conception of politics. Although the Marxist critique of liberalism is very telling in many respects – showing as it does that the organization of the economy cannot be regarded as non-political – it is ultimately of limited value because of the direct connection it draws between political and economic life. By reducing political to economic and class power – and by calling for 'the end of politics' – Marxism itself tends to marginalize or exclude certain types of issue from politics. This is true of all those issues which cannot, in the last analysis, be reduced to class related matters. Classic examples of this are the domination of women by men, of certain racial and ethnic groups by others, and of nature by industry (which raises ecological questions).

The narrow conception of 'the political' in both liberalism and Marxism has meant that key conditions for the realization of the principle of autonomy have been eclipsed from view – conditions concerning, for instance, equal rights and obligations in the organization of economic life (essentially unexamined by liberalism) and equal rights and obligations with respect to the household, child-rearing and many aspects of human reproduction (essentially unexamined by liberalism and Marxism). (I am not saying, of course, that no liberal or Marxist has been concerned with these things; rather, I am arguing that their perspectives or frameworks of analysis cannot adequately encompass them.) In order to grasp the diverse conditions necessary for the adequate institutionalization of the principle of autonomy, we need a broader conception of 'the political' than is found in either of these perspectives.

In my view, politics is a phenomenon found in and between all groups, institutions (formal and informal) and societies, cutting across public and private life (Held and Leftwich, 1984, p. 144). It is involved in all the relations, institutions and structures which are implicated in the activities of production and reproduction in the life of societies. It is expressed in all the activities of cooperation, negotiation and struggle over the use and distribution of resources which this entails. Politics creates and conditions all aspects of our lives and it is at the core of the development of problems in society and the collective modes of their resolution. Thus, politics is about power, about the forces which influence and reflect its distribution and use and about the effect of this on resource use and distribution; it is about the 'transformative capacity' of social agents, agencies and institutions (cf. Giddens, 1979).

If politics is understood in this way, then, the specification of the conditions of enactment of the principle of autonomy amounts to the specification of the conditions for the participation of citizens in decisions about the use and distribution of resources in relation to affairs that are important to them (i.e. us). Thus, rather than striving toward a world in which there is an 'end of politics', we should strive toward a state of affairs in which political life – democratically organized – is an essential part of all people's lives.

Can we specify the nature of this state of affairs more precisely? How can 'the state' and 'society' (or 'civil society' as I shall refer to it) be combined to promote equality and liberty, i.e. the principle of autonomy?

In my view, the principle can be realized only by recognizing the need for reforming and restricting state power and radically transforming civil society.[7] What is meant by civil society? By civil society I certainly do not mean only what liberalism generally, and the New Right in particular, takes it to mean: a non-state sphere dominated by privately owned enterprises and patriarchal families. Civil society in this sense is real enough today. But civil society has a vital additional meaning. For it has the potential to become a non-state sphere comprising a plurality of social institutions, such as productive units, households, voluntary organizations and community based services, which are legally guaranteed and democratically organized; that is, protected by a constitutional framework which recognizes the right of those in social institutions to control the resources at their disposal, the organizational structure, etc. without undue interference from the state or political parties.

Understood in these terms, the path to a new democratic order would entail the attempt to redifferentiate civil society and the state through two interdependent processes: the expansion of social autonomy *and* the restructuring and democratizing of state institutions. Two conditions would be necessary: (1) curtailing the power not only of capital but also of patriarchal institutions and the state over civil society through struggles that enable citizens to equalize their power and, thereby, their capacities to act in civil society; and (2) making state institutions more accountable by recasting their functions as accessible coordinators and regulators of social life. Such an attempt would reject the assumption that the state could ever replace civil society or vice versa; it would thereby defend, on the one hand, the liberal principle that the separation of the state and civil society must be a permanent feature of any democratic social and political order and, on the other, the Marxist notion that this order must be one in which productive property, status and the power to make decisions are no longer subject to the inequalities of private appropriation.

Civil society and the state must become the condition for each other's democratization. State institutions must be viewed as necessary devices for enacting legislation, promulgating new policies, containing inevitable conflicts between particular interests within well defined legal limits, and preventing civil society from falling victim to new forms of inequality and tyranny. Institutions of representative democracy are an inescapable element for coordinating and authorizing these activities. In this scheme of things, on the other hand, a multiplicity of social spheres – including socially owned enterprises, housing cooperatives, independent communications media and health centres (all organized according to the principle of direct democracy) – must secure enhanced powers to check and control their own projects. In short, without a secure and independent civil society, goals such as freedom and equality cannot be realized. But without the protective, redistributive and conflict-mediating functions of the state, struggles to transform civil society will almost inevitably become fragmented, or the bearers of new forms of inequality of power, wealth or status.

The principle of autonomy can only be enacted through a 'two pronged' strategy of democratizing the state as well as civil society. The perspective I have offered on the future of the state departs from both liberal and Marxist perspectives and yet draws upon aspects of both. The central issue today is not the old alternative between liberal reformism and Marxist revolution to abolish the state. Rather, it is the question of how to enact the 'two pronged' strategy of creative reform protected by state action and innovation from below through radical social initiatives. One way of conceiving this is set out in Figure I.

Concluding questions

I think the position sketched above offers a fruitful way to think about the future of state–society relations; you may well disagree. You might contend that far from combining the best of both liberalism and Marxism, the position does nothing of the kind – combining perhaps the worst of both, or sacrificing the essential integrity of each tradition. You might charge that the general argument says very little about such fundamental things as, for instance, how the economy is actually to be organized and related to the political apparatus, how institutions of representative democracy are to be combined with those of direct democracy, how households and childcare facilities are to be related to work, how those who wish to 'opt out' of the political system might do so, how the problems posed by the ever changing international system of states could be dealt with. You might add, moreover, that the arguments pass over the question of how the 'model' could be realized, over the whole issue in fact of transitional stages and over how those who might be worse off in some respects as a result of its application (those whose current circumstances allow them to determine the opportunities of others) might react. Furthermore, you might maintain that the position assumes a mistaken conception of human nature: what if people do not really want to extend the sphere of control over their lives? What if they do not really want to participate in the management of social and economic affairs? What, in short, if they do not wish to become creatures of democratic reason?

These are difficult questions. To respond to them would take more space than is available in this chapter.[8] But questions like these are not just difficult questions for me; they are the kind of issues raised by the elaboration and defence of any perspective on the desirable future relationship between state and society. Issues concerning the nature

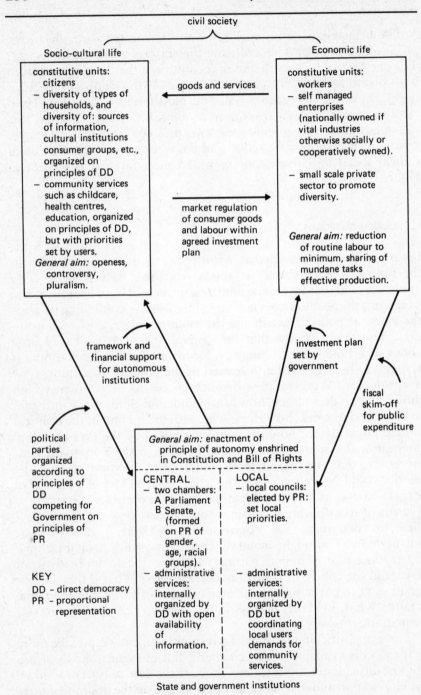

FIGURE I.   *A Future Perspective on State and Civil Society?*

and justification of principles, the conditions of enactment of such principles and the feasibility of implementing the conditions at political, economic and social levels must always be confronted, although the exact type of issue raised will of course vary from one perspective to another.

What, then, is the status of 'models' like the one I have just presented? They amount to a series of arguments which suggest *directions* for political life. Whether one explicitly acknowledges adherence to a political perspective or not, our activities presuppose a particular framework of state and society which does *direct* us. Even the actions of the apathetic are political; for they leave things as they are – a political stand if ever there was one. Perspectives on the future of the modern state are vital reflections on that 'peculiar mix of force and right' that constrains and shapes the lives of generations.

Notes

1. While these three groups are extremely important, they do not fully embrace, it might be noted, the diversity of views found among writers and activists of different revolutionary movements, communist parties, social democratic parties (especially before the First World War) and the many relatively small political groups and organizations (the Socialist Worker's Party, the International Marxist Group, for instance) which have all claimed Marx's mantle. Such diversity testifies to the fact that the history of Marxism is much less monolithic and far more fragmented than is often thought.
2. Unless I indicate to the contrary, I shall use liberalism here to connote both liberalism since Locke and liberal democracy. See Chapter 2 for a discussion of these terms.
3. This is, of course, subject to all the same problems as Mill's principle of harm. I would wish to follow the interpretation set out on page 225.
4. Note that Mill and Marx (in characteristic nineteenth-century and ethnocentric style) held this for humans in 'advanced stages' of social development: Mill sought to justify at some length the British rule of India and Marx was convinced of the 'progressive' impact of capitalism on countries with less 'advanced' social and eocnomic systems.
5. See Beetham, 1981 and Cohen and Rogers, 1983 whose writings have directly informed the argument set out below.
6. I have tried to demonstrate this thesis in relationship to Britain since the Second World War in 'Power and Legitimacy in Contemporary Britain', in McLennan *et al* (eds), 1984.
7. The following three paragraphs are adapted from Held and Keane (1984). John Keane's ideas were decisive in developing these arguments.
8. I am writing about these issues at greater length in *Bureaucracy, Democracy and Socialism*, Cambridge, Polity Press, forthcoming.

References

Bahro, R. (1981). *The Alternative in Eastern Europe*. London, New Left Books and Verso.
Beetham, D. (1981). 'Beyond Liberal Democracy', *Socialist Register*.
Cohen, J. and Rogers, J. (1983). *On Democracy*, New York, Penguin.
Draper, H. (1970). 'The Death of the State in Marx and Engels', *Socialist Register*.
Giddens, A. (1979). *Central Problems in Social Theory*. London, Macmillan.
Green, P. (1981). *The Pursuit of Inequality*. New York, Pantheon Books.
Held, D. 'Power and Legitimacy in Contemporary Britain', in McLennan *et al* (eds) (1984).
Held, D. and Keane, J. (1984). 'Socialism and the Limits of State Action', *New Socialist*, March–April.
Held, D. and Leftwich, A. (1984). 'A Discipline of Politics?', in Leftwich, A. (ed.), *What is Politics?*, Oxford, Basil Blackwell.
Hesse, M. (1974). *The Structure of Scientific Inference*. London, Macmillan.
Macpherson, C.B. (1977). *The Life and Times of Liberal Democracy*. Oxford, Oxford University Press.
Marx, K. (1970a). *Capital*, vol. I, London, Lawrence and Wishart.
Marx, K. (1970b). *The Civil War in France*. Peking, Foreign Language Press.
Marx, K. and Engels, F. (1969). *Selected Works*. three vols, Moscow, Progress Publishers.
Mill, J.S. (1965). 'Principles of Political Economy' in *Collected Works of John Stuart Mill*, University of Toronto Press.
Mill, J.S. (1972). 'Representative Government' in *Utilitarianism, Liberty and Representative Government*, London, Dent and Sons.
Mill, J.S. (1982). *On Liberty*. Harmondsworth, Penguin.
McLennan, G. *et al* (eds) (1984). *State and Society in Contemporary Britain*. Cambridge, Polity Press.
Nozick, R. (1974). *Anarchy, State and Utopia*. Oxford, Basil Blackwell.
Ollman, B. (1977). 'Marx's Vision of Communism: A Reconstruction', *Critique*, Summer, 8.
Poulantzas, N. (1980). *State, Power, Socialism*. London, New Left Books and Verso.
Vajda, M. (1978). 'The State and Socialism', *Social Research*, vol. 45, no. 4.

Index